Authentic Spirituality

Dr. Schmacker,
Thank you for sharing
your building with
our church.

Vernon Maddox
Ohio Ministries

Barry L. Callen holds earned doctoral degrees from Chicago Theological Seminary and Indiana University and masters degrees from Anderson University School of Theology and Asbury Theological Seminary and is Professor of Christian Studies at Anderson University. He has been editor of the *Wesleyan Theological Journal* since 1992 and is the founding editor of Anderson University Press. He has written or edited more than twenty books, including *Clark H. Pinnock: Journey toward Renewal, God as Loving Grace,* and *Radical Christianity: The Believers Church Tradition in Christianity's History and Future.*

Authentic Spirituality

Moving beyond Mere Religion

Barry L. Callen

Published by Baker Academic
a division of Baker Book House Company
P.O. Box 6287, Grand Rapids, MI 49516-6287

Published in the United Kingdom by
Paternoster Press, an imprint of Paternoster Publishing,
P.O. Box 300, Carlisle, Cumbria CA3 0QS UK
www.paternoster-publishing.com

Printed in the United States of America

Library of Congress Cataloging-in-Publication Data

Callen, Barry L.
Authentic spirituality : moving beyond mere religion / Barry L. Callen.
p. cm.
Includes bibliographical references and index.
ISBN 0-8010-2288-6 (pbk.)
1. Spiritual life—Christianity. I. Title.
BV4501.3 .C35 2001
248—dc21 2001043049

British Library Cataloguing in Publication Data
A catalogue record for this book is available from the British Library.
ISBN 1-84227-130-X

For information about Baker Academic, visit our Web site:
www.bakerbooks.com/academic

Contents

Foreword 7
Preface 9
Introduction 11

1. Truly Open: The Spirit's Reaching 23
2. Truly Summoned: The Spirit's Presence 53
3. Truly Amazed: The Spirit's Extravagance 79
4. Truly Belonging: The Spirit's Act 107
5. Truly Knowing: The Spirit's Eyes 131
6. Truly Living: The Spirit's Way 157
7. Truly Abiding: The Spirit's Assurance 183
8. Truly Growing: Paths to Sanctification 207

Glossary 225
Notes 237
Select Spiritual Leaders of the Christian Tradition 255
Select Bibliography 257
Index of Subjects and Persons 263
Index of Scripture 269

Foreword

Christianity started out as a transforming movement of the Holy Spirit. On the day of Pentecost, the Spirit became a fact of experience before it became a doctrine. Nevertheless, it was not long until the apostle Paul could speak of believers who held to an outward form of godliness but denied the power or held to what Barry Callen calls "mere religion" (2 Tim 3:5). How easy it is for the Spirit to become a concept to be believed rather than a baptism of power and love. Why are we afraid of the Spirit? Is it our fear of subjectivity and loss of control? Is it the unpredictability and the revolutionary potential? Thanks be to God, this is changing. We have witnessed a remarkable growth of interest in spirituality in recent years and a greater willingness to be open to the Spirit without reservation. Perhaps it is a disillusionment with rationality and with material possessions that has led people to pay more attention to the spiritual dimensions of life as that which fosters personal fulfillment and well being.

To speak candidly, I have wrestled with spirituality as an evangelical scholar. Like so many others, I have often depended on the grace of God as something in the past (salvation) and in the future (last things) but not as the transforming experience in the present, which it can be and should be. Typically evangelical, I have loaded my mind with intellectual analysis and have been deficient at the affective, everyday level of walking with God. Like many others, I have substituted the knowledge of the Bible for the skills of interacting with God himself. I did not trust personal experience but have relegated matters of the heart to an inferior place. I have valued doctrinal formulation but have been less sure-footed when it comes to issues of the soul. Fortunately, I was touched by God in many contexts of renewal, and the Lord has drawn me higher up and deeper into his trinitarian love, which embraces us all. I have been enabled to go beyond mere thinking and to become an intimate with Christ himself.

We are indebted to Barry Callen for this solid and well-researched book on Christian spirituality from the perspective of Wesleyan holiness in the context of the ecumenical church. He points the way to an enriching and ongoing relationship with the Holy Spirit. He takes us close to the passionate flame of God's loving presence and gives us much help in devising a rule of the spiritual life that will surely lead us to growth in Christ.

Clark H. Pinnock
McMaster Divinity College
Hamilton, Ontario

Preface

To be an available instrument of the Spirit of God, the church in every generation must recall and apply the "Protestant principle." This principle focuses on the spirit of creative protest and prophetic criticism. The revelation of God in Christ has a living character that calls on the church to constantly reexamine its ideas, institutions, and programs and to be renewed according to Scripture and by the wisdom and power of the Spirit. This book is dedicated to the divinely intended goal of believers being well formed as possessors of holy love reigning in the heart.

To be well formed spiritually by the Spirit of God is the biblical goal for all believers. We all are to be maturing as children of the faith who increasingly are growing into the image of the Christ (Phil. 2:1–2). These pages are dedicated to better understanding and then furthering this growth. True disciples are servants of Christ and students of the Spirit.

Spiritual growth and mature Christian disciples are especially crucial today. We live in a generation that is sated with possessions and starving for God, swimming in data and desperate for wisdom. May these pages help to point out God's way, the only way where there is real food for the soul's desire and wisdom for life now and eternally.

The listing of select spiritual leaders at the end of this volume points to numerous saints of God who have followed God's Spirit and have helped to show others the way. I am in debt to them all. One person who has gained no such notoriety in the annals of church history nonetheless deserves some recognition. Evelyn (Jeffreys) Cooley is an exceedingly modest saint who has opened herself to God's Spirit and has been an inspiration to me and my family. Her reward will be great one day.

I also extend a word of thanks to my first semester 2000–2001 class in Christian Spirituality at Anderson University. These nineteen young students of the way of Christ read through an early draft of this book and offered honest and helpful responses. The book is better because of them.

Introduction

> A theology of Word and Spirit . . . challenges both rationalist and spiritualist theologies. It seeks for the unity of wisdom and spirit, *logos* and *pneuma*. It is both logocentric and pneumocentric in that it discerns the gospel as both a rational message and the power unto salvation (Rom. 1:16).[1]

> The basic core of spiritual formation is an enabling relationship with God based upon grace alone. Spiritual formation occurs through a dynamic, growing relationship with God. The only norm or standard for measuring spiritual formation is *Christlikeness* [Gal. 4:19].[2]

This book is designed for two groups of readers. First, it is for Christian believers in general who have no extensive knowledge of theology or church history but do have a desire to better understand and pursue the Christian spiritual life. The resources for this pursuit are here and can be sampled at personal and devotional levels. Second, this book is intended for students who need to acquire significant theological and historical background related to Christian spirituality. Individual students or class study leaders can make use of the extensive notes, glossary, list of select spiritual leaders, bibliography, and index of subjects and persons. For both groups of readers, advancing in spiritual maturity requires being committed to a journey with the Spirit of God as opposed to engaging merely in an academic exercise.

Journeying with the Spirit has great potential for life here and hereafter. Any isolated intellectualism locked into only abstract ideas tends to remain fixed in that limited and relatively arid arena. Moving another way, these pages form a guided journey into the world of Christian spirituality that deliberately extends beyond the abstractions and conventions of mere religion. The purpose is both to inform the reader and encourage actually taking the journey with Jesus, the one who said he *is* the way (John 11:25–26). Walking this way is to grow into the image of Christ through the power of

Christ's Spirit. As theologian Thomas Aquinas said many centuries ago, the entire purpose of Christian theology is to raise believers beyond themselves to a transforming union with the God who cannot fully be grasped, but who nonetheless can be known through divine grace by the open human heart.[3]

Journeying with the Spirit

How important is the subject of Christian spirituality? Pentecostalism joins ecumenism (Christian unity) as the two great movements within worldwide Christianity across the twentieth century. Pentecostal churches presently constitute the largest family of Christian churches after Roman Catholicism. Renewed spirituality among Christians has been the passion of this massive Spirit-movement. Karl Rahner believes that "the Christian of the future will be a mystic or he or she will not exist at all."[4] I agree, although *mystic* is a word requiring careful definition (see glossary). Numerous theologians are now insisting that the only theology that will be meaningful for the church in the near future will be rooted deeply in spiritual commitment and actual life. Such an assumption does not clarify the meaning of *mystic* or *spirituality,* but it does urge a serious search for definitions. Whatever these words mean, they are involved in the very foundation of Christian life, and they focus on the present ministry of God's Spirit. They call for taking a crucial journey. Today this journey proceeds in a postmodern environment where human reason is known to have limits and truth cannot be reduced to verbal formulas. Believers proceed in relational contexts, and thinking about Christian faith requires the supplements of experience and living out belief perspectives—actual life transformation and discipleship in the world.

How might today's data-deluged and spirit-starved people begin the spiritual journey? The nonphysical dimension of human life is parched by neglect and even denied through unbelief. The need is obvious. What is the solution? Christian spirituality seeks to identify the only adequate resource for addressing the human need. The Spirit of God is present, is none other than the Spirit of Jesus, and is now ministering redemptively to a troubled creation. The hope is that "all things are being made new." There is the living water of restored relationship with the God who is made known in Jesus Christ. Long ago a woman from Samaria thirsted for such divine water without being conscious of the real nature of her need or the availability of the solution standing right in front of her. Jesus offered her the liquid of life, the Spirit of the living God (John 4). We still thirst for this amazing liquid and hope for a present renewal of the divine offer to fill our empty selves and our hurting and thirsty world.

This Spirit way of viewing Christian faith and discipleship is distinctly Christian and is elaborated in each chapter of this book, especially by means of four sources of consensual or classic Christian interpretive wisdom. Chapters 2 through 7 each draw first on select language and teaching of the Bible itself, then on the related key elements of the Christian year, one of the six spiritual traditions of the church,[5] and finally on the theological teaching of the Apostles' Creed. This rich church heritage provides the crucial sources, rhythms, rivers, and substance of Christian spirituality. Each is used as commentary on the several dimensions of the contemporary ministry of the Spirit of God—who, of course, is the source and power of all that is authentically Christian. When these spiritually rich Christian sources are taken together, the believer has the necessary elements for an appropriate solution to the typical vagueness about what it means for a Christian to be truly spiritual in our time. One also has access to the church's treasured resources for maturing in Christ, viewing life through Christ, and living life for Christ. Accordingly, the last chapter focuses on practical paths to sanctification.

People strain to hear and believe Jesus when he says, "Let anyone who is thirsty come to me, and let the one who believes in me drink. As the scripture has said, 'Out of the believer's heart shall flow rivers of living water'" (John 7:37–38). Experiencing the grace of God in Jesus Christ is key to understanding the doctrines about God in Christ. Indeed, "The relations between doctrine and worship are deeper rooted and further reaching than many theologians and liturgists have appeared to recognize in their writings."[6] Belonging closely together are *being* and *believing* the good news of God in Christ, adoring and analyzing the God who both stands above the creation and has stooped to be lovingly available in its midst. Worship and study, believing and becoming are so closely intertwined as to be almost one thing. Revealed Word (*logos*) and revealing Spirit (*pneuma*) are twin necessities for Christian faith.[7]

Getting beyond mere religion is a spiritual quest with a long history among Christians. Following the Protestant Reformation of the sixteenth century, there emerged a series of renewal movements hoping to bring new life to Protestant bodies that yielded too easily to the deadening influences of religious formalism. For instance, Pietism (among Lutheran and Reformed churches in Europe) and Puritanism and Wesleyanism (among Anglicans in Great Britain) shared an emphasis on heart religion. A theoretical knowledge of the faith must be supplemented by life-changing experience of the faith. Johann Arndt (1555–1621), father of Pietism, added to his staunch defense of Lutheran doctrine the need for personal appropriation of the truths of faith.

Founded by English layperson George Fox (1624–1691), the Quakers believed that a new age of the Spirit was dawning and urged Christians to come out of apostate churches and form fellowships of true devotion that would cross all denominational lines.[8] The final criterion for true faith, Fox taught, was the inner light of the indwelling presence of the Spirit of God—not creeds, traditions, or even Scripture. John Wesley (1703–1791) laid the theological foundations for Methodism, the nineteenth-century Holiness movement, and even many aspects of twentieth-century Pentecostalism. Wesley's heart was "strangely warmed" after listening to an exposition of Martin Luther's preface to the Book of Romans. This experienced warmth of God's assuring presence sparked the fires of dramatic church renewal.

God's Spirit still warms and enlivens. All who are chilled by mere religion and numbed by excessive formalism ought to set out on a journey with the Spirit. The journey leads to real life. It is the quest to become spiritual in the Christian sense.

Being Religious and Christian Spirituality

A heroic figure in the Christian theological world of the twentieth century was Dietrich Bonhoeffer. He was hanged by the Nazis in 1945 after he actively resisted the German madness of that time. His radical thought renounced the temptation of "cheap grace" and the common preoccupation with the forms of traditional religion. To him, the world could do without an otherworldly religiosity that exhausts itself in confessions and rituals instead of sacrificially investing itself in being truly for others. Jesus calls to new life, not to more religion, to participation with God in all aspects of our personal and social existences, not to huddling in the halls of the sacred while avoiding or attacking the secular. To be authentically Christian is to be fully human and to join God in the costly ministry of redemption and justice. Nothing less is worthy of being called "Christian spirituality."

The enemy of Christian faith often wears a cloak of decency. The greatest opposition to Jesus appeared in religious clothes and carried impressive religious titles. What, then, does it mean for a Christian to be spiritual? Whatever the answer, it will be much more than what usually passes for being religious. Little has changed since 1948 when A. W. Tozer observed that the masses of American people had not gotten beyond mere religion.[9] For them, God was a logical inference, not a living reality. God was a moral ideal, just another name for goodness, beauty, or truth. The possibility of intimate acquaintance and life-changing relationship with God had hardly entered their minds. If religion was respected—and it typically was by most people in the 1940s and 1950s—it nonetheless usually functioned as mere religion.

A mechanical, secondhand, self-serving, or ritualistic approach to God is typical of religious people. In North America and Europe, today's churches too often are seen mostly as custodians of positive cultural values. They are treated as humanitarian centers that provide ties to the past, care for needy people, and ensure social harmony. Rarely, however, are they respected as faith communities of supernatural redemption that carry a message of judgment on all human endeavors that deny the presence, power, and ultimate authority of God. In fact, churches sometimes do not function in ways that encourage anyone to notice them as anything other than benign carriers of mere religion. They may represent welcome ties to the past and comforting adjustments to the present, but too many churches foster little that actually challenges the distorted status quo and alters life in fundamental ways. What about the nature and purpose of religion?

Saying that a person is religious is not saying very much. The current marketplace of faith alternatives is a virtual shopping mall of spirituality, with many of the offerings imported, mass-produced, and certainly on sale. The fine print on religion labels—if there is any—should be read with care. There is, for instance, the individualistic religion of Sheila Larson: "I believe in God. I'm not a religious fanatic. I can't remember the last time I went to church. My faith has carried me a long way. It's Sheilaism. . . . It's just try to love yourself. . . . You know, I guess, take care of each other."[10] Our current cultural setting breeds Sheilas who limit religion to self-love and kindness to others and think of well-being as personal fulfillment. This view assumes that people have a right to feel good and have their needs met—while the mass media attempts to create new needs all the time. But surely there is a difference between personally convenient arrangements and true hope, between autosuggestion and divine revelation, between mere religion on one's own and what Jesus had in mind for us by the Spirit.

Today there are numerous religious systems, traditions, and institutions with which a person may be identified. The common choice is to disassociate from them all and try to be religious privately. So, to know a person's religious label and association (or lack thereof) is to know something, but not the most fundamental something about the person. Much religion-related reality involves outward factors of organization, custom, creed, liturgy, and traditional practice. Religion, however, typically is thought to be something inward. Whatever the outward associations, the key question finally focuses on an individual's spiritual experiences, values, and life commitments. Christian faith in particular seeks to move beyond the outward incidentals to inward realities. The goal, however, is not just any comfortable and satisfying spiritual inwardness. To avoid the heresy (serious deviation from classic belief) that now often emerges from postmodern considerations of spirituality, we need a fresh focus on the person and work of the Holy Spirit, a consideration rooted in biblical testimony about the definitive revelation of God in Jesus Christ. *Logos* and *pneuma* are coordinate, not separable.

One would think that persons of faith would be protective of all things religious. Not so. Certainly, many Christian voices lament the presumed loss of a Christian America, but others insist the United States never was Christian and that the primary goal of the church is not to Christianize culture. So we ask two questions among the many others addressed in this book: What were the politics of Jesus?[11] What has such a question to do with being spiritual in a sense supported by Jesus? As prophetic Christian voices like Dietrich Bonhoeffer have often said, Christians should welcome a religionless world, that is, one freed of the dominance of mere religious conventions so there might be fresh opportunity to receive Jesus Christ in an inwardly transforming way. Jesus said the pure in heart will be blessed and what defiles is what comes from inside an individual (Matt. 5:8; 12:34).

Martin Marty has written about religion in America during the period of 1893–1919 when social analysts frequently feared the coming loss of religion both in the culture and in the meaning of private life as the country rapidly urbanized and industrialized. What really happened? Religion prospered in multiple ways: "Instead of dissolving in the face of the jostling and erosion caused by American diversity, it relocated more than it declined. Instead of assuming a single non-religious style of rationality and life, . . . citizens kept inventing protean ways to pursue their spiritual questions."[12] In fact, the persistent role of religious faith has been key to the American experience since the founding of the country.[13] Today, despite the secularism and pluralism on every hand, religion flourishes in a bewildering range of forms. It is dispersing rather than dissolving. We now have reached the twenty-first century and find ourselves living in a time that is being called "postmodern." Whatever else this means, it clearly rejects the conventionally outward in all religious claims. It is open only to what is inwardly authentic and translates into effective and fulfilling patterns of actual life.[14] Religion still lives on in the context of our global and technological times.

What, then, is spirituality? First, it is a transreligious word. There are Hindu, Muslim, and numerous other traditional spiritualities and brands of spirituality not rooted in any organized religious tradition. Being religious or spiritual today can mean everything from a renewal of high-church Christian liturgy to a flight from religious institutions and dogma to New Age therapies designed to overcome boredom and addictions and to offer a substitute for lost families. Experimentation is rampant. Spirituality, variously defined, is definitely in vogue. The atmosphere is often a supermarket of options catering to personal preferences. For example, I live in central Indiana near Camp Chesterfield, a large spirituality center that focuses on deepening human spiritual growth through recognition of the afterlife and psychic readings. One of the resident ministers explains the camp's philosophy: "The concept of spiritualism encompasses all religions—Christianity, Buddhism, Judaism, Islam—as equally valid points of view from which wisdom can be gained." She adds, "It's like the circle in downtown Indianapolis. No matter what road you take, you're arriving at the same destination. . . . There is no wrong road to take when your goal is to reach God. Spirituality is in all religions."[15]

Spirituality has become more than an attempt to reach God or to find oneself. It is also an emerging academic discipline and a lucrative industry in North America and Europe. Many Christians, especially conservative Protestants, fear it is just another self-improvement fad, a subjective do-it-yourself effort at salvation without the necessary truth and disciplines of church and creed. Christians have long known that the focus of the faith should go far beyond merely being religious. Human need includes much more than achieving social peace, psychological health, and ecological balance in our polluted physical environment. Definitions of spirituality must be more precise than merely "whatever gets me in touch with my true self or the larger reality outside myself." Here is the important question: Is there anything that makes spirituality distinctively Christian? Kenneth Collins edited the book *Exploring Christian Spirituality* in part to bring greater clarity to the meaning of spirituality today, particularly the distinctive meaning of Christian spirituality.[16] A similar motive lies behind this present book.

A useful definition of spirituality is "the experience of consciously striving to integrate one's life in terms, not of isolation and self-absorption, but of self-transcendence toward the ultimate value one perceives."[17] If the ultimate value perceived is God as revealed in Jesus Christ and experienced through the gift of the Holy Spirit, the result is Christian spirituality. It necessarily has certain theological foundations. While the dimensions of Christian spirituality are identified and explored throughout this book, three preliminary things should be stated here, things commonly assumed by Christians who think of themselves as orthodox.

First, the image of God implanted in humans by the divine creation means we are enough like God that communion with him is possible. Christian spirituality involves the quest to realize this potential communion. Second, Christian spirituality is lived experience of God in Christ through the Spirit and reflection on this experience. It has been defined briefly as "the lived encounter with Jesus Christ in the Spirit."[18] Given the divine-human communion possibility and the lived-experience emphasis, the third assumption emerges. Theological language should be understood as reflection on the primary experience of actual relationship with God. A theolo-

What Is a Christian?

Being a Christian is "knowing Father and Son and walking along the pathway of cross and resurrection through the power of the Spirit. . . . We must be personally crucified and buried with Christ and rise with Christ to new life in the Spirit."

Clark H. Pinnock, *Flame of Love*

gian who does not actively worship God is hardly a Christian theologian, regardless of constantly quoting the Bible and regularly handling orthodox traditions and doctrines. Outward rightness in belief and practice may be judged orthodox, respectable, and readily acceptable to religious insiders; formal rightness by itself, apart from the immediacy of experience with God, will not lead to effective Christian living and evangelism.

The nature of the faith to which Jesus calls and that our times demand is a religion *of the heart*. Note this wisdom from a sermon of John Wesley: "A man may be orthodox in every point; he may not only espouse right opinions, but zealously defend them against all opposers; he may think justly concerning the incarnation of our Lord, concerning the ever blessed Trinity, and every other doctrine contained in the oracles of God. . . . He may be almost as orthodox as the devil . . . and may all the while be as great a stranger as he to the religion of the heart."[19] Wesley certainly was not demeaning proper belief in concert with biblical revelation and the teaching tradition of the church. What he was demeaning, as did Jesus long before him, was dead orthodoxy. Mere religion consists of inherited faith, formal commitment, distant memory, and routine practices that have become so institutionalized, intellectualized, and socially adjusted that they have lost vital touch with the very purpose of the faith itself. The challenge is to get beyond such mere religion!

The question then becomes, What is a real Christian?[20] One good definition of Christianity is "knowing Father and Son and walking along the pathway of cross and resurrection through the power of the Spirit. . . . We must be personally crucified and buried with Christ and rise with Christ to new life in the Spirit."[21] Beyond the mere knowing and believing of church teachings (primarily intellectual functions), the Christian life also is journeying with the Spirit along Christ's path and into Christ's mind and image—a journey requiring personal transformation and serious discipleship.

Enduring wisdom for living the Christian life comes from the Book of First Thessalonians. Early Christians were instructed to rejoice and give thanks in all circumstances (5:18). The joy comes as believers accept by faith and live out what is truly good. And what is truly good? It is the enduring and enabling paradox of Christian truth, what has been called the *text-context* poles of Christian believing and living. The *text* is the fixed givenness of the faith, what has been expressed once and for all by the "will of God in Christ Jesus" (5:18). The critical *context*, the dynamic ongoingness and contemporaneity of the faith, resides in the presence and power of Christ's Spirit. These are not to be despised or quenched (5:19–20)—although they always are to be measured by the *text* of God in Christ. Accordingly, the individual who would be authentically Christian must remain both anchored in the text and enlivened by the context, rooted in the Word of God in Christ and open to the current work of God in Christ's Spirit.

Admittedly, among today's Christians too much of what is considered traditional theology has been heavily influenced by alliances between the church and the power structures of the world. For the church to be authentically Christian, spiritual as God intends, the primary influences must be an intentional alliance with Jesus Christ and a genuine openness to the power of the Spirit. Fortunately, the success of the church does not ultimately depend on its members, but on the power of the Spirit graciously at work in its midst. Can the church be reformed into its true nature? Yes, "not because we trust our own programs of reformation, and even less because we trust its structures and committees, but because we trust in the Holy Spirit."[22] The Spirit wants to move the church beyond the spiritual deadness of mere religion.

The Present Challenge and Plan

The challenge of this book is to show the way beyond dead orthodoxy to the authentic Christian faith of the heart, a faith that is both text anchored and Spirit enlivened. The goal of wholeness in Christ reflects John Wesley's understanding of salvation as divine therapy. God's redeeming work came to full expression in the death and resurrection of Christ and then in the outpouring of the Holy Spirit at Pentecost. In this redemption and outpouring resides the divine potential for the healing of human sin.[23] The challenge before us, despite the distractions of the many church personalities, denominations, creedal controversies, and cultural accommodations, is to explore Christian spirituality through the lens of Jesus Christ as illumined and empowered by God's Spirit and envisioned by the universal church across the centuries.

Always at the center is the Spirit of God, who defines and enables authentic Christian spirituality by reaching, calling, acting, amazing, adopting, illuminating, empowering, commissioning, and assuring—the vital Spirit functions that form the chapter divisions of this book. Each of these Spirit activities is explored as it has been experienced and presented in the Bible and in the rich Christian tradition over the centuries. It is assumed that Christian spirituality is rooted deeply in Hebrew soil and is enriched when made aware of the stream of Christian tradition that has sought to understand and live it out in the changing realities of our troubled world. Also explored here are the key activities of the Spirit of God as viewed in light of the times in which we now live. The church today exists "as resident aliens, an adventurous colony in a society of unbelief." Therefore, "no clever theological moves can be substituted for the necessity of the church being a community of people who embody our language about God, where talk about God is used without apology because our life together does not mock our words."[24] Now is the time for a sturdy spirituality that is distinctly Christian, is full of new life, moves well beyond mere religion, and is serious about witnessing for Christ with the testimony of transformed life in the Spirit—not merely with traditional words of orthodox belief.

To avoid mocking the intended nature and mission of the church, Christian believers must demonstrate with their lives what they affirm with their mouths. Bill and Gloria Gaither are the leading Christian gospel songwriters of the twentieth century and are friends of mine. Their personal lives have added credibility to their many songs. Bill once told me, "We've tried to put serious faith ideas into words that regular people could understand and believe. . . . I don't like a lot of things that are 'religious.' I like things that are real."[25] This preference points to the heart of authentic Christian spirituality.

In order to discover what authentic spirituality is, this book is divided into four parts. First, this introduction explores basic definitions and directions essential for a proper beginning. Next, chapter 1 focuses on the key issue of openness, God to us humans and Christians to the whole of their spiritual heritage. Chapters 2 through 7 examine the dimensions of the present ministry of God's Spirit and the rich resources of Christian faith and tradition that illumine each of these dimensions. Finally, chapter 8 suggests helpful paths for personally maturing spiritually in light of all these Spirit ministries and heritage resources.

In these pages, readers will encounter the Christian spiritual masters of the centuries, be they Methodist, Eastern Orthodox, Quaker, Pentecostal, Roman Catholic, Presbyterian, Lutheran, Baptist, or Church of God (see the listing of select spiritual leaders at the end of the book). What is val-

The Plan of This Book

First, this introduction explores basic definitions and directions essential for a proper beginning. Next, chapter 1 focuses on the key issue of openness, God to us humans and Christians to the whole of their spiritual heritage. Chapters 2 through 7 examine the dimensions of the present ministry of God's Spirit and the rich resources of Christian faith and tradition that illumine each of these dimensions. Finally, chapter 8 suggests helpful paths for personally maturing spiritually in light of all these Spirit ministries and heritage resources.

ued is spiritual substance, not denominational labels. There is "a river whose streams make glad the city of God" (Ps. 46:4). Cited often as part of these beautiful streams are the Christian spiritual classics. What constitutes a classic? It is a Christian publication that seeks to lift the heart to the eternal, is ecumenical in outlook, and has stood the test of time by long contributing to the central aim of Christian spirituality, finding a way of daily living that leads increasingly toward union with God's nature, grace, and present purposes in this world.

Each of the chapters is well documented for the information and guidance of serious students of the Christian faith. The many notes, however, are placed at the end of the book so that readers whose main interest is more devotional than academic will not be burdened by their presence on every page. There is a bibliography rich with resources for further reading about Christian spirituality and an index to allow easy access to any person or subject found in this book. These pages seek to take into account many streams of Christian spirituality. My own tradition is Wesleyan/Holiness, a wonderful base from which to explore the breadth and lived meanings of Christian life. Like John Wesley's work in the eighteenth century, this work in the twenty-first century resists being a provincial prison house of inert ideas and instead hopes to be a living launching pad for believers in Jesus who seek real life in the Spirit of the Christ.

The first phase of the development of this book came when I delivered the S. R. Belter Annual Lectures at Gardner College in Camrose, Alberta, Canada, in January 1987. I focused these lectures on a series of "wonderful words of life," trying to unfold for both a lay and academic audience the foundations and real-life implications of biblical spirituality. Since the early 1990s, I have taught the course "Christian Spirituality" offered by the department of religious studies of Anderson University. My concern and writing about the Christian spiritual life grew over the years until now it is presented in this form. An early draft of these pages was studied and critiqued by seven wise and trusted Christian colleagues. I am in debt to Donald G. Bloesch, Kenneth J. Collins, Dwight L. Grubbs, Fredrick H. Shively, James Earl Massey, Clark H. Pinnock, R. Eugene Sterner, and Wesley D. Tracy.

My hope is that Christians who care about God's will for their lives will read these pages with care and benefit. Teachers of new Christians should find this a ready resource. Ministers who need biblical perspectives on the Christian life should be able to find them here. I hope that college and seminary students will take seriously the references, bibliography, glossary, and index. May all who read find wonder in the Christian faith through the presence and power of God's Spirit. May the faith find root in head and heart and practical relevance in today's world. May you come to realize the following, which can open the way out of mere religion: "Orthodoxy is about being consumed by glory: the word [orthodox] means not 'right belief' (as dictionaries tell us) but right *doxa,* right glory. To be orthodox is to be set alight by the fire of God."[26] To be spiritual in a Christian sense is to be rightly related to God so that God is inspiring, enlivening, illuminating, re-creating, and commissioning. The quest we now begin is a search for this right relationship made available through the presence and ministries of God's Holy Spirit.

Questions to Pursue

1. Is the subject of Christian spirituality important for the life of the church in today's world?
2. What is the key difference between being merely religious and participating in genuine Christian spirituality? How did Dietrich Bonhoeffer model authentic spirituality?
3. Do you understand the central purposes and plan of this book?
4. Are you willing to take the Christian journey that leads to life in the Spirit and maturity in the image of Jesus Christ?

1

Truly Open: The Spirit's Reaching

> God loves us and desires for us to enter into reciprocal relations of love with him and with our fellow creatures. . . . God has sovereignly decided to make some of his actions contingent on our requests and actions. . . . God freely enters into genuine give-and-take relations with us.[1]

> Orthodoxy becomes barren and deadening unless it is nurtured by an abiding seriousness concerning personal salvation and the life of discipleship. What is called for is a *live orthodoxy*, which is none other than a biblically grounded and theologically robust Pietism.[2]

In all human traditions of life-wisdom, including many non-Christian faiths and philosophies, is an underlying assumption: An essential part of human nature seeks relationship with the purpose of existence. As Job said long ago, "There is a spirit in man." For the Christian, this spirit is part of the divine creation. We are made to belong to God, to live in right relationship with God, to know that God intends such a relationship. Even more important than awareness that the human spirit reaches out is the basic Christian belief that God first reaches toward us hurting humans.

The Biblical God and the Christian Way

No Christian teaching is more central than the nature of God. How we understand God deeply affects our understanding of creation, the incarnation, grace, election, sovereignty, salvation, prayer, suffering, and the future. To be spiritual in a truly Christian sense rests squarely on the perceived identity and intentions of the divine Spirit.[3] If God has created humans for special relationship with the divine, then a God-determined spirituality becomes possible. The leading word of the Apostles' Creed is the Latin *credo*, "I believe." When we begin the Christian spiritual journey, it is crucial to clarify in what and especially in whom we believe. Hans Küng says that Christians believe

> Not in the Bible (which I say against Protestant biblicism),
> but in the one to whom the Bible bears witness;
> Not in tradition (which I say against Eastern Orthodox traditionalism),
> but in the one whom the tradition hands down;
> Not in the church (which I say against Roman Catholic authoritarianism),
> but in the one whom the church proclaims;
> So . . . *"Credo in Deum,"* "I believe in God."[4]

Christian spirituality refers constantly to the Holy Spirit. The meaning of this reference is essentially that God is presently at work in the world. The Spirit is invisible yet powerful, like the air we breathe or the energy of the wind. The Spirit is holy because he is the Spirit of God. The Spirit is truly open to the creation and reaches toward it in loving concern. This reaching makes possible human responding. Christian spirituality lies in the arena of this reaching and responding.

The fundamental Christian belief is reported in Colossians 1:15–23. Not only does God exist, but we sinful humans have been visited and touched by the divine. In Christ, all was created, and in Christ all things now hold together. The fullness of the divine essence dwells in Christ, and this fullness is the agency by which God desires to reconcile all things to himself. People are alienated from God—but now God has reached savingly to all people, indeed, to the entire creation. Therefore, in Christ, through the Spirit, God is at work, reaching in forgiving love and restoring relationships. No Christian belief is more basic than that the God who called the creation and then Israel into being millennia ago is the same God who now calls for re-creation and promises a new heaven and a new earth.

Fundamental to any biblically based spirituality is the underlying view of God. J. B. Phillips explains in his book *Your God Is Too Small* how our concepts of God relate directly to the way the Christian life is perceived and lived. For instance, if God is thought of as a heavenly police officer, Christian life tends to be lived as a cringing compliance to a strict set of divine rules that threaten heavy consequences if not followed carefully. Perhaps you have heard this painfully perverted proverb: "If you see a blind man, kick him; why should you be kinder than God?" It is crucial that one's conception of God conforms to his self-revelation. Otherwise, all that follows, including this proverb, is distorted. The graffiti that says, "God is not dead—he just doesn't want to get involved," is very wrong. The God of Christian prayer is the involved God. Prayer is a living encounter with the living and sharing God. God reaches out—that is the incarnation. When we pray, we make life-changing contact with God. We love only because God first loves. The Word once incarnate in Jesus Christ is now to be enfleshed in us.

An essential aspect of Christian theology leads into the world of Christian spirituality. The God revealed in the Bible is a living God, the divine person, not the abstraction of a philosophical first principle or a mere moral ideal. God is not an impersonal Brahman or the arid Aristotelian concept of an unmoved mover. The biblical picture of God as the creating Father emphasizes a loving grace that acts in accord with its own nature. The occasional biblical likening of God to the role of a divine mother focuses on the protection and nurturing of children as a hen would gather the brood under her wings (Matt. 23:37). This parent God is no static absolute beyond human history, but a dynamic, interactive reality who first launched the history we know and now chooses ongoing involvement in its fallenness by seeking its highest well-being. Thus, the prayerful interaction of the wills of Creator and creature are to remain open to real relationship, genuine transformation, even a dynamic partnership leading to communion, human liberation, and mission with God in the world. To think and become in this biblical arena of understanding is to be spiritual in the Christian sense.

To conceive of the possibility of a Christian spirituality requires that a person think of God in truly biblical ways. William Temple once said, "If you have a false idea of God, the more religious you are, the worse it is for you—it were better for you to be an atheist." It is true that no one has ever seen God (John 1:18; 1 John 4:12). God lives in an unapproachable light (1 Tim. 6:15–16). The great mysteries of the faith are more matters for adoration than analysis. Always to be joined together are reason and experience, theology and spirituality, cognition and mystery. The Bible recounts a long pattern of God's actions in human history and through them a growing human awareness of who God is and how he chooses to work for and with a fallen creation. This divine work is accomplished by the Holy Spirit of God, the Spirit of Jesus Christ in whom God is known and made present. We know God best through the divine self-disclosure in Jesus, not through any system of human speculation.[5] To be spiritual in the Christian sense is to be so aware of Jesus and so influenced by his Spirit that all aspects of life become Spirit-shaped and Spirit-directed (which is the same thing as being hid in Christ with God and having the mind of Christ).

Our human need is clear. By the grace of divine revelation, just as clear is the wonderful reality that God is truly open to our need and actively

God Is Truly Present

Before it is possible to breathe, one must be surrounded by atmosphere, and atmosphere must *be in one*. Likewise, before it is possible to commune with God, which is a more conventional way of characterizing the deep breathing of the soul, one must know that God surrounds all and God is in all; that the Kingdom of Heaven is *here* and *now*.

Glenn Clark, *The Soul's Sincere Desire*

reaching to redeem and satisfy. Central biblical images unfold both the limit of our human capacity to fulfill our deepest needs and the unfathomable ability and desire of God to satisfy them. At Meribah a desert rock produces water to soothe parched throats (Exod. 17:6); at Bethlehem a virgin womb bears a spring that nourishes the new creation (Matt. 1:18–25); at Jerusalem a stone tomb brings forth living water that eternally fills all who hunger and thirst for righteousness (Luke 24:1–12; Matt. 5:6). As Jesus hung on the cross and announced "I am thirsty" (John 19:28), a profound part of his meaning surely went beyond his physical circumstance. In this voluntary suffering was dramatic evidence of how much God thirsts for us, for all who thirst for life, eternal life, real life, life cleansed, forgiven, and made whole.

The first reality is that God truly is. The next reality is that God reaches redemptively toward all else that is. J. B. Phillips gained numerous spiritual insights as he completed his famous translation of the New Testament into modern English. He wondered about the "fear and trembling" in Paul's instruction to the Philippians. Joy came to him when he realized that the Greek word translated "fear" can equally mean "reverence" or "awe."[6] Phillips rejoiced and worshipped the great God who is "rich in mercy" (Eph. 2:4). To be spiritual as a Christian is to reverence this existing and reaching God as biblically revealed and to respond properly to God's offering of love and calling to mission. The good news is that God *was* before the world was created and *will be* even if this physical universe runs down, blows up, or is rolled up like a scroll (Isa. 34:4). This eternal God is personal—not an "it" to be surveyed or an abstraction to be manipulated.[7]

Being personal, God can be encountered in prayer and in long-standing relationships with faithful disciples across the centuries. When so encountered, believers learn that God is open, active, reaching, and accessible. God desires real, loving, reciprocal relationships with sinful humans. Because of this, life can be redeemed, prayer can be real conversation, and the future, though largely unknown, can nonetheless be full of hope. A key biblical foundation for such hope is found in Romans 5:1–5. There has been a Pentecostal outpouring of the Holy Spirit on the people of God that fulfills divine promises and ushers in the last days of salvation history (Acts 2:16–21). God's Spirit poured out love upon the apostles in the upper room and infused them with a holy passion to burn up their lives for Christ and the gospel. When the Father pours divine love into our hearts by the Holy Spirit, we also are inflamed with a holy passion to give our lives for Christ and the gospel.

One way to know the biblical God is to explore the many facets of God's nature as identified in the biblical record. Kenneth Leech has attempted this exploration, noting the mobile God, the God of the desert, the God of suffering, and so on.[8] Each of these divine facets should be allowed to accumulate into the larger divine reality. Each builds a broader base for Christian spirituality. Taken together, they lead to the conclusion that God is transcendent and immanent, stands above and stoops below, reaches and risks,[9] searches and suffers, loves and redeems. All these facets can be explored helpfully in light of the distinctive Christian doctrine of the Trinity. Each of the elements of the Trinity highlights a distinctive pattern of Christian spirituality. Since God is actually one, whatever the multiplicity of descriptive meanings, the Christian way is best seen as one, with many interrelated dimensions. Simon Chan observes that a Christian spirituality focusing exclusively on Father, Son, or Spirit is inadequate because it fails to reflect the full range of God's self-revelation. He concludes that Christian spirituality is characterized by "a sacramental understanding of created things," seeks a personal relationship with God through the person of Jesus Christ, and is open to the powerful workings of God the Spirit.[10]

To be a spiritual Christian, one must be aware of and celebrate the presence of God. God is open, reaching, risking on our behalf, available for real relationships. God does not remain at a safe distance protecting the divine honor, but comes near because of love. We may say that "God is so transcendent that he creates room for others to exist and maintains a relationship with them, that God is so powerful as to be able to stoop down and humble himself, that God is so stable and secure as to be able to risk suffering and change."[11] Worship is celebration in honor of this open God. The believer who celebrates has in clear view the work of God in nature, the unique deeds of God in human history, and the reconciling operations of divine grace. In all of this, the one who truly worships is a viewer, a rememberer, an experiencer, and a grateful responder. Celebrating God's active presence is to be energized, summoned, instructed, changed, and sent.

Current Times and Needed Definitions

The fullness of trinitarian theology is needed for any adequate Christian spirituality, but much today pulls the other way. Spirituality is in vogue, although often it is not shaped by the biblical God as known through the Spirit of Jesus Christ. The cult of materialism in the West and the collapse of Marxist ideology in the East have brought fresh and often experimental and frustrating searches for the truly meaningful in human life. There is growing reaction to the depersonalization of modern society. The sheer fright of nuclear weapons, the world's growing population, and ecological crises call for new ways of being human and living in community. Cults have become distressingly common, and books on angels, reincarnation, out-of-body experiences, yoga, and witches have become best-sellers. Trends in popular culture like the New Age movement often mimic Christianity in a variety of non-Christian ways. They speak of a significant shift of perception among the secular public. The shift is from atheistic secularism to a mystical but amorphous spiritual view of reality, what *Christianity Today* disparagingly calls "spirituality without religion."[12]

In October 1999, a large festival of music from many of the world's spiritual traditions was staged in Los Angeles. The organizers and participants hoped the richness, haunting beauty, and universality of sacred music could bridge the gap between culturally conditioned worldviews and dogmas, thus encouraging more understanding and tolerance and helping to bring about a better world. To be spiritual is headline news in the twenty-first century and is accepted as a sensitive stance of progressive life in a technologically advanced world. There is a hunger to be satisfied. Presumably, many creative and equally valid ways satisfy the hunger as long as the satisfaction is subjectively contained and pliable to the fluidity of today's pluralistic, relativistic world.

The election of Bill Clinton and Al Gore in the 1990s brought baby boomers to the highest political offices in the United States. Born between 1946 and 1964, these many millions of Americans are often characterized by optimistic dreams and increased material and spiritual choices. They lived through and significantly shaped the turbulent 1960s, the depressing 1970s, the expansive and bloated 1980s, and the transitional 1990s.[13] Note this about spirituality and the current status of this large generation of Americans:

> Why ask about religion and spirituality? Because there is widespread ferment today that reaches deep within their lives. . . . They are still exploring, as they did in their years growing up; but now they are exploring in new, and, we think, more profound ways. . . . Many within this generation who dropped out of churches and synagogues years ago are now shopping around for a

> congregation. They move freely in and out, across religious boundaries; many combine elements from various traditions to create their own personal, tailor-made meaning systems.[14]

Since the 1800s, the modern world has tried to believe that a human being is a body that has evolved from lower forms, is available for comprehensive scientific analysis, and is able to rise above environment to view truth rationally and objectively. At the opening of the twenty-first century, however, there is much postmodern thinking to the contrary. People must be understood as living souls far more complex than the mere material. We are spiritual beings who are heavily conditioned in thought and belief by immediate genetic and social environments. Somehow we need to be enabled by God's grace to transcend the merely material and the negatives of environmental and genetic heritages and be raised into the redeeming environment of God's presence. The times are open to such questing.

Within the Christian community itself, many renewal movements (often charismatic in nature) have gained dramatic attention worldwide. Living reality is being sought underneath the frequently deadening institutions and creeds of traditional faith communities. We are witnessing the emergence of grassroots gatherings and down-to-earth faith. However, the dynamic and diverse nature of the spiritual revivals now underway too often leaves vague the precise meaning of being spiritual. Often spirituality seems to mean no more than whatever is found to be personally satisfying. The Unitarian Universalists, for example, do not follow a fixed creed or set rituals. People of any faith—or no faith—are free to join congregations. The following is the list of principles and purposes for the Unitarian Universalist Associations:

1. The inherent worth and dignity of every person.
2. Justice, equity, and compassion in human relations.
3. Acceptance of one another and encouragement of spiritual growth in congregations.

While these principles and purposes are worthy, by themselves they are hardly adequate for establishing the meanings of Christian spirituality as pictured in the New Testament.

There is much at stake here for Christians. It is costly to be ambiguous about something so central as what it means to be renewed by and live in Jesus Christ. For Christians, spirituality should not be conceived and pursued outside of "the matrix of core biblical theology."[15] Spirituality does not define itself, is not an end in itself, and must not deteriorate into merely the pursuit of experiences. Essential doctrinal clarity is available. Note, for instance, this definition: "Christian spirituality is best construed as a way

Questing after Holiness

Spirituality is the quest, under the direction of the Holy Spirit but with the cooperation of the believer, for *holiness*. It is the pursuit of the life lived to the glory of God, in union with Christ and out of obedience to the Holy Spirit.

Stanley Grenz, *Revisioning Evangelical Theology*

of life as disciples of Jesus Christ in the Spirit."[16] Assumed here is that God is revealed in Jesus Christ and is mediated through the ministry of the Holy Spirit. To be truly spiritual in the Christian sense is to treasure this historic revelation and to be in the process of personal transformation at the hand of the Spirit. Anything affirming less than this is hardly adequate Christianity.

All spirituality, of course, is not Christian in character. To be truly Christian is to be a follower of Jesus Christ. Christians look to Jesus, "the pioneer and perfecter of our faith" (Heb. 12:2). Real discipleship is not just a one-time conversion but a way of life; it is not just an intellectual consent to a body of beliefs but an actual new existence made possible by the presence and power of the living Spirit of Christ. The Christian story is primarily about "God's work of initiating us into a fellowship and making us true conversational partners with the Father and the Son through the Spirit and, hence, with each other (1 John 1:1–4)."[17] God is known best by looking at Jesus. Life is lived best by intimate relationship with Jesus through the ministry of the Spirit who brings Jesus into every present and transforms obedient believers into his image. Christian spirituality is a consciously chosen relationship to God, in Jesus Christ, through the indwelling of the Spirit, in the context of the community of other believers. Theologically speaking, being spiritual in the distinctly Christian way is explicitly trinitarian, christological, and ecclesial (the fullness of God seen in Christ and realized together in the whole church).

So we who wish to be real Christians today are faced with a delicate balance. On the one hand, Christians are informed by divine revelation. They are not free to think and do as they please. Biblical bounds give definition to the faith. On the other hand, the faith is much more than a shared theological language or a common religious heritage. Stanley Grenz has encouraged viewing contemporary evangelicalism as properly moving from a creed-based to a spirituality-based identity. Rather than preoccupation with systematizing a body of doctrine assumed to be found in

Scripture, there should be a biblically informed quest for holiness. Spirituality, he says, "is the quest, under the direction of the Holy Spirit but with the cooperation of the believer, for *holiness*. It is the pursuit of the life lived to the glory of God, in union with Christ and out of obedience to the Holy Spirit."[18]

We should be suspicious whenever there is a preoccupation with elaborate and mandatory systems of religious thought that fail to engage the whole person with an active and liberating sense of God's transforming presence. The Spirit lives in, leads, and testifies to believers that they are children of God (Rom. 8:9, 14, 16). Caution about wrong preoccupations is featured, for instance, in the Christian renewal tradition known as Pietism. Believing that the Protestant Reformation had itself become bogged down in "dogmatics, polemics, and institutional rigidity,"[19] the Pietists emerged in the seventeenth century with new proposals for serious Bible study that involved increased lay participation and a strong focus on devotion and life implications. Though Pietism is often viewed today in negative ways (emotionalism, subjectivity, individualism, legalism, etc.), Donald Bloesch rightly recognizes it as one of the "wellsprings of new life in the church."[20] A Christian spiritual classic is the 1675 tract *Pia Desideria* by Philipp Spener (1635–1705). In a setting of constricted confessionalism where clergy seemed intent on disgracing Reformed, Roman Catholic, and Anabaptist wings of the church, this book challenged the faithful to get beyond a crusade to protect pure doctrine. The church exists by godly lives as well as by orthodox doctrine.

Themes of this Pietist tradition are now resurfacing, such as the new birth, sanctification, cell groups, house churches, gifts and fruit of the Spirit, and practical discipleship. These are key elements of authentic Christian spirituality. To be oriented to the presence and work of God's Spirit is to move away from theological nit-picking and to avoid becoming mired in subjectivism or committed to anarchy in church life. It is to be committed to spiritual reality and serious discipleship within the context of the church's historic teaching and present life. Something John Wesley said about the early Methodists in his 1746 *The Principles of a Methodist Farther Explained* is insightful: "Our main doctrines, which include all the rest, are three—that of repentance, of faith, and of holiness. The first of these we consider, as it were, the porch of religion; the next, the door; the third, religion itself." Christian spirituality is concerned with no less than holiness—religion itself, the life-changing dynamic that moves well beyond mere religion.

Christians today frequently want to be more spiritual and in a truly Christian manner. What is the best way to proceed? Centuries ago, Bernard of Clairvaux noted that people who try to be their own spiritual directors have fools for disciples. In other words, no one should proceed alone, relying only on personal experience and private reading of the Bible. Christian discipleship is a call to belong to a community of believers. This community, the church, is the primary context of the Spirit's ministry (the primary, not the only context). In its long history, and despite its human frailty, the church has developed much treasured spiritual wisdom.[21] Christian spirituality should be life in this community of faith, the story-formed community of Jesus journeying through time. It is crucial for a believer not only to be in this community but to learn the Jesus story and allow life to be shaped increasingly by this story.

Foundational to Christian spirituality is the Bible itself, the authoritative record of God's actions in human history. Even so, the Scriptures are not to be read and interpreted outside of the church's life—even though the church is always at the service of the revealed Word. As Christians have interpreted the Bible together in search of its enduring meaning from generation to generation and culture to culture, they have developed patterns of insight that have come to enjoy wide and long-term acceptance. Western and especially Protestant Christians need to escape the tendency to extreme individualism and immerse themselves in the broad spectrum of Christian wisdom.

Maturing as Christian believers depends in large part on being open to the community of Christ's disciples, both past and present. To be one with Christ is to seek oneness with those who are Christ's and to learn from their accumulated insight into the faith's resources and implications. Believers should be caught up in a movement characterized by its warm biblical faith, its vital spiritual experiences, and its passion for mission and evangelism. This movement is composed of spiritually journeying people who "want Christ to be central, not the sectarian debates that led to wars of religion in the past." This vision of openness, growth, community, and unity hopes for spiritual existence together "on the basis of a living faith in mere Christianity in a holy catholic church."[22]

This book itself is a journey into the accumulated spiritual wisdom of the Christian community. It is a response to the biblical call to "look to the rock from which you were cut" (Isa. 51:1 NIV). The approach shares the general intent of Thomas Oden as he wrote his three-volume work on Christian theology: "I view my task as an extraordinary privilege—that of unapologetically setting forth in an undisguised way the apostolic testimony to Christ in its classic consensual form," based on the assumption that on most crucial matters "there has generally been substantial agreement between traditions of East and West, Catholic, Protestant, and Orthodox."[23] To be specific, the Christian life is viewed in relation to the person and work of the Holy Spirit, the Third Person of the Trinity that is God. The common cause is for believers to be people of God's

Sources of Spiritual Wisdom

This book draws on (1) select language and teaching of the Bible itself, (2) related key elements of the Christian year, (3) the six spiritual traditions of the church, and (4) the theological teaching of the Apostles' Creed. This rich church heritage provides the crucial sources, rhythms, rivers, and substance of Christian spirituality. Each is used as commentary on the several dimensions of the contemporary ministry of the Spirit of God—who, of course, is the source and power of all that is authentically Christian.

reign, by the power of the Spirit, in the now of Christ's mission in the world.

There are necessary foundations for Christian spirituality. These center in God's Spirit who is present, calls, and enables transformation, belonging, knowing, living, and abiding. Since we have the promise that the Spirit will lead us into all truth (John 16:13), we are to begin the spiritual journey with the whole church, led always by the Spirit. To be spiritual in a distinctly Christian way, one must remember, believe, be changed, and be active in the believing community—thus the importance of giving careful attention to key biblical materials, seasons of church remembering and celebration, vital Christian spiritual traditions, and the long believing consensus of the church. There must be no sentimental or merely intellectual remembering of the past. Essential to the vitality of the faith in our postmodern setting is the fact that people need and want to know God as much as they want to know about God. The current challenge is present participation in new life found in the ministry of the Spirit of God.

We seek to move forward with the Spirit into the unknowns of the twenty-first century, keenly aware that an age that has experienced the "death of God" (or, at least, so it often tells itself) needs to experience the power of the resurrection of the Son of God in the lives of believers. So, "the remnant of the faithful need to be filled and empowered by the Spirit of God so that they can give an intelligible and compelling witness to a world groping in the darkness of sin and plagued by the anxiety of meaninglessness."[24] Such filling and empowering, reports Richard Foster, is happening: "Today a mighty river of the Spirit is bursting forth from the hearts of women and men, boys and girls. It is a deep river of divine intimacy, a powerful river of holy living, a dancing river of jubilation in the Spirit, and a broad river of unconditional love for all peoples."[25]

God and a Living Orthodoxy

When the Great Depression was at its worst and the young Quaker D. Elton Trueblood was acting dean of the chapel of Harvard University, this prophetic Christian voice gained attention with his book *The Essence of Spiritual Religion* (1936). Forty years later he reaffirmed the book's content and wrote a new preface for the paperback edition, then still in print. He said, "So far as religious experience is concerned, the supreme paradox of our time is that of the combination of obvious spiritual need with the failure to provide reasonable answers. It is part of our contemporary tragedy that, just when the world is becoming more aware of its need, the Church is becoming less sure of its mission."[26] Trueblood's 1969 book *A Place to Stand* insists that we need to know our faith and mission before we can engage in effective witness. The standing place is the person of Jesus Christ, and true spiritual life is enabled only by Christ's Spirit.

Even though it is fashionable today, nonetheless it is foolish to call for religion without theology. If there could be such a thing as spirituality without a theological spine, it surely would degenerate into little more than pious sentimentalism. The current postmodern inclination is toward a religion that rests on the thin base of cynicism and personal preference. It is widely assumed that the only wrong idea is to believe in any universal truth, and the only recognized sin is actually to believe in sin. In this setting, the self becomes god, truth is relative, and objectivity is an illusion. Ideas, doctrines, and religious forms are accepted or rejected on the basis of whether or not persons like them and whether they are found useful and personally fulfilling.

In contrast, the Christian tradition rests on the firm foundation of an assumed divine revelation—even if we humans apprehend it only in part. Theology is essential, although admittedly it is never enough. James Stewart is right: "Personal experience is indeed the primary, the *sine qua non* of the Christian life; but experience begets reflection. . . . Life to Paul was a unity. Salvation must also be truth."[27] Paul's letter to the Romans is especially theological in nature. Nonetheless, it deals with vital religion rather than advancing a compendium of abstract doctrine. A key New Testament concept is being "in Christ," actually communing with and being transformed by new life in the Son. Paul's theology was forged on the anvil of active missionary service. The fire in his preaching and writing came from his heart and experience as much as from his head.

The Believers Church tradition represents a distinctive theological vision that highlights Christian spirituality.[28] It insists on biblical revelation and the centrality of serious discipleship realized in covenant community, not in the settledness of church structures, traditions, or systems of theology.

Prayer: Self-Delusion or Sublime Joy?

Prayer . . . is either the primary fact or the worst delusion. If God is not, and the life of man, solitary, poor, nasty, brutish, and short, prayer is the veriest self-deceit. If God is, yet is known only in vague rumor and dark coercion, prayer is whimpering folly: it were nobler to die. But if God is in some deep and eternal sense like Jesus, friendship with Him is our first concern, worthiest art, best resource, and sublimest joy. Such prayer could brood over our modern disorder, as the Spirit once brooded over the void, to summon a new world. Prayer would not then dispel the Mystery: worship requires Mystery. . . . But the Mystery then would be a gracious Mystery, inviting and needing the friendship of our humanity, granting us light for life here and "authentic tidings" of life hereafter.

George A. Buttrick, *Prayer*

This focus lies well within the orthodox faith boundaries established ecumenically by Christian leaders over the centuries. Orthodoxy, however, is viewed less as compulsory tradition and more as Spirit-directed faithfulness in the context of the serving community of true believers in the Jesus of New Testament history who now is freshly present in the ministry of the Spirit of God. Christians who view the faith this way tend to approach Christian theology like Alister McGrath defines spirituality: It "designates the Christian life—not specifically its ideas, but the way in which those ideas make themselves visible in the life of Christian individuals and communities. Spirituality represents the interface between ideas and life, between Christian theology and human existence."[29]

The biblical faith, rooted in the Hebrew tradition, sees authentic religion as far more than a code of conduct or a correct creed. The Hebrews understood faith not as mere religion but in terms of a journey, the way a person of faith actually walks in light of belief in the ever-present God. No creedalism or ceremonialism alone will ever meet God's requirement for the good life (Isa. 1:11–17; Amos 5:21–24). Those who please God are those who act justly and love mercy and walk humbly with God (Mic. 6:8). Therefore, "the essence of religion is relationship; it is walking with God in his path of wisdom and righteousness and in his way of service to others."[30] Young theologians bent on comprehensive definitions and rigorous adherence to the traditional fine points of a given doctrinal system have been warned: "Even an orthodox theologian can be spiritually dead, while perhaps a heretic crawls on forbidden bypaths to the sources of life."[31]

Very early on, Christianity was called "The Way," a way of Christ-infused living. It is not merely a correct way of thinking. Christian spirituality assumes sound Christian theology or it is not truly Christian; but Christian spirituality is much more than focusing only on well-disciplined doctrinal correctness. It is nothing less than real life in Christ that shapes all of life. For spirituality to be Christian, it must be Christ-centered. When it is, it opposes any smothering overlay of the formal, literal, legal, ceremonial, hierarchical, sacerdotal, creedal, material, external, or traditional. There is, of course, potential value in all of these adjectives if—and only if—they nurture rather than suffocate real life in Jesus Christ. Christianity is more than hymns, sermons, pilgrimages, creeds, denominations, dinners, and committee meetings. It is about loving God out of gratitude for God first loving us. According to Jesus, "God is spirit, and those who worship him must worship in spirit and truth" (John 4:24).

Unfortunately, the needed breadth and balance is often lost. A seasoned Christian pastor and seminary professor concluded his academic career by expressing a deep concern that many evangelical Protestant pastors are quite well prepared in terms of knowing (history, theology, Bible) and doing (homiletics, counseling, administration), but sometimes are lacking in terms of being (self-awareness, personal integrity, spirituality). Leaders "are often more motivated to action than to prayer." His point was that "effective ministry requires the establishment of a vital spiritual center. . . . One cannot give what one does not have."[32]

Some years ago the English theologian Alister McGrath took a lecture tour of the United States and commented on what he perceived to be the dynamic character of American evangelicalism. One of his hosts cynically responded, "Huh! American evangelicalism may be three thousand miles wide, but it's only six inches deep." McGrath agreed and later wrote that evangelicals have done a superb job of evangelizing people, "but they are failing to provide believers with approaches to living that keep them going and growing in spiritual relationship with [God]."[33]

John Wesley once struggled with similar concerns. In 1790, late in his long life and ministry, he wrote the sermon "The Wedding Garment." In this pivotal work, he said that "orthodoxy is a small part of religion and must not be mistaken for the very substance of the Christian faith, which is not a string of ideas or speculation of any sort, but holy love reigning in the heart."[34] To be holy is more than to think correctly and believe standardly; it is to *be* rightly, to have matured in the faith by God's love reigning in one's life.

The need to focus on being seems perennial. Joseph Driskill, writing about Christian spirituality from the perspective of mainline Protestantism at the end of the twentieth century, admits that there is a general discomfort in this arena of the Christian community with things identified as spiritual. Even so, he argues for seriously addressing "the need to nurture an experiential relationship with the holy and the need to recover practices that invite spiritual growth and development." Driskill makes clear, however, that any renewed emphasis on spiritual practices "must not become narcissistic, self-absorbed practices devoid of concern for the outer world." Given this caution, he actively advocates a challenge to the deadening notion that "only analytical—in contrast to devotional—approaches to biblical texts and Christian classics have merit." Since explicit focus on spirituality is relatively new for mainline Protestants, he hopes to provide encouragement and resources for this crucial journey of faith.[35]

A troubling tension has developed recently between Christian spirituality and a modern Western concept of theology. This concept views theology as a professional academic discipline set apart from the actual life of the church. But this view impoverishes both theology and the church, which by their very natures belong together. Says Thomas Merton, "Unless they are united there is no fervour, no life and no spiritual value in theology; no substance, no meaning and no sure orientation in the contemplative life."[36] J. I. Packer rightly challenges any conceptualizing of the subject matter of theology as merely revealed truths about God. There must be no wedge driven between "knowing true notions about God and knowing the true God himself."[37] When one adds actual life in the Spirit to orthodox faith, one has the desired live orthodoxy, what Donald Bloesch calls a biblically grounded and theologically robust Pietism.[38]

In the following chapters of this book, there is regular reference to the elements of the Apostles' Creed. These references assume an important connection between the great doctrines of the church and the believer's inner life. In her classic 1934 book *The School of Charity*, Evelyn Underhill explains:

> The Christian creed is a hand-list of the soul's essential requirements: the iron ration of truths, the knowledge of mighty realities, which rightly used is sufficient to feed and safeguard our supernatural life throughout its course. When Christians say the Creed, they say in effect, "This is what we believe to be the truth about existence; about God and the things of God, and so by implication about our own mysterious lives." For the whole of life, visible and invisible, is governed by these statements; which come to us from beyond our normal radius, entering the human scene in their penetrating truth and majestic beauty, to show us how to live.[39]

The spiritual life is not to be viewed as an alternative to orthodoxy. In fact, orthodoxy is food for the contemplative soul. Across the centuries, leading teachers of Christian spirituality have taught from within the church and have been affirmed and nourished by its central beliefs and practices. They ask us to probe the depths of the doctrines, not move away from them. They call for a move beyond the doctrines (mere religion) to the actual life of the soul that the doctrines are intended to signify and encourage. More than right structure in church life or correct opinion on a range of complex doctrinal issues, a higher orthodoxy of holy love should be reigning in the human heart. Spiritually mature believers will be known by their holy love for other believers and for the whole world (John 15:12). In fact, the only thing that really counts is faith expressing itself through love (Gal. 5:6).

The most important teaching of the Bible is about the existence and nature of God and how God relates to what humans experience as everyday reality. Humanity has been created in the image of God. This means that we have been created by God and for God, with our true goal and only ultimate satisfaction in this life and in the next lying in a right relationship with God. Many spiritualities are in the Christian tradition, but they all share at least the norm of Jesus Christ, "who endows each of these forms with its own particular meaning derived from the unity of God's triune love."[40] Any spirituality that is authentically Christian seeks to bind us to Christ and lead us through the power of the Holy Spirit to God the Father. Therefore, all Christian spiritualities should be christological (Christ-centered), pneumatic (Spirit-driven), and trinitarian (leading to the Father through the Son by way of the Spirit).

Where do we get the necessary orientation for such a relationship? Our immediate source is biblical revelation—all of it. Christians too often devalue the Hebrew Scriptures (Old Testament), when in fact there is the deepest of spiritual links between every Christian and the Jewish heritage. Gentile Christians are grafted by faith into Israel (Rom. 11:17–24). Those who believe in Jesus as the Christ are "children of Abraham" (Gal. 3:7 NIV), who is the father of us all (Rom. 4:16). To be ignorant of this ancient family of faith is to be spiritually impoverished. Christians who now are grafted into the spiritual family are to "look to the rock from which you were cut . . . look to Abraham, your father" (Isa. 51:1–2 NIV). The whole Bible is best understood in light of Hebrew thought and culture. While Paul wrote in Greek, the language of his day, "his inner world of the spirit reflects primarily his Hebrew heritage, fed from sources that originally flowed from Jerusalem."[41] To be anti-Jewish is to be anti-Christian. The church was built on the foundation of Jewish apostles and prophets, with a Jewish Lord as its chief cornerstone (see Eph. 2:20).

The God Who Superintends and Reaches

Drawing on this rich spiritual heritage, read Psalm 114 prayerfully, and then consider my paraphrase below. The questions the psalmist poses are about what is most real in life despite the confusion of surface observations. Where does final control lie in this chaotic world? Is it human politics or God's providence that finally prevails? What is worth remembering, believing, and living for? Here are the answers from Psalm 114:

> Dear Lord, since confession is good for the soul, I'm prepared right now to do my soul a big favor. I confess that I and humans generally seem to see only what is on the surface of things and remember only what we choose to remember. I readily admit how easily this subtle process of selecting our memories can serve selfish ends. Please forgive my inability to perceive the depths of what is real.
>
> Here is the big question: What is really worth perceiving and then remembering? What escapes mere self-service and lies beyond the prejudice of my private bias and personal circumstances? What pinpoints actual reality rather than being infected by how we humans are fond of naming and recalling it? What has happened on the human scene that is so important, so intentional on your part that it should shape us? If you, O God of Abraham, Father of Jesus, and Lord of nations, were to show us the real truth and focus our blurred memories on the really important, what would we see and remember most of all? This question is my most profound prayer.
>
> I know something that would be emphasized. You, the gracious and revealing God, would teach that our human history—all those events, generations, battles, sufferings, joys, and questions—has not been a random and empty process. What has happened has or still can have meaning because you, the ruler of nature and nations, have put a God-shaped plot into the drama of history, making it truly *his*-story, *your story* of a good creation, a costly involvement, and a glorious redemption. We are obligated, therefore, to do more than just sing about this being "our Father's world." We must remember that it actually is.
>
> Let's get specific. When the ancient Israelites escaped their Egyptian bondage, it wasn't just one of those numerous and annoying slave revolts. It wasn't even an escape. It was a deliverance. The Egyptians were baffled, the mountains trembled, and the sea had to get out of the way as you, God, made for yourself a people. Moses may have been up front, but you were the leader. The Egyptians may have seen nothing divine about it at all, but that doesn't alter reality. Surface observations may have concentrated on human determination and opportune events of nature. An adequate understanding, however, brings one back to you.
>
> What really has happened? Where is the wisdom in all the data of our modern days, the right perspective in the pluralistic maze that prevails in the early years of the twenty-first century? It has always been you, my God, hasn't it? Now I am remembering rightly. There is you and there is your plan. Behind the sound and fury of world events, somewhere in the shadows of time,

stands the One who created the world and remains Lord over its peoples and events. Even though you, dear God, are anything but a cold, calculating manipulator, you nonetheless are the chief architect of time and eternity. In the final analysis, your providence is more potent than our politics. Your love will outlast our evil wars. Your sovereign will superintends our fragile and often foolish human ways. You graciously grant us freedom, but you also hold us responsible for its use.

O, that your people could comprehend their divine birthrights and the potential always latent in your creating and leading. Let the mountains dance again! May the rivers that still obstruct and the captors who still enslave bow before the design that is deepest in things. And when it happens, may I and all others recognize your hand and gladly join the trail of destiny. You, my God, are still making history, not only by establishing a special people, but by ministering through this people. To see and know and be transformed by this ultimate reality is hope and life itself. What a realization! What a memory! What a responsibility!

Let all things their creator bless,
And worship him in humbleness,
O praise him! Alleluia![42]

Lead on, O King Eternal,
The day of march has come;
Henceforth in fields of conquest
Thy tents shall be our home.[43]

God's history making continues. As it does, it is crucial to be aware that the center of all God's work is the fullness of divine revelation in Jesus Christ. The Christian spiritual life, especially as presented by the Gospel of Matthew, could be called story-shaped. What story? The story of Jesus, of course. Christian discipleship is following the person identified in the story who, raised from the dead, goes on leading the community. There is a sense in which spirituality, according to Matthew, is something to be worked out. Given as foundation for belief are the story of the Messiah and of the kingdom of heaven breaking into the present.[44] Much is to be received, believed, and embodied. All is rooted in the God who comes in Jesus Christ and remains through the ministry of the Holy Spirit.

Hope in Transitional Times

Given the continuing presence, providence, and gracious purposes of God in human affairs, hope remains, whatever the circumstances. At the

God and Authentic Spirituality

An authentic "Christian" spirituality is one that binds us to Christ and leads us through the power of the Holy Spirit to God the Father. It must therefore be both christological and trinitarian. Within that essential framework there are innumerable ways of meeting Christ, and these are often described as "schools" of spirituality or spiritualities (e.g., Wesleyan or Benedictine spirituality).

Robin Maas and Gabriel O'Donnell, eds.,
Spiritual Traditions for the Contemporary Church

opening of the twenty-first century, the circumstances are dramatic and troubling. What has been known as Christendom in the Western world (Christianity as culturally and even politically dominant) has virtually collapsed. This collapse need not be read as all negative, however. Even it rests in the hands of God. Being marginalized as sincere believers in Jesus Christ tends to return the church more to its apostolic beginnings when it was a tiny and often persecuted community.[45] Observes Howard Snyder, "Perhaps Western culture is nearing a point where the Christian faith can be successfully reintroduced. Maybe the collapse of the present order will lead to a new outbreak of revolutionary Christianity."[46]

Today is surprisingly like the England of John Wesley more than two centuries ago. Wesley witnessed his nation going through the throes of transition from the age of agriculture to the age of industry. The twenty-first century is seeing the transition from the age of industry to the age of information. Kipling once said of major transitions in human society that between the dying of the old and the dawning of the new is that awkward time when "one is dead; the other is helpless to be born." Today is an awkward time as we talk of the passing of the modern period and the beginning of a postmodern time. The former is not quite dead; the latter is trying hard to be born.

Wesley saw traditional Christianity being undermined in his day in a way that compromised the credibility of religion in general. But he also saw the providence of God at work. Maybe the very undermining of what had become so traditional as to be largely inauthentic was preparing Christians "for tolerating, and, afterwards, for receiving, real Christianity . . . [by] causing a total disregard for all religion, to pave the way for the revival of the only religion which was worthy of God!"[47] Perhaps enough darkness finally allows whatever real light there is to be seen more clearly. David

McKenna concludes that "under the mandate and motivation of the Holy Spirit, John Wesley saw in the chaos of his time the challenge of spiritual regeneration for individuals and moral transformation for society."[48] The challenge surely remains in today's troubling transition.

Now is the right time to make a bold affirmation. God's Spirit is present and very much at work in our day. The rootlessness and emptiness of modern materialism and the pluralistic confusion on the religious scene have created a vacuum, a dark cynicism, moral chaos, and spiritual hunger. Into this consumer-driven marketplace of competing values and many faiths comes the faithful God. Stephen Seamands has pictured it as a holiness renewal. He turns to Isaiah 6:1–8 and sees a vision of God's people newly open to God's presence and transformed by that presence into a people of power and purity whose integrity is measured by their love.[49] Clark Pinnock rightly says that today we should heed the East's complaint that Western Christianity has confined the Spirit to the margins of the church. So he earnestly prays, "Welcome, Holy Spirit, come and set us free! Let each one catch the living flame and be ravished by your love! Let our souls glow with your fire. Help us overcome our forgetfulness of the Spirit."[50]

So, where should we begin in reconsidering Christian life in the twenty-first century? We should begin with the Spirit of God who is with us now, who is active among us now, and who is our only real resource and hope.[51] The Spirit's presence should be of central concern for every Christian believer. What is the Spirit's intent among us? Church institutions evolve, generations change, and traditions solidify, but holiness should be central. Wesley and the early Methodists were sure that Methodism had been raised up to promote holiness in every sphere of life. Holiness was the hub of the wheel that held all the spokes together. It was the burning focus and driving force of the revival movement.[52] The final end of the Christian spiritual quest is for the believer to be taken up into the transformative circle of love that exists within God. Jesus prayed to the Father, "As you, Father, are in me and I am in you, may they also be in us, so that the world may believe that you have sent me" (John 17:21). The Eastern Christian tradition makes the helpful distinction between the *essence* and the *energies* of God. The essence is the very being of God in sovereign transcendence; the energies are God in action on our behalf. Through the energies, there is a path to the essence. God became one with us in Christ's incarnation so that we might become one with God through new life in the Spirit. That is holiness.

There is no pantheistic danger here (see glossary), that is, no temptation to claim that through spiritual life believers can actually become part of God or the same as God. We do not become one with the essence of God (a fully arrived union with God), but we can be touched and changed into real Christlikeness by God's active energies. These energies are the Spirit

Types of Christian Spirituality: The Categories of H. Richard Niebuhr

World-Affirming . . .

Christ *of* culture
Christ *above* culture
Christ the *transformer* of culture
Christ and culture *in paradox*
Christ *against* culture

. . . World-Denying

of God with us.[53] Real holiness is the goal of Christian spirituality. It is personally transforming and community creating. To be reunited with God is to be united with all who are in Christ.

Relating Faith and Culture

As Holy-Spirit renewal comes, there are several options for how Christians living beyond mere religion might relate to this present world. The options are seen in the differing emphases of the Christian spiritual traditions highlighted in the following chapters. They also are summarized in five Christ-culture categories. H. Richard Niebuhr has described the historic patterns of Christians relating to culture, and Geoffrey Wainwright has used these patterns to understand types of Christian spirituality.[54] These five types are explained and illustrated in various ways in the rest of this book. The first two are the extreme opposites, both being seriously deficient views of Christian spirituality. Each of them, however, holds some worthy value that is championed in the other three mediating types.

Christ of Culture

The Christ-of-culture spirituality views Christians as appreciatively affirming and embracing the prevailing culture. In the early fourth century, there came a dramatic change in the political stance of the Roman Empire that shifted from actively opposing Christians to actually embracing the Christian faith. Persecution ended, and official establishment began with Emperor Constantine. Christianity soon became institutionalized along Roman lines with the blessing of the emperor. Inevitably, there were strong cultural influences on the faith, even an absorption of the faith by the prevailing political and social realities. The danger here is a subtle move to merely external observance of the faith and even an altering of the faith to fit the current value system of the world. Christ becomes defined by the culture, becoming part of it. *Liberalism* may be defined as an alignment of the faith with the world to the degree that the world is shaping the faith more than the faith is shaping the world. For example, the early Christian theologian Origen used Neoplatonic philosophical concepts so extensively that it sometimes is difficult to decide whether he was a Platonic Christian or a Christian Platonist. Many liberal Christians of the nineteenth century overlaid their ideal of an ethical teacher on the Gospels and came up with a Jesus mostly of their own making and in their own image. Some presentations of today's process theology appear so reflective of a current secular philosophy that the result leaves little that is distinctly Christian.

Christ above Culture

The Christ-above-culture spirituality views Christians appreciating and emphasizing the positive elements in human nature and culture, while recognizing that even these need to be purified and lifted by divine grace. Such grace comes not to destroy nature and culture but to perfect them. Leaders like Clement of Alexandria and Thomas Aquinas were academic theologians exhibiting the intellectual and aesthetic character of this spirituality. Clement (c. 155–220) taught that Christ frees humans from bondage to sin and the power of death and the devil. By using philosophy, he believed he would be able to demonstrate to the cultured despisers of Christianity in his time the intellectual and moral superiority of the Christian worldview. Christian spirituality is more than human wisdom, but rational thought can be employed in engaging the world. Clement incorporated the cultural milieu of Hellenism so profoundly that his thought can appear almost as a branch of Greek philosophy. Sin, for instance, is anything that goes against right reason. Even so, he taught that the life of the Christian is dependent on what Christ has done for the Christian. Christ is immersed in and yet ultimately above the culture.

Christ the Transformer of Culture

Transformationist spirituality affirms the positive doctrines of creation and incarnation while insisting on the radical corruption of sin. Only the redeeming grace of God can cleanse the corruption. Coupled with the realism about sin is an optimism about the potential of divine grace. God has come in the incarnation of Jesus and still comes sacramentally in baptism, the Lord's Supper, and the wonderful work of the Holy Spirit (see *sacraments* in the glossary). There is a principle of reciprocity in the Christian saving process. John Wesley was fond of quoting this statement of St. Augustine: "He [God] who made us without ourselves will not save us without ourselves." Wesley taught that "entire sanctification" or "perfect love" is in some real sense attainable in this earthly life, evidencing itself in pure love of God and neighbor. While believers always must press on toward the goal (Phil. 3:14), some genuine realization is being made possible by the work of the Spirit. The church is called to be a realized anticipation of the final reign of God—and it is in the church's life that the vocation of Christian spirituality is to be shaped. John Calvin, more than Martin Luther, looked for the present permeation of all life by the Christian gospel.

Christ and Culture in Paradox

Martin Luther exemplifies a spirituality of conflict and paradox featuring the persistent polarities of law and gospel, the God who reveals and hides, the God of wrath and grace, and the two kingdoms of Christ and the world. All of these are the homes of the Christian, at least for now. Believers have the firstfruits of the Spirit and yet groan inwardly as they await final redemption (Rom. 8:23). The two kingdoms in which Christians live simultaneously are the kingdom of God (God ruling all regenerate believers through Christ and the gospel by personal faith and love) and the human kingdom (God rules all sinful creatures through Caesar and the law by civil justice and order). God is at once Lord of both kingdoms, and Christians are at once subjects of both. Dietrich Bonhoeffer vigorously opposed "cheap grace" and lived in paradox, seeking reconciliation and deciding that killing Hitler would be a Christian ethical act. First Corinthians speaks of the folly of the cross and of being fools for Christ's sake in a troubled world (1:18–31; 4:10). There is struggle, but in Christ believers can be more than conquerors (Rom. 8:37) as they are grateful for the unmerited grace of God and are freed to do good works of service for their neighbors.

Christ against Culture

The reign of Christ and the realities of this present world are sometimes set in sharp contrast, so much so that the true Christian views this world as something to avoid and even escape. First Peter 4:12–5:11 makes clear that Christians will suffer in this world, thus sharing in the sufferings of

Jesus and maybe even experiencing the baptism of blood that would usher persecuted believers into the heavenly feast of the coming better world. In its earliest generations, Christians often faced severe persecution and sometimes violent death. There is a spirituality of martyrdom. The world is hostile to Christians, but another world waits to welcome the faithful. Believers are to stand against the world at whatever cost is necessary. Tertullian rejected participation in political life and strongly rejected the use of Greek philosophy as a tool to expound Christianity, asking, "What indeed has Athens to do with Jerusalem?" More recently, Carl F. H. Henry helped contemporary evangelicalism rise above the severe cultural isolationism typical of fundamentalism in the first half of the twentieth century. Many believers are tempted to think that "worldliness" is *the* great temptation for true believers and that to be spiritual is to be set against all accommodation with the world.

Coming from these various ways of relating the faith to the world, the following is suggested as wisdom. Patterns of Christian spirituality range from substantial world affirmation to severe world denial, from continuity to discontinuity with the created order as it now stands. Christian missionaries have translated the gospel of Christ into a multitude of human languages. Likewise, the Holy Spirit can and does work creatively in a variety of human cultures (Col. 1:27–28; 3:11; Rev. 5:9). For the Bible message to be meaningful today, believers who seek to live out and proclaim a relevant Christian spirituality must (1) understand the cultural settings of the original biblical passages; (2) understand the current cultural setting being addressed; and (3) apply the supracultural biblical message in culturally relevant ways. This assumes that the Bible is not merely the product of given times, places, and people (Christ *of* culture). Somehow it is divine revelation for all times, standing above the human scene even while it obviously participates in it. The Christ-of-culture approach is mere religion, since it reflects the world instead of speaking prophetically to it. When the faith is seen as at least above and in real tension with culture, there is the potential of transformation. Sometimes the faith must stand firmly against elements of culture; but even then it must retain a constructive interaction with culture for the sake of relevant witness.

Conclusions and Beginnings

Much follows when minds and hearts are open to the work of the Spirit. The result might be called maturity in Christ, the fullness of the indwelling Spirit, the people of God becoming the light of Christ to the nations. The many-faceted consequence of the Spirit's work is reviewed in the follow-

The Apostles' Creed

I believe in God, the Father, the almighty,
creator of heaven and earth.

And in Jesus Christ,
his only Son, our Lord,
conceived by the Holy Spirit,
born of the Virgin Mary,

Suffered under Pontius Pilate,
crucified, dead, and buried,

Descended into the realm of death,
on the third day risen from the dead,
ascended into heaven;
he is seated at the right hand of
God, the Father;
from there he will come
to judge the living and the dead.

I believe in the Holy Spirit,
the holy catholic church,
the communion of saints,
forgiveness of sins,
resurrection of the dead,
and eternal life.
Amen![55]

ing pages as a way of illuminating the essential dimensions of Christian spirituality. Each essential dimension is developed biblically, historically, and theologically. The ancient Apostles' Creed is a brief narrative of Christian faith based on apostolic preaching[56] and is held in high regard by both the Roman Catholic and Protestant traditions. It is not an expression of mere religion, a set of religious propositions that are just to be accepted intellectually. The wisdom of the church's whole spiritual history says that this creed represents the dramatic reality that confronts us all in Jesus Christ. We can know this truth only insofar as we know this Christ and are drawing our life from the Spirit of this Christ. As the church restates this pattern of belief and recalls its biblical foundation, it keeps alive the vital experience of the living God known especially in the risen Christ and in the present work of the Spirit.

Recalling biblical and theological foundations must include personal and present participation in the formative realities of the faith. The ancient Hebrews set the pace with a paradigm of patterned memory and praise that Christians are to understand and follow in light of Jesus Christ. Life flows in natural cycles, both seasonal and historical. Jews would pilgrimage to Jerusalem for the annual festivals of Passover, Pentecost, and Tabernacles. Agriculturally speaking, they were commemorations of spring beginnings, the firstfruits, and the autumn's final harvest and end of toil. Historically speaking, they recall the exodus from Egypt, the receiving of the law at

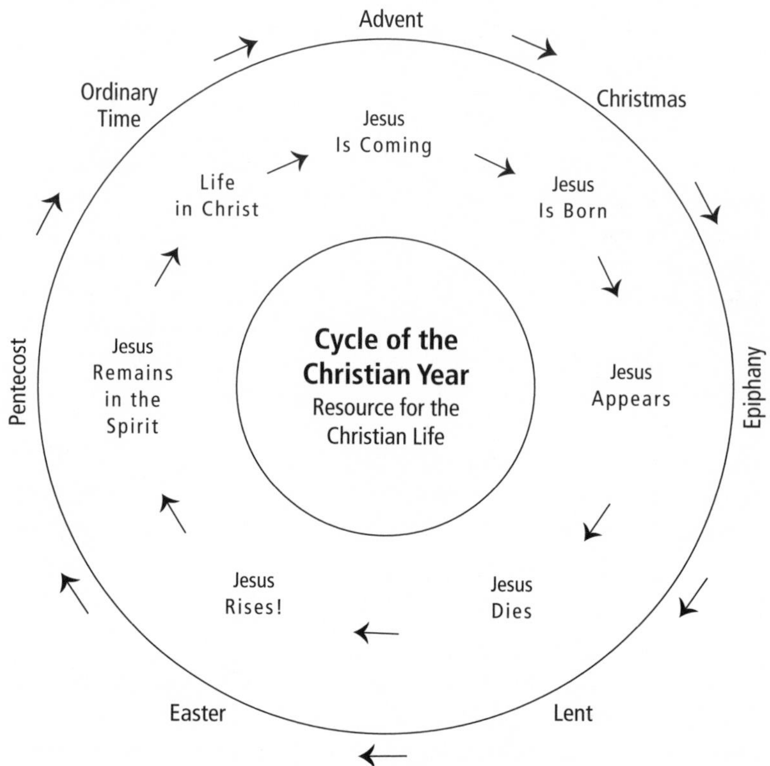

Figure 1.1 The Christian Year

The Christian year is a distinctive way of marking time. It is the Christian's pattern of essential memories that inspire spiritual growth and joy.

Mount Sinai, and the wilderness wandering. Likewise, Christians each year celebrate the Easter spring of redemption victory (the faith's dramatic beginning with an exodus from the grave), the Pentecost provision of the first-fruits of the Spirit (the Spirit's launching, gifting, and governance of the church), and the summer/fall ordinary time of wandering the world in pilgrim faith that culminates in Advent (God comes and the promise finally is fulfilled).

Says Jacob Neusner, "To be a classical Jew is to be intoxicated by faith in God, to live every moment in God's presence, and to shape every hour by the paradigm of Torah." The day with its worship in the morning and evening, the week with its climax at the Sabbath, the season marked by nature's commemoration of Israel's sacred history all "shape life into rhythms of sanctification and thus make all of life an act of worship."[57] For Christians now grafted into this grand Hebrew tradition, there should continue to be the remembering, the seasonal rhythm, the annual celebration of beginning (Easter), presence and provision (Pentecost), and coming fulfillment of hope (Advent, Christmas).

By looking at figure 1.1, readers can see that the Christian year begins and ends with Advent. Christian faith began with God's coming in Jesus Christ and will be consummated when Christ comes again. Framed by these comings is the work of the Spirit and the life and mission of the church—with Pentecost in the middle of it all. The sacred cycle of seasonal rejoicing is that of God's saving so that God might indwell and one day God's glory might fill the whole earth. The Christian year is the cyclic celebration of Advent, Christmas, Epiphany, Lent, Holy Week, Easter, Pentecost, Ordinary Time, and back again to Advent. Why highlight this annual pattern of celebration for Christians on journey with the Spirit? There are four valuable insights into how this pattern encourages believers to best proceed together in the Christian spiritual quest.

1. Being Balanced

The recurrent seasons of the Christian year provide a rounded balance of Christian remembrance, celebration, and guidance. Every year each part of the Christian faith receives its due weight of emphasis. Annually, believers follow the footsteps of our Lord and keep company with fellow Christians who are engaged in the same spiritual pursuit. There is a pattern of biblical reading and spiritual challenge that is symmetrical in proportion and true to the whole faith. The use of a lectionary guarantees a diverse biblical diet for God's people, and it can help protect the congregation from the prejudices and blind spots of pastors and other worship leaders. The Christian message "is not seasonal, but the seasons help to hold to the light the varied facets of its one jewel."[58]

2. Being Catholic

The difference between a denomination and a sect is that the former is concerned about its catholicity while the latter, in its presumed self-sufficiency, does not care whether or not it is catholic. A practical point at which church leaders can start practicing catholic Christianity is the church calendar. The calendar is thoroughly catholic in the sense that it arranges for the proclamation and observance of the whole biblical message in yearly sequence, as the church in many ages, lands, and branches has best learned to ensure that nothing essential to the Christian witness is overlooked. The calendar is something all Christians can follow together, gaining fellowship with one another in a common catholic practice without losing any special denominational values. A good lectionary guides a reader of the Bible through an ordered sequence of key passages whose cumulative force is broadly representative of the total biblical message. To pursue such a plan together as believers is to nurture the oneness of Christ's people.

3. Being Community

Richard Adams's novel *Watership Down*, on the surface an adventure story about rabbits, is really about the conditions necessary for viable community, namely, the ability to sustain the narrative that defines a group's life. *Watership Down* begins with an exodus, a hazardous journey in search of a new home. The rabbits move out as a group, but each individual has his or her own reasons for leaving. They become a people, a community, as together they acquire a story. They then remain a community so long as they retell and live out their story. So it is with Christian believers. To be a community of faith requires a shaping story commonly held. For Christians, it is the biblical story of who God is and who we are supposed to be in light of God's redeeming work in Jesus Christ. People live out of this divine story when they have a common memory and vision, common rituals or symbolic actions expressive of the community's memory and vision, and a common life together that manifests the community's memory and vision. The most important and fundamental task as Christians is to learn God's story and become part of it. The cycle of the church year, with its representation of God's story in interaction with our human story, effectively orders the lives of believers within a Christian faith community.[59]

4. Being Charismatic

The word *charismatic* has negative connotations for many Christians, but the fact remains that the Christian life is a life in and by the Spirit of God. It is the Spirit who keeps believers balanced, catholic, and in the true church, the community of the Spirit. Many Christians have called for spiritual renewal over the centuries. When Wesleyans and Pentecostals, for instance, speak of restoration in church life, they usually do not mean restoring some outward characteristic of the early church. They mean a contemporary renewal of apostolic purity, power, and expectancy.[60]

For much too long the subject of holiness has been hushed even in holiness denominations because being perfect got embarrassingly lost in a sea of legalisms or overwhelmed in distracting preoccupations with institution building, church planting, and becoming respectable in the eyes of mainstream evangelicalism. But such silence must be stopped because the subject of holiness is the central theme of the entire biblical revelation.[61] Perversions and substitutes are common, but none justify avoiding serious engagement with a subject of such importance. I commend *Weavings: A Journal of the Christian Spiritual Life* for dedicating its 1999 issues to uncovering contemporary images of Paul's ancient phrase "holiness of spirit" (2 Cor. 6:6). Recalling the 1790 sermon by John Wesley titled "The Wedding Garment" and seeing the great spiritual need as the twenty-first century starts to unfold, David McKenna is surely right—it is a wonderful time to be a Wesleyan![62]

More important than championing any given stream of the Christian tradition is a renewal of the call to be authentically Christian. Once the spiritual foundations are securely in place, believers today are invited on a journey of transformation. Along the way will be a series of realities about the person and work of God's Spirit. Each of these is interpreted by the rich tradition of God's people, including the guidance of pivotal Bible words, particular streams of Christian experience and wisdom, emphases that constitute the Christian year, and teachings that form the substance of the ancient Apostles' Creed. While wisdom collected in many places will be discussed in the chapters to follow, the basic truth is that the Spirit of God is the only source of true life.

The last written words of the great reformer Martin Luther were found scrawled on a piece of paper lying by his deathbed. They concluded with this: "We are beggars. That is true." His reference was to the stance of humans before God. We can achieve no merits that establish a favorable standing before God. We are beggars—needy, guilty, vulnerable—totally lacking resources to save ourselves. But Luther knew some good news. God in Jesus Christ, by an amazing divine choice, had become a beggar too. Like the Good Samaritan who exposed himself to dangers in order to save an abused man in the ditch, God has come to where we are so that we may truly be with him. Such graciousness is overwhelming. So, as we now consider God's presence and extravagant love, we humbly pray as human beggars before a loving and saving God:

Come, Holy Spirit of God!
Come: As fire and set our hearts ablaze with love.
Come: As silence to sharpen our readiness to hear the Word of God.
Come: As light and illumine our searching minds.
Come: As wind and move us toward each other and toward our neighbors.

Come, Holy Spirit of God!
Come: To consume all sin that may exist among us.

Come: To convert us to the will and way of Christ.
Come: To gift us with yourself and whatever gifts of service we need.
Come: To consecrate us to the mission of God's church in this needy world.

Questions to Pursue

1. If not all spirituality is Christian, what theological foundations are necessary for it to be truly Christian?
2. What do you understand as the meaning of the "openness" of God?
3. Are you really open to moving beyond your own limited experience in the heritage of the Christian faith and sampling the riches available from other streams of Christian spiritual wisdom?
4. What is meant by a "living orthodoxy"?
5. Recall the five types of Christian spirituality (Niebuhr's categories of Christ-culture relationships). Which describes you best at present? Are you satisfied to stay where you are?

2

Truly Summoned: The Spirit's Presence

> The Spirit sets this life in the presence of the living God and in the great river of eternal love.[1]

> O my God, since Thou are with me, and I must now, in obedience to Thy commands, apply my mind to these outward things, I beseech Thee to grant me the grace to continue in Thy Presence; and to this end do Thou prosper me with Thy assistance, receive all my works, and possess all my affections.
>
> Brother Lawrence

Chapter 1 addressed the first key question: Is God both truly sovereign and reaching out in love to lost humanity? We said yes and thus identified the foundation for authentic Christian spirituality. The second key question follows: Is God really present and readily available in the midst of our actual living? How is this divine presence known and nurtured? Believers occasionally experience God as seemingly absent. Sometimes awareness of God's presence comes suddenly and at first is unrecognized.

God's presence was experienced the breezy night of February 9, 1709, at the Epworth rectory in England. The big Wesley family was asleep, including five-year-old John and eighteen-month-old Charles. Suddenly, all was consumed in flames. People ran into the night cold. By God's grace, the family survived. Charles, later to become a great Christian hymn writer, frequently would employ the metaphors of wind and fire in his lyrics, though he did not consciously remember this awful night from his childhood. John did remember. When all the desperate family members were outside except for John, who thought at first the bright light was just the morning sun, cries from upstairs made it clear that the little boy was in grave danger. His father, Samuel, tried to get to him, but the burning stairs collapsed under his weight. Samuel knelt down and commended John's soul to God, thinking he was lost. But the boy was spotted in his bedroom window on top of a piece of furniture. A ladder was fetched, one man stood on the shoulders of another, and they rescued John just before the flaming ceiling of his room crashed inward. Samuel cried out in relief, "Come, neighbours, let us kneel down: let us give thanks to God! He has given me all my eight children: let the house go, I am rich enough." John grew up with an unshakable feeling that the fire had shown the providence of God, who perhaps had a special plan for his life. God did! The saving divine presence had a great divine purpose.

Often, however, keen awareness of the divine presence is largely lacking. Many Hebrew and Christian prophets have challenged the communities of faith they knew, scolding them for being stale pools of mere religion. Some communities speak routinely about God and yet rarely encounter the divine. One prophetic voice was Søren Kierkegaard (1813–1855), who was bluntly clear about why the Danish clergy of his day should be shunned. They lived "by presenting the sufferings of others, and that is regarded as religion, uncommonly deep religion even, for the religion of the congregation is nothing but hearing this presented." This shallow religion, he said, was "just about as genuine as tea made from a bit of paper which once lay in a drawer beside another bit of paper which had once been used to wrap up a few dried tea leaves from which tea had already been made three times."[2] Beyond such distance and secondhand dryness, such unsatisfying mere religion, how can believers who are spiritually hungry and thirsty find satisfaction? The answer lies in sensing the graciousness of the divine presence. People are much like the two blind men sitting by the roadside in Jericho as Jesus came by. They shouted to the Lord for mercy: "Lord, let our eyes be opened" (Matt. 20:33). We easily sympathize with Jacob when he awakened from sleep and declared, "Surely the Lord is in this place—and I did not know it!" (Gen. 28:16).

Most of the time, we are blind to God's presence and gracious working. Let us pray for spiritual eyes that can really see. Given the two quotations that open this chapter, it appears that being aware of God's presence requires both divine grace and human attention. The Spirit sets us in the river of God's eternal presence and love, but our awareness of this may require "sinking" and seeking God among the suffering, erring, and the downtrodden. Sight is especially impeded by pride.

Sensing the Divine Presence

God has been called "uncanny," since the God who appears in Jesus Christ is surprising, captivating, alluring, but not always predictable and never controllable. Whatever we can think or say about God falls short of who God actually is. Indeed, the best and only proper response to the divine is the silence of awe, reverence, gratitude, and hope.[3] Howard Thurman said, "What we most want to know about God is whether He is present in the commonplace experiences of ordinary living, available to ordinary people under the most garden variety of circumstances."[4]

Is this awesome God available to mundane me? Anthony Bloom, a Russian Orthodox priest, once described God as "extremely sensitive, vulnerable, and shy."[5] Shy? The Bible speaks of God as all-powerful and everywhere present. It also suggests that, in love, which is the divine essence, God's power is intentionally present in particular ways, ways that often are gentle, risking, nonmanipulative, and not obvious except to eyes of faith. The Bible frequently depicts God as approaching humans indirectly—concealed in a burning bush, whispering in a still small voice, appearing as a baby in Bethlehem and an ordinary carpenter in Nazareth. Job's anguished search for God represents a common human experience: "If I go forward, he is not there; or backward, I cannot perceive him; on the left he hides, and I cannot behold him; I turn to the right, but I cannot see him" (Job 23:8–9).

It is relatively easy to be confident of God's presence when the experiences of life are good. We find God nearby as we find many good reasons to sing, "Praise God from whom all blessings flow." But there is this sober verse: "Moses drew near to the thick darkness where God was" (Exod. 20:21). Harry Emerson Fosdick reported the following in 1955 when the fearsome atomic age had dawned. One Englishman had seen too much of life and admitted this: "I don't know what I believe, but I don't believe all this God-is-love stuff. I have been in two world wars. I have been unemployed eighteen months on end. I have seen the Mrs. die of cancer. Now I am waiting for the atom bombs to fall. All that stuff about Jesus is no help."[6] For this man, if God really exists, he is well hidden in a thick darkness. His song was more like, "Please, God, why do not at least some blessings flow?"

Locating God is difficult in the midst of human tragedy, although Helen Keller said this about her deafness and blindness: "I thank God for my handicaps for through them I have found myself, my work, and my God." It was in Gethsemane that Jesus said, "Not my will but yours be done" (Luke 22:42). Martin Luther wrote "A Mighty Fortress Is Our God" when his life was in grave danger. It was on the scaffold that Sir Thomas More said, "I

Bless Me, Lord!

"Jabez called on the God of Israel, saying, 'Oh that you would bless me and enlarge my border, and that your hand might be with me, and that you would keep me from hurt and harm!' And God granted what he asked" (1 Chron. 4:10–11). Paul instructed the Christians at Ephesus to make it a priority to be "filled with all the fullness of God" (Eph. 3:19), a filling that would bless and strengthen them "with power through his Spirit" (Eph. 3:16). Regarding the Jabez prayer, Bruce Wilkinson observes: "When we seek God's blessing as the ultimate value in life, we are throwing ourselves entirely into the river of His will and power and purposes for us. All our other needs become secondary to what we really want—which is to become wholly immersed in what God is trying to do in us, through us, and around us for His glory."

Bruce Wilkinson, *The Prayer of Jabez*

die, the king's good servant, but God's first." It takes time, experience, and maturity in Christ to be able to testify like Fosdick: "My deepest faith in God springs not so much from my Galilees, where God clothed the lilies. . . , but from times when the rain descended and the floods came and the winds blew and beat, and God *was there* so that the house fell not."[7]

To pray sometimes means to wait expectantly and invitingly for the God who surely will come. And God does come, thrust onward by divine love in spite of a complete lack of our merit or worth (Rom. 5:20–21; Eph. 2:1–5). God arrives in the everyday of our lives, often coming quietly, gently, largely unseen and unheard.

Our world is full of voices clamoring for attention in ways that are not shy at all. Some loud voices are angry or ridiculous; many are trying to wield power and sell products for their own selfish ends. Can you identify with this desperate prayer composed in the midst of the Vietnam War when the United States had put men on the moon while many of its cities were in violent social turmoil?

> Lord, I see satellites flying like kites so close to earth they seem anchored to the string fingers of March children. They hover above my head like fallen saints trying mightily for heaven. Man is in orbit, Lord; man is in orbit around the earth searching for God among the flying debris of civilization thrown-up. Come close, Lord, for we are getting our kicks by shooting rats on the man-made garbage dumps of the world. Come close, Lord, and see how mer-

ciful we are, how clean the shots, how deadly. Come close, Lord; we recite our prayers between crucifixions. Amen.[8]

God does come close and cries with us over wayward human wills and social tragedies (Luke 19:41–44). The still-coming God is the one who was with Jesus on the cross, although the presence seemed like absence (Matt. 27:46). God went with Jesus into the valley of death with this result for us: "His darkening passage into death illumines with the intensity of a lightning bolt God's pledge to be unconditionally present for us. In that molten moment, the cross of God's most unbearable absence is also the cradle of God's most intense presence, the birthplace of a new creation."[9]

Where can God's presence and peace be found? The beloved Quaker Thomas Kelly (1893–1941) wrote in his classic *A Testament of Devotion* (1941) that each person can know a "light within." By focusing on this light (practicing the presence of God), faithful Christian believers can be wonderfully guided into both detachment from and reattachment to the world. The fruit of such obedient awareness will be humility, holiness, suffering, and simplicity. Kelly found the urban life of his day too frantic and hectic, leaving people weary and unfulfilled. How contemporary! The solution is not to flee the world, he concluded, but to slip into the center where God is—and thus contact amazing peace, power, serenity, integration, confidence, and "simplified multiplicity."

Fundamental to Christian life is the belief that the divine voice appears, informs, invites, disturbs, quiets, and potentially transforms. This belief is rooted in the Hebrew Scriptures. A key verse is Deuteronomy 6:4, referred to as *Shema*, literally meaning "hear!" and based on the verbal imperative at the beginning of the verse. Knowing God starts with listening and responding to the God who has graciously chosen to come close and speak. God is wholly above and beyond us; God also chooses to be truly open to us, truly close, and constantly calling us to the possibility of our mystical union with the divine. When we sing "Draw me nearer, nearer blessed Lord," we should not be thinking of the nearness of place, but of the intensity of relationship. We sing and pray for greater degrees of our awareness of what already is, for a more perfect consciousness of the divine presence. There is no need to shout over some big expanse of space to a distant God. He already is nearer than our most secret thoughts. The need is for us to choose greater nearness to God, a need that can be met because God graciously takes the initiative.

We are being summoned! The Spirit of God is truly present with us, even though we are so undeserving. God's summoning can be heard clearly in a faithful reading of the Bible. There is a deep and pivotal paradox in regard to inspired Scripture. The human words of the Bible, written in particular places at particular times by particular persons, somehow reveal to us the awe-full mystery of God in Christ. The divine Word comes through human words. The Scriptures are like Christ. They are incarnate in time and place, yet transcendent, spiritual, and beyond the merely human. There is a textual revealing of the divine mystery, words from God embedded in human words, a divine voice coming through human voices and communicating messages of forgiveness and life. We humans are being addressed from beyond ourselves. May we seek God like Solomon did and come to have a listening heart and an "understanding mind" (1 Kings 3:9).

We read in 2 Timothy 3:16 that all Scripture is God-breathed. Note that Paul was not wrestling with the questions about biblical infallibility, inerrancy, and technical accuracy on all subjects addressed, religious or otherwise. He was an ancient Hebrew, not a modern scientist and literary critic. He meant simply that the Spirit of God resides behind and within the sacred text as its life and power in a way that gives the text the potential of spawning life. God's breath originally brought humankind into being (Gen. 2:7). Now the same divine breath hovers over this sacred text to offer new life. Therefore, read the Bible humbly and openly, listening for God's voice and the movement of the Spirit. "God-breathed" is more a spiritual than a technical or mechanical claim about the biblical text itself. We are not being called to argue about details, but to adore the graciously present God who resides in and through the text in order that we might be changed.

If believers wish to sense the divine presence, to read the biblical text rightly, and to have listening hearts and understanding minds, it is essential that they join the church at worship on a regular basis. Worship is a rehearsal of God's saving actions in history. It is active participation in the Christian story that shapes the meaning of history, forms authentic spirituality, and motivates for God's redeeming mission. In worship, believers are assisted to recall, remember, proclaim, and enact God's mighty deeds. Today's postmodern world is turning away from rational rigidities and is newly open to the mysterious spiritual nature of reality. People are willing to consider modes of communication that are more symbolic than verbal, and they are prepared to value worship that calls for significant participation and not merely the witnessing of religious performance—mere religion. Christian worship is to be the informed participation of believers in the ancient and still alive good news about God. We are not to be passive witnesses to programs of religious hype and entertainment. Worship is to be Scripture-laden and not market-driven.

Christians who wish the benefits of being spiritual must get beyond the hectic life, beyond only playing religion, and really sense God's presence. Seekers need the confidence that they actually are in conversation with their heavenly Father, that they are being heard, that God really exists and is close at hand. A contemporary classic of Christian spirituality is *Centering Prayer* by the Trappist monk M. Basil Pennington. He describes centering prayer as the process of putting aside all thoughts and images so the senses and mind are stilled in favor of being one with God in the center of one's existence. The intent is to be present to God as God wishes to be present to us. The 1692 classic *The Practice of the Presence of God* by Brother Lawrence views prayer as a continual sense of the divine presence. This simple lay brother counted on God to give him whatever he needed as he lived in the present—and in the presence. We are not to *have* a spirituality but to *be* spiritual as a state of mind and a habit of life. This constancy of intentional life in the Spirit is a major New Testament theme (Rom. 12:12; Eph. 6:17–18; Phil. 4:6; 1 Thess. 5:17; Heb. 13:15).

Why is this so? Because God closely ties together *revelation* and *residence*. God has expressed a passion to be with his chosen people. Only two chapters in Genesis are devoted to the divine creation of all things, but it takes thirteen chapters in Exodus to detail the proper construction of the house in which God's special presence would be. This was to be a place of constant divine-human meeting. God brought the people to himself so that he could give himself to the people. He had carried them to himself on the wings of eagles (Exod. 19:4). Now his people are to join this relating process by dwelling in God's house all their lives (Ps. 27:4). When times of crisis came, God's message to the people was the same as to Moses when he asked who he should say had sent him to Egypt to bring out the Hebrew slaves. The message was: What is God's name? God's answer was a relational marvel that lies at the base of all Christian spirituality: God is "I AM" (Exod. 3:14). In other words, "I will be present with you and there for you." Therefore, disciples of Jesus will not learn this through a discipleship correspondence course with certificates awarded when they get all the required information. They are rather to be with Jesus, residing with his Spirit, engaging in revealing relationship so they might be changed into Christ's likeness. What is the right response to the presence of the high and holy God? Get as low as possible because God discloses himself to the humble.

According to Psalm 46, "God is our refuge and strength, a very present help in trouble. . . . The LORD of hosts is with us. . . . 'Be still, and know that I am God!'" (vv. 1, 7, 10). When one is still and comes to really know, what happens? A heightened awareness of the Spirit's presence occurs and helps believers recognize that "because the Holy Spirit brings the life of the kingdom of God into the present, passivity and cultural pessimism are minimized as people are empowered for ministry."[10] To know that God is truly present is to awaken and become empowered, meaningfully active, and full of hope. To realize God's presence involves intentionality in prayer. Saint Francis seemed "not so much a man praying as prayer itself made man." Frank Laubach reported gratefully, "Oh, this thing of keeping in constant touch with God . . . is the most amazing thing I ever ran across."[11]

God comes in Jesus! The announcement of this glorious coming was first made to shepherds busy about their mundane work. They heard, they came, they saw, and they believed. We all are hoping to hear and need to see and believe. Howard Thurman said wisely that there "must be always remaining in every man's life some place for the singing of angels, some place . . . [that] glows in one bright white light of penetrating beauty and meaning." Despite all the crassness and harsh discords, "life is saved by the singing of angels."[12] When God speaks, the chords of creation sound and divine music is heard. One contemporary book on Christian preaching is titled *Sharing Heaven's Music.*[13] To hear the rhythms of heaven should cause a grateful and enthusiastic hearer to share the good news in a world full of discord.

Christian believers should feel the vital vibrations from their Hebrew roots and react accordingly. In their religious thinking and language, the Hebrews leaned toward the concrete instead of the abstract. Rather than being inclined to doctrinal formulation, they viewed true godliness as tied primarily to a proper set of relationships. "Shalom" is life in balance, whole, at peace. Israel was privileged by divine grace to be the people of God (2 Sam. 7:24; Jer. 31:33; Heb. 8:8–12). The Torah tells Israel how to relate to both Creator and creation. Theology in the New Testament is also relational or existential, always more than propositional or creedal. It is ethical rather than ceremonial. To respond to the calling God is to repent, re-relate, love, and serve. As John says, we realize we have come to know God when we willingly obey the divine commands. Living in Jesus Christ necessarily means walking with him and loving like him (1 John 1).

What, then, is a real Christian? According to John Wesley, being a real Christian means responding to the prior overtures of God that enable one "to love the Lord our God with all our heart, and to serve him with all our strength; to love our neighbour as ourselves, and therefore do every man as we would he should do us."[14] Being an authentic Christian means hearing God's call, realizing God's presence, and responding to God's reaching love by loving others as we have been loved. Because God really is present with us, we can be changed into the divine likeness. As A. W. Tozer says in his 1948 classic *The Pursuit of God,* God's presence is our natural habitat. Church leaders must help people experience the divine presence. Rather than the object of a creed or the subject of a philosophical argument, God wishes to be a present and personal reality.

The Wonderful Bible Word

A wonderful biblical word opens to human understanding the amazing choice of God to be lovingly and redeemingly present with a lost creation.

The word is *paraklētos*. The divine calling of a person, *klētos*, is richly intensified when the one who calls also comes alongside and is with, *para*, and obviously for the one called to a new life and joyous destiny. From the New Testament comes the word that all sinners are truly summoned by God. Lost humanity has a divine presence by its side, a loving presence that is prepared to advocate for the well-being of the guilty and lost. *Paraklētos* is a prominent word in the Johannine writings. In the fourth Gospel, it is virtually a title for the Holy Spirit (John 14:16, 26; 15:26; 16:7). In 1 John this word is used of Jesus, who now pleads our cause with the Father (2:1). Here is a word rich in meaning for the believer who wants to know what God is doing and is prepared to do. God's presence is full of stabilizing, clarifying, and empowering potential. God comes, calls, and comforts. Will we hear, respond, and be transformed?

We Are Not Alone

The Holy Spirit is the fulfillment of the promise, "And remember, I am with you always, to the end of the age" (Matt. 28:20). The Greek word *paraklētos* characteristically referred to a legal setting where the accused had a special friend, an advocate who had come to stand in the place of the guilty one and plead his cause. In 1 John 2:1 we learn that Jesus is the prisoner's friend. He chooses to counsel for the defense, to come to the repentant sinner's aid by making intercession. God is a very present help in time of need (Ps. 46:1; Rom. 8:39) and is attentive to those who call upon his name (Matt. 18:19; Acts 17:27). The technical word for God's amazing availability is *omnipresence:* God is everywhere at once (Jer. 23:24). Explains one theologian, "No atomic particle is so small that God is not fully present to it, and no galaxy so vast that God does not circumscribe it. . . . Only God is able to *be* without being in some specific location to the exclusion of all others."[15] Wherever we are, we are not alone.

John Calvin once said, "As long as Christ remains outside us, and we are separated from him, all that he has done and suffered for the salvation of the human race remains useless and of no value to us."[16] John Wesley developed a theology that focuses on the transforming consummation of creation in and through the Holy Spirit. The God who is sovereignly *over* and actively *for* us (the creating God the Father and the redeeming God the Son) is truly available to be *in* and *through* us (the immediately present and ministering God the Spirit). The biblical story of God-with-us moves from the event of the risen Christ to the ongoing reality of the ever-present Spirit of the Christ.

The events of that first Christian Pentecost are a central part of the drama of the incarnation. The whole story of Jesus is the historic baseline, the fulfillment of God's promises through the prophets (Heb. 1:1–2). But the fullness of the good news about the coming of Christ is that the incarnational work of God extends from the first-century Jesus to this very moment. The announcement that now brings great joy is a continuing narrative of what God did and is doing. The full gospel is the news that in Christ the "power of God for salvation" (Rom. 1:16) can become present reality for all who receive. The relevance of the historic gospel is that it can be accepted and activated now. The ministering presence of God's Spirit makes this possible. As a sheer act of God's grace, we are not alone.

We Are Called

Paraklētos literally means "one who is called in to be alongside." The purpose of the calling is to summon the called one to a special service as a helper. The prime biblical example of God's calling is Abraham, who was called by God to journey to an unknown place (Gen. 12:1–4). He was in no position to know the stunning role that he would play in God's salvation plan for lost humanity. He went because of the profoundly spiritual experience of having been called to go. By faith he went (Heb. 11:8). Destiny depends on a faithful response to God's call.

Genesis features four key descriptions of the calling that comes to humans from God. Knowing these features of the divine address and invitation is to know much about God's will and ways in our world.[17] God's call is (1) *sovereign,* bringing worlds, including Adam and Eve, into being. Such creative calling once did and yet should bring forth a doxology of human praise (Rev. 11:15–19). God's later call to a new future beyond human fallenness must be (2) *embraced* as a call of promise. The One who first called creation into being now calls into existence a special community of obedience. Through Israel and the church, God wishes to work for the redemption of a lost world. Obedience in the midst of a fallen world, however, inevitably brings (3) *conflict* to the right hearing and faithful doing of God's call. As the journey of faith encounters the activity of darkness, the web of resisting evil weaves its sinister way into even the elect community. Finally, God's call, although sure, remains (4) *hidden,* not fully clear or ever controllable, just as once it quietly worked through the surprising turns in Joseph's life (Gen. 37–50).

God's ways are as sure as they often are inscrutable (Isa. 55:8–9). God will accomplish the divine purpose through faithful persons or in spite of them. In all the dramatic events and lives reported in Genesis, God's marvelous and mysterious ways can be seen. The four features of the divine calling continue, beckoning us with loving grace and inviting our faithful response. God's call is sovereign, embraced, conflicted, and hidden. The promise is clear and the possibility assured. The question concerns the nature of human response to the gracious calling of God.

Ironic indeed and almost shocking is the fact that God came, called, and was refused. Seen within the context of ancient Near Eastern hospitality, such rejection is beyond imagination. Israel once had been aliens in Egypt and thus was repeatedly called to extend hospitality to strangers (Deut. 10:19). The idea of an earthly sovereign entering his own kingdom and being refused even minimal hospitality was unthinkable. What about the arrival of the very source of life, the sovereign of sovereigns? God in Jesus Christ came to the lost creation in an unexpected way and was not even recognized by many of the divinely elect people. Blame is not the right agenda now. In our own ways, we all were there and participated in that awful crucifixion.[18] The wonderful opportunity is to recognize that, in the redeeming action of God, the excluded became included despite their inattention and blindness. Those at fault can be those who find forgiveness and resurrection life. In reality, the coming God is the great host who invites to the divine banquet both the privileged and the destitute (Luke 14:16–24). The wonder of the divine calling goes on.

We Are Comforted

When God stands alongside and calls, something special can happen. The person who embraces the divine presence and yields to the tender divine calling becomes fortified for courageous living. Jürgen Moltmann says, "By experience of the Spirit I mean an awareness of God in, with, and beneath the experience of life, which gives us assurance of God's fellowship, friendship, and love."[19] The *paraklētos* of John's Gospel, according to many English translations, is our "comforter." This rendering of the word is often thought to mean that the Holy Spirit sympathizes with and consoles the believer in times of trouble. The Septuagint translation uses this Bible word in its rendering of Psalm 71:21–22 ("You will increase my honor, and comfort me once again. I will also praise you with the harp for your faithfulness, O my God") and in Isaiah 40:1–2 ("Comfort, O comfort my people, says your God. Speak tenderly to Jerusalem, and cry to her that she has served her term, that her penalty is paid").

The Spirit certainly is tender and sustaining, speaking gently and being faithful, but there is more to being comforted than receiving sympathy. Long ago John Wycliffe translated *paraklētos* as comforter, but he also worded Ephesians 6:10, "Be ye comforted in the Lord." Here the word in question is *endynamoun*, from which English derives the word *dynamite*. The primary meaning is "strength, power, enabling, bravery." So, one who is filled with the Spirit's presence is comforted by the grace of God's power that fortifies the believer with the ability to cope triumphantly with whatever life brings. With God by one's side and filling one's heart, the breaking point of any crisis can be passed without breaking.

Note that this Bible word was used in classic Greek to exhort troops who were about to go into battle. Aeschylus (*Persae* 380) says of the ships as they sailed into battle, "The long galleys cheered [*parakalein*] each other, line by line." To be comforted by God is to be encouraged for the task, to be rallied from all hesitancy and fear, to be fortified with a hope that sends one forward into the mission of God. To be summoned by God is to have the very presence, power, and rallying encouragement of the risen Christ. It also is to be surrounded and cheered on by a great cloud of witnesses (Heb. 12:1) who help those still in the heat of battle to lay all the negative aside so they can fight the battle and run the race with perseverance. As we fight and run, with the church of all ages supportingly by our side, we also know who else has come to be with us and to whom we should always be looking for strength and assurance. It is none other than the Spirit of the Christ, the very Christ who now "has taken his seat at the right hand of the throne of God" and who is "the pioneer and perfecter of our faith" (Heb. 12:2).

The Rich Christian Tradition

The Christian past is a rich treasury of spiritual tradition. Since not all its lessons are positive, constant caution is in order. Christians who think of themselves as Protestants typically have protested when established forms of the faith have relied excessively on the traditions of the church. They choose to be perpetual reformers who resist any premature solidifying and institutionalizing of the beliefs and practices of the faith. They tend to see such tradition not as accumulated wisdom from the long experience of the church's life but as mostly a thick overlay of human sediment that burdens and suffocates the real life and revelation of God. Is it not true that Jesus had to resist the traditions of the elders so the revealed wisdom of God could be known?

Much has gone on in the name of Jesus that has not been Christlike in nature. Apostasy from biblical truth has a long and sad history. Christians repeatedly have taught opposite viewpoints on the same subjects. The order of every day should be vigilance lest the authentic be buried in layers of the merely human. We hope for more than mere religion, even more than mere Christian religion. Nonetheless, Christian faith necessarily involves a community of memory and rightly believes that God always has been at work in the church. The church is newly formed in each generation by remembering what God has done in the past and how the faithful have understood and lived out of the formative influence of these memories of God's revelation in Word and Spirit. To forget is to cease to exist.

When we hear nostalgia about the "old-time religion," we need to ask with care which "old" is best. Robert Webber has argued well that the best for the church's future lies in its common era of the past, the classical period A.D. 100–600 when the Bible and the great creeds of the church were formalized. The early church was in such close historical, geographical, linguistic, and conceptual proximity to the New Testament era and to its parent faith tradition, Judaism, that it captured for all time the enduring essence of the faith.[20] The journey into the church's intended future necessarily involves an appreciative journey back into the church's ancient tradition. The spirituality of the ancient church was closely related to the perceived conflict between God and the powers of evil. Christian spirituality was located in Christ, who defeated the powers of evil by his death and resurrection. New believers were baptized into Christ's death and united to him in his resurrection. To be spiritual was and still should be to live in the Christ-pattern of death and resurrection as empowered by the presence and fruit of the Spirit of Christ.

The great tradition of the Christian faith did not cease with the year 600, however. The quest to interpret the faith and apply it properly to ever-changing circumstances has never ceased. Richard Foster has identified six rich streams of Christian spiritual tradition, each different in emphasis and all exhibiting essential aspects of Christian life and faith as it ought to be.[21] These streams are intended to flow together into the richness and wholeness of the river of God (the "Mississippi of the Spirit"). Christians individually and denominations corporately often are seriously out of balance, stressing one of the streams primarily or even exclusively. Apart from the witness of the others, any believer or body of believers is stunted in spiritual growth and mission because avoidance of the other streams shuts out important voices that belong to the church's past and are crucial for its future. Each tradition is susceptible to perversions. Nonetheless, each is a treasure of biblical truth that must not be lost by any believer who hopes to be the disciple of Christ's intention.

Growth in the life of faith is more likely when deliberate attention is given to spiritual traditions not previously considered, not natural to one's personality type, or not often appreciated by one's denominational environment. Believers are called to swim the wide river of God's Spirit, maturing into the fullness of life in Christ as lived in the context of the whole body of Christ (the church "catholic"). To encourage such maturation, the pages that follow explore the entire range of the Christian spiritual traditions. Openness to the speaking of the Spirit is required if benefit is to be received.

The remainder of this chapter gives attention to the opening season of the Christian year, the first of the six spiritual traditions (the Evangelical), and our first sampling of the related theological instruction from the Apostles' Creed. All of these contribute significantly to understanding the Spirit's presence.

The Church Year: Advent, Christmas, Epiphany

The Christian year begins with a "cycle of light" that includes Advent, Christmas, and Epiphany (see the graphic in chapter 1). These closely related seasons all involve the coming of Jesus Christ and the illumination that proceeds from the presence of Christ, who is the light of the world. The Advent season begins with the Sunday nearest to November 30 and launches the drama in which the mighty acts of God pass in annual review for observant Christian believers. This is the season when we who hope and believe approach a vast spiritual frontier, something new, something wonderful and yearned for, something long in coming, something known to be well beyond human capacity to bring about. The primary question of the season is not, How can a virgin bear a child? The virginal conception of Jesus in Mary's womb points to the larger mystery. What happened in Bethlehem lies outside the bounds of previous human experience and defies any of the usual explanations that arise on a merely human level.

What has happened? The Creator has come as creature! The One who is life itself submits to fleshly birth and death so that sinful humans can experience rebirth and eternal life. This is the larger and wonderful mystery, the truly amazing Advent expectation. Advent provides the time to consider life anew in light of a gift that God is about to give. The Hebrew hope had long been for peace, justice, and well-being—*shalom*. Advent begins with a vision of this hope's fulfillment. The New Testament declaration is that prophecies are being fulfilled and the new age of God is being inaugurated in the coming of the Christ child. It is the Isaiah gospel come true as a fragile baby. "Here is your God!" proclaimed Isaiah to waiting exiles (40:9). On the one hand, this amazing event is full of power and might (40:10). On the other hand, "He will feed his flock like a shepherd; he will gather the lambs in his arms, and carry them in his bosom" (40:11). The awesome Creator and the gentle shepherd, the paternal and the maternal, the coming king and the baby born into poverty and great danger—"Here is your God" who has come!

Advent is the time annually when believers are reminded that God comes! The most important truth of the divine coming is that, in the appearance of Jesus Christ, God comes to do for us what we could never do for ourselves—and God will come again to vindicate the faithful and become all in all. History is headed somewhere. It finally will be God's somewhere. Jesus Christ was and always will be the focus of this somewhere. The Gospel readings of Advent begin with a mature Jesus teaching about the reign of God and close with the unborn Jesus still in Mary's womb. The sacred story, to be understood properly, has to be read backward: "Just as the birth and ministry of Jesus are incomprehensible until we know of the Lord's death and resurrection, so too the whole of the past is muddled unless first we have a grasp on the nature of the future."[22] After the resurrection of Jesus, his true identity and the full meaning of his birth finally dawned on the amazed disciples. Then they knew the future was also in his hands.

Advent is about God's presence and especially the presence of God's grace. The season begins with a note of despair because we know we are lost and helpless without a dramatic intervention of God. The prevailing prayer of the season is that finally Christ will come and rule the troubled creation in love, power, and justice. There is hope in the midst of hopelessness. It is birth time in Bethlehem. Something old is dying, and the newness of God is breaking over the human horizon. The good news is that we are being met, being visited. The very God who created in the beginning and will consummate all things at the end has joined us in our troubled present—and he has come to save. So the church humbly prays:

Come, thou long-expected Jesus,
Born to set thy people free;
From our fears and sins release us,
Let us find our rest in thee.
Israel's strength and consolation,
Hope of all the earth thou art;
Dear desire of ev'ry nation,
Joy of ev'ry longing heart.[23]

Christianity began as an Easter faith, with little Easters celebrated weekly as the Lord's days. So central was this pattern of grateful remembering and worship that the birth of Jesus was hardly an issue of particular note for the first generations of believers. But that changed by the fourth century when a date in late December was adopted and celebrated as the holy birthday. Was Jesus born on December 25? Probably not. Is accuracy important here? No. While the actual birth date is unknown, the annual Christian observance of the nativity was inserted into the church calendar where people of the northern hemisphere had celebrated since ancient times the return of the invincible sun. Late December includes the shortest day of the year and the winter solstice when the sun begins to grow again. Days lengthen, hope is refreshed, and the spring of new life is not far away. What a wonderful symbol of the coming of the Christ, the true light of the world and the source of eternal re-creation! The Roman emperor Aurelian in A.D. 274 declared a pagan festival on December 25 in honor of the sun god, but Christians soon transformed such a perverted public practice into a sacred observance of the birth of the sun of righteousness (Mal. 4:2).[24]

Many people are comfortable with where and how they are. They are the privileged of the world, the ones with power, resources, and control. For them, God's coming is more threat than promise. It suggests change from the status quo. They join Herod in hoping for the death of the divine child. When Jesus comes, old things are in danger of becoming new. At least for the lost, hungry, poor, and humble, this coming is good news. The big challenge for God's people is the formation of a faith community that lives by an alternative, liberated imagination, a way of looking at things that is very different from that of the privileged of this world.[25] Such a different view brings the courage and freedom to act in ways that appear foolish to the world. It allows one to see in a baby born in a desperate set of circumstances the very appearance of God. Those now in charge of this world rarely understand or accept such marvelous things. The story of Jesus' birth is incredible to them—and unacceptably threatening. While they will do what they can against the Christ child, they will not have the last word and finally do not define reality or control history. Ready or not, welcome or not, God comes!

For today's believers, Advent is a time to anticipate and prepare. Anticipating God's arrival requires sobering self-examination and a necessary pattern of preparation. An old story makes the point well. A conspiring uncle was the center of a popular tale in sixteenth-century England. He would inherit a wealthy estate if he could dispose of the rightful heirs, a young boy and girl. So he hired two men to do away with the children. One of these men, just not able to do the awful deed, killed his partner and left the children on their own in the woods—a supposed act of kindness. However, despite avoiding being killed, the children could not survive the harsh environment. Each, a mere "babe in the woods," eventually died. This sad tale has become a symbol of anyone who is naively innocent, who is unprepared to handle a situation and thus pays a heavy price. Survival calls for proper preparation. We all are babes in the woods of this world—that is, until a babe in Bethlehem comes to show us the way home.

The manner of waiting on God's coming should be one of penitence and discipline. After all, the wood of Jesus' cradle foreshadows that of the inevitably coming cross. Representing God in this world will exact a cost. Today's secular culture exploits Christmas well in advance of the December date, romanticizing the birth of Jesus for maximum commercial benefit. Why kill Christians if they can be bought? True believers in Christ, however, should use the time of Advent anticipation for something more

Mystery of the Spirit's Comings

The Spirit is intrinsically a mystery, like the wind, whose movements are too complex and hidden to predict. It is easy to know that the wind is moving, but difficult to tell precisely from where to where. . . . However evident may be the work of the Spirit to the heart, it is not visible to the eye or audible to the ear or tangible to the touch. The fact that we cannot see the wind does not mean that it does not exist. We hear it, feel it, observe its results. At times the unseen wind is capable of uprooting giant trees and swelling vast ocean waves—visible effects of a less visible operation. It was by a strong wind (*ruach*, Spirit) that the Red Sea was divided at the Exodus (Exod. 14:21). The work of the Spirit everywhere leaves footprints, traces, signs, and symbols. These are best expressed not in flat empirical descriptions but in powerful metaphors as indirect and hidden as the work itself: breath, dove, fire, oil. Some works of the Spirit apparently are intended to remain veiled, whereas other works of the Spirit have been openly revealed in history, recorded and recalled in scripture.

Thomas C. Oden, *Life in the Spirit*

than gorging on commercial goods. It is to be a time for maximum spiritual benefit, adopting the mood of this twelfth-century hymn-prayer:

O come, O come, Emmanuel,
And ransom captive Israel.

John the Baptist is a good model of how to prepare for the Lord's coming. He came to the public's attention after he had disciplined himself (Luke 7:33) and created space in himself and in Israel for the prophetic Word of God to be spoken and really heard. Here is the point: "The silence, the fasting and other practices that intensify solitude are for the sake of the emptiness to be filled by the overshadowing by the Holy Spirit who brings about the fullness of Christ within the human person."[26] Soon Jesus himself became a model of the wilderness experience (Matt. 4:1–11), after which he was "filled with the power of the Spirit, returned to Galilee, and a report about him spread through all the surrounding country" (Luke 4:14). The desert is the place for serious dialogue with the Holy Spirit, who then makes the desert bloom (Isa. 35:1–2) with good news and inspired ministry.[27]

The Lord has come! He is present with his people. Following the birth of Jesus is Epiphany ("appearance" or "manifestation"), second only to

Easter as an annual Christian time of remembrance and celebration. The word is found in 2 Timothy 1:10, speaking of the power that God now has brought to visibility in Jesus Christ. This powerful appearance radiates with the fulfillment of Isaiah 60:1, "Arise, shine; for your light has come, and the glory of the LORD has risen upon you." Epiphany resounds with the theme of John's Gospel: "The light shines in the darkness, and the darkness did not overcome it" (1:5). The focus is on the important question about the birth of Jesus: Just who is this one who has come? Confusion, denial, unbelief, and fear led to the mass murder of young children in Bethlehem (Matt. 2:16–18). We contemporary believers need to get beyond the surprise and romantic delight of a helpless baby in poverty and move on to an understanding of how and why a sovereign God would choose to come this way, despite contrary human expectations and all the other options presumably available to God.

The New Testament materials to be studied during Epiphany include the coming of the shepherds to Bethlehem, the arrival of the Magi, the eventual baptism of Jesus, and the first miracle of Jesus at the wedding in Cana. These pivotal appearances speak directly to the issue of the true identity of Jesus. The news of Jesus' arrival came first to shepherds, clarifying that Jesus is committed to and will elicit faith from the despised of the world (fulfilling the words of Mary's song in Luke 1:46–55). After the lowly shepherds, the mighty Magi came, Gentiles from afar. Speaking further to the identity of Jesus, these men brought the monarch's gift of gold, the deity's incense of presence, and the myrrh related to death. Thus, the Magi identify Jesus as the supreme ruler of the world, the anointed high priest of God (Messiah), and the suffering servant who would die as a fragrant and beautiful offering of God.

Beyond the appearances of the shepherds and Magi came the baptism and first miracle of Jesus. These were also key epiphanies of identity. Jesus was to be known as the Son of God (Mark 1:11; Luke 3:22). He is the lamb of God who takes away the sin of the world and will baptize with the Holy Spirit (John 1:29, 33–34). With mention of water and dove, it is suggested that Jesus is inaugurating a new creation. He is the new Noah and the new Moses. Adding the miracle at Cana clarifies that Jesus is God actually present and at work, sometimes dramatically and often in the ordinary lives of everyday people. In contrast to the teaching of early heretics called "Gnostics" (see glossary), there is a real incarnation to celebrate, the actual enfleshment of God in our sordid human world.[28] Jesus was fully human and fully divine, God with us in our frail flesh—only without sin. Such news must be shared.

The Evangelical Tradition

The first of the Christian spiritual traditions to be considered is the Evangelical. God calls, arrives, appears, and comforts. These are the marvelous announcements of Advent, Christmas, and Epiphany. We humans are not alone after all. We have been addressed and visited. The herald angels sang long ago about a miracle birth in Palestine, and those who hear with obedient appreciation in every generation themselves become heralds of this wonderful good news.

The dynamic shift from the historic fact of being called by God to becoming callers of others is at the heart of the Evangelical tradition of Christianity. We who have received Christ gratefully pass along the good news. An evangel is a herald prepared to deliver an urgent gospel message. The word of witness is about the greatest news ever spoken or heard. Evangelicals are "people with passion to know the living God—the Father, the Son, and the Holy Spirit—and to make his grace and love known to every person on earth."[29] We who believe are enabled by the power of God to take the word of the gospel into our hearts in such a transforming way that others want it for themselves. The apostle Peter was primarily a preacher of good news, a fisher of men and women who needed to hear that God had come for them and wished to be with them. The day of Pentecost culminated with the waiting of Jesus' first disciples, the coming of the promised Spirit, and the inspired preaching of Peter to the gathered crowd.

What should people do and what will they receive in light of God's redeeming presence? Announced Peter, "Repent, and be baptized every one of you in the name of Jesus Christ so that your sins may be forgiven; and you will receive the gift of the Holy Spirit" (Acts 2:38). Peter represents well the Evangelical tradition. He models the believer who is faithfully "holding forth the word of life" (Phil. 2:16 KJV). Jesus said, "I am the way, and the truth, and the life. No one comes to the Father except through me. If you know me, you will know my Father also" (John 14:6–7). Since Jesus is the door into the transforming love of God, the evangelical message is clear and compelling: "So if anyone is in Christ, there is a new creation: everything old has passed away; see, everything has become new! All this is from God, who reconciled us to himself through Christ, and has given us the ministry of reconciliation" (2 Cor. 5:17–18).

Following the marvelous example of Peter, there now have been many other outstanding models of the Evangelical tradition lived out at its best. One is a North African, Augustine (b. 354), and another is a North American, Billy Graham (b. 1918). St. Augustine's coming to the faith is one of the most well-known conversion stories in Christian history, while Graham "has traveled to more places and preached to more persons than anyone in history."[30] A third evangelical, one of the most influential of all Christians across the centuries, is Martin Luther (1483–1546), a faithful but troubled Roman Catholic priest. His was a difficult search for a personal assurance of faith. He struggled with his own efforts and finally was granted a wonderful liberation through the Word of God. Luther realized that the assurance of salvation will not come by outward acts, such as disciplined eating and drinking, wearing sacred vestments, living in holy places, and going on pilgrimages. Relying on such things usually produces hypocrites. What the soul needs is the gospel of Jesus Christ, incarnate, suffering, risen, and glorified. Only by receiving this good news in faith can the soul be assured of right standing before God. Here is the heart of evangelical faith. God and God's grace are truly present and fully adequate.

Martin Luther and John Calvin reacted negatively to the dominant pattern of Western Catholic spirituality in their time. This pre-Reformation pattern lacked proper focus on the justification before God through the sinner's act of faith in response to God's gracious offer of forgiveness. This absence had led to widespread spiritual dysfunction. Believing they were justified in God's eyes only in the process of being sanctified (considered an ongoing and never completed process in this life), Christians were striving and never arriving, struggling but never assured of salvation. They assumed that such lack of assurance could be addressed by martyrdom or a laborious cultivation of the questing human spirit. But the Reformers came to view any exercises for achieving salvation as inadequate. It was unacceptable to have only a partial assurance of faith that grew out of vigorous self-denial on the way to sanctification. Both salvation and its assurance are gifts of God in response to faith. Such grace-gifts are not the fruit of vigorous self-denial.[31] Those who are called to preach must truly preach the present Christ, not only talk about Christ in an historical manner. Christ should be proclaimed in such a way that faith is created in the hearts of hearers. Beyond the historical realities, Christ must become the living God of present experience.

These insights were key to launching the Protestant Reformation of the sixteenth century and remain critical for the church's spiritual life. As recurrent patterns of institutionalism and creedalism cool and depersonalize church life, the vital witness of the Evangelical tradition reemerges as a revival or awakening. For example, the First Great Awakening came in the religious life of the American colonies in the eighteenth century (see glossary). It revitalized traditional conceptions of entrance into the Christian life. Like Pietism in Germany and the evangelical awakening in England (Wesleyan revival), new emphasis was placed on conversion, a transforming life change accepted by faith. A key leader of this first awakening was the influential Congregationalist preacher Jonathan Edwards in New England (1703–1758). His most famous sermon was titled "Sinners in the Hands of an Angry God."

The evangelical witness to Jesus Christ is defined in part by its emphasis on the authoritative biblical record. While significantly personal in impact, Christian faith does have a particular content. The modern mania for relativizing all belief is not shared by the mainstream or orthodox tradition of Christians. On the other hand, the peril of numerous Christians in the Evangelical tradition has been the persistent temptation to fixate on nonessential matters, failing to distinguish between the primary and the secondary in belief.[32] This can lead to a loveless legalism in the name of truth, a sectarian arrogance, and an isolation of believers from the world and even from each other.

What is best in the Evangelical tradition are the calls to conversion and the sharing of the good news with all people. This tradition features central themes that interlock and need not be lost in distractions that might emerge. These themes are (1) a call to faithful proclamation of the gospel of Jesus (evangelism), (2) an acceptance of the central importance of Scripture for rightly interpreting this gospel, and (3) a grateful acceptance of the confessional witness of early Christian generations to the meaning of the gospel message.

Evangelism is viewed as the key mission of the church. Billy Graham reports that when World War II ended, he became a full-time evangelist. In the uncertainty of those troubled times, "many people were ready for a message that pointed them to stability and lasting values. In the providence of God, we were able to take advantage of the spiritual hunger and search for values that marked those years." Even though times change, leading to new challenges and opportunities for evangelism, Graham insists that one thing will not change: "God's love for humanity and His desire to see men and women yield their lives to Him and come to know Him in a personal way. The human spirit is never satisfied in a lasting way by anything less than God."[33] Saint Augustine prayed this to God many centuries ago: "You have made us for Yourself, and our heart is restless until it finds rest in You." A marvelous saving message, the biblically defined gospel message is to be proclaimed to all people. This message was formulated very early in a simple creed still affirmed by Christians worldwide.

The Apostles' Creed

There is a range of belief among Christians on numerous subjects. However, this diverse, rich, and sometimes confusing circumstance is not without its common elements that form the foundations of Christian belief. The Apostles' Creed has been affirmed almost unanimously by Christians as containing the essence of what makes faith distinctively Christian (see chapter 1 for the creed's full wording). It is an ancient statement, probably the progressive enlargement of an early pattern of preparation for Christian baptism. Emerging as it did from the worship life of the early church, and particularly the baptismal setting where new believers were committing themselves to the Christian life and the community of faith, the Apostles' Creed played special instructional and affirmational roles. It "served as a means of vowing loyalty in life and in death to the God whom we meet in Jesus Christ."[34]

The general structure of this classic creed reflects the Great Commission of Jesus as found in Matthew 28:19. Its format is built around the particular way in which Christians understand the nature of God (Trinity). The Apostles' Creed may rightly be regarded as a compact summary of the biblical witness to the identity of God as Father, Son, and Holy Spirit. At the center is the historical Christ event. The "I believe" (*credo*) of the creed is hardly a commitment to a religious equation or a rational proof about God. Christian faith is not just a matter of believing something or believing someone, but of believing in someone. The creed is about Jesus Christ. Christian faith is essentially about a living relationship with Christ through the continuing presence of his Spirit.

Believers representing the rich tradition of Christian belief are to be renewed people who form a new community on mission with the good news of Jesus Christ for a lost world. Christians are to confess together the one God who is Father, Son, and Spirit (the eternal, historical, and now-present God). The three articles of the Apostles' Creed match this trifold structure and make clear that the God who is sovereign creator and historic redeemer is the same one who is now by the side of every sinner, enabling human transformation.[35] The good news from God needs sharing. It is news about who God is and what God is doing, especially in Jesus Christ. The phrases of the creed that speak of "conceived by the Holy Spirit, born of the Virgin Mary" intend to make clear that the origin of Jesus was the intentional coming of God. The Christmas story is not the act of humans, but the arrival of God enfleshed on the human scene. In fact, the biblical emphasis on God as creator (Gen. 1:1) is intended to make clear that God is the constant cause and ultimate sustainer of all things. While above and beyond all things (transcendent creator), God also is in all things (immanent redeemer). God is truly present.

For good news about God to be received, God must come to provide the news and enable the reception (revelation and prevenient grace), since we fallen humans are not in a position to discover such news on our own. Our world is not a closed system in which things cannot happen in ways other than what we humans currently recognize as fixed laws of nature. Can a baby be conceived without both a female ovum and a male sperm? No, not in a closed view of a mechanical universe. Yes, conceivably it could, if God should so choose and if those involved are fully obedient to the overshadowing and powerful presence of God's birthing Spirit. Stuart Briscoe properly links the virginal conception of Jesus in the womb of Mary and how God's good news comes to us from God. The point of the unique birth of Jesus is to alert us to the unique person of the Lord. The news is about God's initiative. The birth is about God's grace and power. It is "not of ourselves, but here's one thing that makes it possible. If the Holy Spirit was to come upon Mary. . . ."[36] God summoned Mary and she responded. God continues to call all of us. The news is about God in Jesus Christ. How will we respond?

Truly Alive in God's Presence

It is a vital question indeed: What is possible if the Holy Spirit comes upon us? When the Spirit comes upon us, the fullness of Christian spiritual life can emerge. A central way of viewing the goal of a church or individual believer is through the concept of "being fully alive in the Spirit." The first task in the spiritual quest is not to strategize, as though this process is under human control, or to determine to be relevant or successful as believers in this world. The task is to pursue in God's way the goal of being in Christ and a new creation of the Spirit. Jesus told his disciples that they would do many things in his name, but only after they first waited for power from on high (Luke 24:49). A vital community of Christian faith is one in which spiritual transformation is held in higher priority than congregational structures, staffing, and programming. A wide-eyed waiting should precede and undergird all that is done. Waiting is done well in prayer, praise, and humility. Waiting on the Spirit is not group passivity; it is the people's pointed intention to become God's children and church, living out of God's life toward whatever ends God chooses—and all in God's time and way. The living God chooses to be present and specializes in resurrection life.

The earliest Christian congregations, once having waited and been inflamed with divine life and love, were led in directions often unexpected. For instance, how were they to relate to believing Gentiles (a theological/cultural crisis for those of Jewish heritage)? However surprising may be the stretching called for by the Spirit, fresh life surges only when the breath of the Spirit inspires new frontiers of being and doing. The stretched community is the one most likely to be on mission with God and the one that most fully can convey the vibrant power of God's love to a skeptical world. Some of the earliest Christian congregations (like Corinth) experienced division over loyalty to various human leaders. Paul warned that only God enables real progress; those gifted to guide the church's life play only limited roles that are dependent on the wisdom of God and the faithfulness of others (1 Cor. 3:6–7). There must be an avoidance of ego-centered human leadership and leader-infatuated human following. The Spirit leads, and all disciples, whatever their gifts and functions, are but servants.

A church periodically should consult, research, and reconsider its structures, staffing, and programs. However, foundational to all such activity should be intentional renewal of its Spirit-life. After all, it's God's church! Clark Pinnock is right: "The effectiveness of the church is due not to human competency or programming but to *the power of God at work*. . . . The main rationale of the church is to actualize all the implications of baptism in the Spirit."[37] Such actualization was modeled well by the nineteenth-century Holiness movement. This movement, like all church renewal efforts that champion the marvels of the immediate presence of God, was criticized as too emotional, often anti-intellectual, and lacking in cultured sophistication.[38] Granting some truth to this criticism, the more important truth lies beyond the criticisms. The primary religious phenomenon for these holiness revivalists was the overwhelming grace of God that showed itself in "a love that one could feel and know and participate in, thus creating a spirituality based on relationality."[39] People found themselves being re-related to God in forgiveness and renewal; the resulting wholeness of the divine-human relationship led naturally to fresh unity among Christian brothers and sisters.[40]

Without the immediate and transforming presence of the Holy Spirit, God may be majestic, ideal, before all time, and the center of all perfections, but this God is distant, mostly a grand idea, and too removed to really impact me and my life in the present world. Christ tends to stay in the past, and the good news about God in Christ deteriorates into an old letter from an unknown friend in a forgotten language. The church is mostly another time-consuming organization of nice people hoping to do some good things together with minimal friction and little personal sacrifice. Authority is a matter of domination—which leader or church tradition will be granted the status of being right and official, the person to follow, the dogma to memorize and confess. Mission verges on being religious propaganda, and Christian living is a slave morality where right things are enforced and wrong things condemned and punished.

But with the immediate and transforming presence of the Holy Spirit, the whole creation is being helped to reach for resurrection life. The Christ of Easter glory is present in every moment. The church is the gathering of people who are alive in Christ and full of the fruit of the Spirit. The authority that instructs and directs is the overwhelming and liberating love of God against which there is no law. To be on mission in the Spirit is to be walking in love and sharing gracefully out of love's overflow. When God's Spirit is welcomed in life's everyday experiences, those who do the welcoming learn quickly that God's presence makes all things new. The God who is with us gives in truly amazing ways.

Questions to Pursue

1. Recall the Martin Luther quote that begins this chapter and the prayer of Jabez. What does it take to be aware of God's presence?
2. What answers can you find in this chapter to the key question, How is the divine presence to be known and nurtured?
3. Have you ever experienced God as "extremely sensitive, vulnerable, shy," and even apparently absent? What were the circumstances?
4. Taking the advice of Brother Lawrence, how might a Christian go about "practicing the presence" of God?
5. What do *paraklētos,* Advent, and the evangelical spiritual tradition have in common?
6. What is the spiritual significance of the Apostles' Creed focusing more on a present someone than an abstractly true something?

3

Truly Amazed: The Spirit's Extravagance

> I shall use the word mysticism to express the type of religion which puts the emphasis on immediate awareness of relation with God, on direct and intimate consciousness of the Divine Presence. It is religion in its most acute, intense and living stage.[1]

> Christianity is not a philosophical school for speculating about abstract concepts, but is essentially a communion with the living God. That is why . . . the fathers of the eastern tradition . . . never allowed their thought to cross the threshold of the mystery, or to substitute idols of God for God Himself.[2]

It is one thing, one truly amazing thing, to realize that we humans are not alone in this vast universe. There indeed is an eternal One who is and who chooses to come alongside us humans. This divine presence calls and comforts, but much more needs to be known. Who really is this God? What is the divine nature, intent, and way of relating to humans who have defied their Creator and are selfishly trying to find their own sinful way through life? How grand is the majesty of God, and how unmerited and extensive is God's power and grace? The biblical answers given to such questions are themselves amazing. They are truly extraordinary and world-changing. While we humans approach the marvels of God, we only touch and never grasp. We glance, but barely see. If the reality and mystery of God were small and simple enough to be fully comprehended by humans, then God would neither be great enough to be worshipped nor wonder-full enough to be adored. But such is not the case.

The Christian faith is filled with superlatives. God, of course, is the greatest of all, surpassing the analytical and descriptive abilities of human language. The devotional classic by Oswald Chambers, *My Utmost for His Highest,* stretches to the limit what we humans hope to be in light of the wonders of who God is. The faith of Christians began when a shocked and scattered band of depressed disciples got the news that was too good to be true. Their beloved Jesus had been cruelly killed. Hope had been dashed. Faith apparently had been folly. But wait! There was news, news so good that at first it could not be believed. He was risen! Jesus had conquered death. The power of death had itself died. God was in Christ, and it all was for us. God wants to bring resurrection life to each one of us who will believe. What power and extravagant love. It is truly amazing!

Christian spirituality is not speculation about abstract religious concepts. That would be too impersonal, only intellectual religion at best. It is about actually communing with the living God. We humans will never exhaust the mystery of God, but we are privileged by God's grace to participate in the life-giving presence of this vast mystery. True faith kneels amazed at the feet of the risen Christ. True faith involves actual relationship with the God who spoke the worlds into being, who called Jesus from the grave, and who invites us to new life. We now can be intimate with God. When true faith comes, religion moves from its creeds, ceremonies, and traditions to its most acute, intense, and living stage.

The Wonder of It All

One of the more recognized and beloved Christian songs in the world is "Amazing Grace." The dramatic story of its composition by John Newton (1725–1807), a former slave trader, illustrates well why the gracious God is truly amazing in a world of sin. When people open themselves to the power of Easter and the filling of Pentecost, they begin walking in the light of the Holy Spirit who guides through the maze of life. The maze can be bewildering, but the holy guide is even more amazing. God pursues, saves, transforms, directs, and causes extravagant rejoicing.

Charles Wesley (1707–1788), the most gifted and prolific of all English hymn writers, gave unparalleled expression to evangelical faith and experience in language both biblical and lyrical. A biography written by T. Crichton Mitchell is titled *Charles Wesley: Man with the Dancing Heart.* The following sample of his thousands of hymn lines illustrates Wesley's lyrics of rejoicing that flowed from a soul's grateful heart: "Hark! the herald angels sing"; "Come, thou long-expected Jesus"; "And can it be"; "Love divine, all loves excelling"; and "O for a thousand tongues to sing."

Consider another Englishman's Christian witness. C. S. Lewis (1898–1963) is one of the more important Christian thinkers of the twentieth century. Born in Ireland, he spent most of his adult life as a fellow of Magdalen College, Oxford, where he taught medieval literature. A sophisticated atheist, he was one day *Surprised by Joy* (the title of his autobiography). What was the surprise? He says that finally he was overtaken by awe. "God closed in on me. . . . I felt as if I were a man of snow at long last beginning to melt. . . . As the dry bones shook and came together in that dreadful valley of Ezekiel's, so now a philosophical theorem [God], cerebrally entertained, began to stir and heave and throw off its grave-cloths, and stood upright and became a living presence. . . . Total surrender, the absolute leap in the dark, were demanded. . . . In the Trinity Term of 1929 I gave in, and admitted that God was God, and knelt and prayed." There was joy, surprising and wonderful joy.[3]

When finite humans approach the infinite God, they must begin with a sense of awe and astonishment. It is truly amazing that God is accessible to humans and humbling to know that God desires nothing short of godlikeness in humans. It is stunning to realize that the biblical call is to holiness for believers. The God who has come now says to us: "For I am the LORD your God; sanctify yourselves therefore, and be holy, for I am holy" (Lev. 11:44). Again, "For this is the will of God, your sanctification" (1 Thess. 4:3). The holy God who comes also calls, invites, and enables. The invitation is to godlikeness or sainthood. The need for divine enablement is obvious. What makes a Christian a saint? According to Barbara Brown Taylor: "*Extravagance*. Excessive love, flagrant mercy, radical affection, exorbitant charity, immoderate faith, intemperate hope, inordinate love. None of which is an achievement, a badge to be earned or a trophy to be sought; all are secondary by-products of the one thing that truly makes a saint, which is the love of God."[4]

How can one recognize a true Christian saint? The best way is not looking for perfection in someone's life. A more likely approach is to observe what happens as a life is being lived. When a saint is present, there often is tension with the ordinary, and problems are being created for the status quo of this world. Children of God have primary allegiance to their Father. On the occasion of his inaugural lecture as the Harry Emerson Fosdick Visiting Professor at Union Theological Seminary in New York in 1961, Douglas Steere announced that saints are persons whose lives have been irradiated by divine grace and who have put themselves at God's disposal. They seek to be faithful rather than safe. They are prayerful, joyful, and "kindlers and purifiers of the dream."[5] What dream? They perceive by faith what God is trying to bring into being in this world, and their posture is, "Your kingdom come. Your will be done, on earth as it is in heaven" (Matt. 6:10).

Jesus and his disciples were always in trouble. They may have been sane and sensible, but they were hardly bland and safe. In biblical faith and in Christian discipleship, there is an important place for a kind of extravagance, a yielding to the excessive, a stepping out of the usual paths. Some things go beyond the ordinary so dramatically that they shout for attention; they call us to radical new ways of thinking and acting. Something in the Christian experience should cause believers to be witnesses, not religious wallflowers, to be apostles of a new world, not recluses meekly retreating from this one. If we do not speak of the glories of God in Christ, the very rocks will cry out. Mere religion ends when true faith comes and God actually transforms. We speak of being "saved." The root of the Hebrew word for *save* means giving room, space, or width. Salvation frees people up, grants them growing space, liberates to widths of spiritual experience previously unknown. It is not giving space for the freedom to be me or the arrogant "I did it my way," but it gives the ability to be all that God intends. The coming of grace looses the potential of love. When this is loosed, people will notice, things will change, even the mundane will ignite with wonder.

Christians have become culturally domesticated. This subtle worldly imprisonment spawns mere religion, a wonder-less world. What we claim to know and possess as Christians too often appears to the general public as ordinary and unremarkable. We fall far short of being sources of amazement to those around us. But we serve a God who is beyond the ability of our minds to comprehend or our language to convey. Vision and adoration should dominate our lives—and spill over to others. When we approach God, it should be humbly, with a sense of awe and even astonishment. What a God we serve! All our years should be like that one when King Uzziah died and the prophet Isaiah "saw the Lord sitting on a throne, high and lofty; and the hem of his robe filled the temple. . . . And I said: 'Woe is me! I am lost, for I am a man of unclean lips, and I live among a people of unclean lips; yet my eyes have seen the King, the Lord of hosts!'" (Isa. 6:1, 5). Having seen, Isaiah became one of God's greatest prophets.

Note the following view of human salvation, featuring divine love and grace in a way that both honors the sovereign but risking God and underlines human responsibility in the process:

> The fellowship model [of God] understands sin as the breaking of a relationship rather than as some sort of entity or condition. God takes it on himself to overcome this breech and restore the relationship through the cross and resurrection of Christ and by giving us the grace that enables us to see the injury we have done, thus making reconciliation possible. God does not manipulate our love but makes himself contingent on our response. Thus it is God who takes the risks involved with our responding to enabling grace

> with trust and love and continuing to mature in the relationship. This does not mean that we merit God's love; we are the recipients of grace. Grace opens up possibilities for us that otherwise would not be open.[6]

Many things are amazing in this fellowship model. God has bridged the gap, restored the relationship possibility, and given to us fallen humans the grace needed to realize this marvelous reconciliation. God risks our human responses, drawing by love rather than manipulating by a carefully calculated providence. God is an awesomely loving and grace-giving God!

Prayer is wonder-full in this view of who God is and how God works. James says that the prayers of righteous people really make a difference (James 5:16). They impact those praying and those prayed for because they also impact the life of God. What a thought! We mere humans are heard, taken seriously, allowed to become love partners and co-creators with God. Some of the future depends in part on our prayers. Amazing! The goal of God's original creation was our participation in the loving triune relationship that God is throughout eternity. We were made to belong and participate. God has granted us the ability to significantly affect the divine working in the world, thus the power that lies in petitionary prayer. God exercises sovereignty "by deciding *not* to always unilaterally decide matters." Our input is enlisted, not because God has no other choice, but because God desires to have authentic, mutually loving, and dynamic relationships with us as real and empowered persons. Like a loving parent or spouse, God wants "not only to influence us but to be influenced *by us*."[7]

To grow up spiritually, then, is to become really alive in a dynamic divine-human relationship. To grow in this divinely graced arena is to be empowered by God to participate with him in our growing into the image of Christ and, together with God, seeking the salvation of the rest of the fallen creation. What a vision of the Christian life this is!

The Wonderful Bible Word

Here is an important question. What was so new, revolutionary, exciting, demanding of the world's attention that it flashed like lightning into ancient cities like Ephesus on the wings of inspired Christian witnesses? The answer can be found by following one word through the New Testament. The Greek word *hyperbolē* comes into English directly as *hyperbole,* meaning an obvious exaggeration (e.g., I just bought a mile-high ice cream cone). A related Latin equivalent word that means "extravagant" is *extravagari,* to wander like a vagabond beyond the usual limits and into uncharted territory.

Used only a few times in the New Testament, *hyperbolē* suggests why the early church turned the world upside down. There are a few essential elements of a much-needed Christian extravagance (exceedingly superlative realities) referred to as *hyperbolē*. This graphic word means a throwing beyond or an excessive statement that seems to so surpass the ordinary that it is almost too good to be true. For example, used negatively, Paul confessed that he once had "persecuted this Way [of Jesus] up to the point of death" (Acts 22:4). He had once violently, excessively attacked the church of God, trying to destroy it (Gal. 1:13). But the negative extremes had been transformed into Paul's positive actions and claims on behalf of the very Christ that he had once opposed.

Something major had changed for Paul. Something happened to him on the road to Damascus that became a wonder almost beyond his imagination (Acts 9). Soon he found himself addressing the young and troubled Christian community in Corinth. Christians there were experimenting with what some of them were judging a superior spiritual experience (tongues) and then placing those not experiencing it into the category of second-class believers. Paul told them, in effect: You think you have found something great? Let me tell you about something that is surpassingly great indeed (1 Cor. 13 on God's love). Paul was now as intensely for this faith in Jesus as once he had been intensely against it. He was concerned, however, that the right things be on the church's center stage.

What had jolted Paul from a very negative to a very positive stance? Whatever it was, it constitutes the keynote of a proper Christian extravagance and a central aspect of Christian spirituality. He had encountered something that in his view went beyond all else. For him, speaking of such extraordinary reality in lavish and superlative terms was not an obvious exaggeration (the usual meaning of *hyperbole*). It was the ultimate and glorious truth. He had learned that a few things about God in Christ are as real as they are extravagant, things demanding that they be proclaimed to the whole world. If a Christian individual or congregation wants to be heard credibly in this world, these are the extravagant things worth announcing and living out. They are the glory of the church and the hope of the world.

What are they? To the midst of the thriving cosmopolitan city of Ephesus, Paul brought news of some things that are excessively positive, truly grand and extraordinary, even explosive in their potential. His extravagant claim was that the gospel of Jesus is the best of the best. As he expresses it in Ephesians 1:15–23, we humans have been confronted with something so outrageously wonderful that it is difficult to put in human language. The divine love, grace, and power resident in Jesus Christ reach well beyond all other events, persons, and truth claims ever encountered by humanity. Let us explore briefly these three wonder-full divine realities.

Divine Love

Humans long for true love in societies where love is perverted constantly on billboards, television screens, and internet sites. Where is real love found? There has never been a love like that of Jesus Christ. His cross was the ultimate illustration of the amazing extent of God's love, reaching to the very bottom of sin's disgrace and extending to the most unlovely person. It is indeed a love beyond all understanding and all deserving. It is without precedent. God has showered us extravagantly with the warmth and acceptance of redeeming love. This love is the expression of God's very essence. A cross was in the heart of God before one was planted in a hillside outside Jerusalem. God's love is, in the literal sense of the word, ecstatic, a love that causes God to go beyond himself and create reality other than himself, including beings endowed with the potential of sharing in the very love and life of God. Amazing!

Paul prays that the Christians of Ephesus might "know the love of Christ that surpasses knowledge, so that [they] may be filled with all the fullness of God" (Eph. 3:19). How do we know this beyond-knowledge love? "We know love by this, that he laid down his life for us—and we ought to lay down our lives for one another" (1 John 3:16). What would be the result of coming to know this incomparable love? Paul says that real sharing in the Spirit of Christ results in a body of believers "having the same love, being in full accord and of one mind" (Phil. 2:2). In other words, the church is to be the body of Christ's love in the middle of an unloving world. It would shock any city of any time if common observation caused this public evaluation, "Behold, how they love one another!" This love of God in Jesus Christ inspires believers to sing the hyperbolic words of Charles Wesley:

Love divine, all loves excelling,
Joy of heaven, to earth come down;
Fix in us Thy humble dwelling;
All Thy faithful mercies crown.

Jesus, Thou art all compassion,
Pure, unbounded love Thou art;
Visit us with Thy salvation;
Enter every trembling heart.[8]

Divine Grace

Paul announced that God has raised us up with Christ and seated us with him in heavenly places "so that in the ages to come [God] might show the immeasurable riches of his grace in kindness toward us in Christ Jesus" (Eph. 2:7). God, because of love, chooses to be exceedingly gracious to us. This is amazing, unprecedented, nearly unimaginable. We who are ravaged by guilt, despair, anger, anxiety, and inadequacy are candidates for a wholly unmerited grace from God. In praising God's glorious grace, which has been freely given to us, Paul tells the Ephesians that in Jesus Christ "we have redemption through his blood, the forgiveness of our trespasses, according to the riches of his grace that he lavished on us." Even more, "With all wisdom and insight he has made known to us the mystery of his will, according to his good pleasure that he set forth in Christ, as a plan for the fullness of time, to gather up all things in him, things in heaven and things on earth" (Eph. 1:7–10). The hymn writer nearly stammers in trying to speak of God's grace in Jesus Christ: "Wonderful grace of Jesus, Greater than all my sin; How shall my tongue describe it, Where shall its praise begin?"[9]

Divine grace is more than a means for our forgiveness and a hope for our future. It is the way that we frail humans can be sustained in our troubled presents. Paul prayed for the thorn that plagued him to be removed, but the Lord said, "My grace is sufficient for you, for power is made perfect in weakness" (2 Cor. 12:9). The Thessalonians were informed about how the love of God issues in a divine grace that becomes comfort and strength for the believer. The grand truth comes almost as a blessing: "Now may our Lord Jesus Christ himself and God our Father, who loved us and through grace gave us eternal comfort and good hope, comfort your hearts and strengthen them in every good work and word" (2 Thess. 2:16–17). God is always adequate. In Christ, so are we.

How can God's grace be described? Its extravagance puts an impossible demand on human language. One beloved song of the church tries to describe divine grace in these wonderful but finally inadequate words: "Marvelous, infinite, matchless grace, Freely bestowed on all who believe."[10] Paul explained to the Romans the astonishing good news that "where sin increased, grace abounded all the more, so that, just as sin exercised dominion in death, so grace might also exercise dominion through justification leading to eternal life through Jesus Christ our Lord" (Rom. 5:20–21). Grace is God's way of empowering the sin-enslaved will and healing the broken and suffering human spirit.

The grace offered is intended for all people. In a fast-paced and lonely culture of self-centered striving, the presence of divine grace that is unmerited and without price is really good news. Apart from such grace, "the task of personal growth turns into a frantic search for innovative strategies. . . . We have tried to manufacture spiritual growth while missing the very grace that would enable it. We have wanted to produce results without a readiness to receive help through the available means of grace—prayer, scripture study, sacrament, and actively serving love."[11] Paul told believers to "work out your own salvation with fear and trembling; for it is God who is at work in you, enabling you both to will and to work for his good pleasure" (Phil. 2:12–13). We bear some responsibility for our own salvation and can succeed for one reason only: God at work in us—grace!

Divine Power

The revealed way of God's exercise of sovereignty refutes humanity's usual view of power. The divine victory that finally overcomes the evil of the world is pictured unforgettably in Christ who, of all places, reigns even from the horror of an old rugged cross. God's weakness is said to be stronger than human strength (1 Cor. 1:25). In light of the biblical witness, to say that God is omnipotent is to say that, with patience and even suffering, God can and will accomplish all that he promised. Such divine power "includes the power of self-restraint; it allows a real drama of invitation, rejection and resistance to unfold; yet it also bespeaks a power of persistence that stubbornly endures until victory is won. . . . It manifests the power of powerlessness."[12] Such is the way of the God of extravagant love and grace.

John reports that "Jesus, knowing that the Father had given all things into his hands, and that he had come from God and was going to God, got up from the table, took off his outer robe, and tied a towel around himself" (John 13:3–4). He, Lord of all creation, washed the dirty feet of the disciples! All who are his are to do the same, realizing that the extraordinary power of God is not available for purposes of dominating others, but for their service. In our power-crazed world, the truth is not readily received. It is not the power of the bullet, the dollar, the mass of information, or the intercontinental rocket that finally will prevail. It is the power of God as seen dramatically in both Christ's great sacrifice and dramatic resurrection. Paul reports this about "the immeasurable greatness of his power for us who believe": "God put this power to work in Christ when he raised him from the dead and seated him at his right hand in the heavenly places, far above all rule and authority and power and dominion, . . . and he has put all things under his feet and has made him the head over all things for the church" (Eph. 1:19–22).

With God in Christ, we are faced with a love beyond description, a grace beyond deserving, and a power beyond comparison. If we know about and have received this love, grace, and power of God through the ministry of the Spirit, what should we do? Paul asks the Corinthians whether all believers are prophets, teachers, miracle workers, and tongues speakers. The implied answer is, Of course not! Instead, when it comes to seeking for the fullness of God's provision, the believer is to desire the greatest gift, the most excellent way, the wonderful love of God that transforms within, radiates hope outward, and builds community rather than fractures it (1 Cor. 13). The Christian's extravagant message for the world, the one message around which all believers can rally in full unity, is expressed in these hymn lyrics:

God's love has no limit,
His grace has no measure,
His power has no boundary known unto men;
For out of his infinite riches in Jesus,
He giveth and giveth and giveth again![13]

How should we who believe respond to the good news of all this amazing divine extravagance that enables the Christian life? Using the words of Charles Wesley, themselves a deliberate hyperbole in relation to extravagant truth, we should offer the amazing prayer: "O for a thousand tongues to sing my great Redeemer's praise." We also should be filled with a hope that the world cannot explain apart from the truth of the risen Christ. In 2 Corinthians 4:17, we find a compounded extravagance, one wonderful hyperbole piled on top of another: "For this slight momentary affliction is preparing us for an eternal weight of glory beyond all measure." Literally, the Greek reads "the excessively to excess." Phillips translates it, "These little troubles (which are really so transitory) are winning for us a permanent, glorious and solid reward out of all proportion to our pain." To know this is to leave mere religion far behind.

The Rich Christian Tradition

A great spiritual resource for Christians is the Book of Psalms. In this collection of Hebrew spirituality, the believer's life is pictured as experiencing two decisive moves of faith.[14] First, there are songs of creation that are spiritually oriented, full of confident faith, and secure (e.g., Ps. 1, 37, 145). Then comes a decisive change, unwelcome but common, to a dark circumstance of disorientation—hurt, doubt, alienation, suffering, even death. This dark night of the soul struggles with faith and yields personal (e.g., Ps. 13) and communal lament (e.g., Ps. 74). Then comes the second shift, the surprise and joy of God's sheer grace that brings into being a new spiritual orientation beyond and tempered by all the negative. Into human despair bursts the new life of God. After defeat and exile, Israel came to know such resurrection grace and gave thanksgiving for it in Psalms 30 and 40. At times God acted so wonderfully that Israel was lost in wonder, love, and praise. For the first-century Jews in Jerusalem who had believed in Jesus as the Messiah (orientation) and then had suffered the loss of their master on the cruel cross (disorientation), it happened again. An apparently tragic Friday of spiritual darkness suddenly became an unbelievably wonderful Sunday of spiritual sunshine. After Easter, however, would come days and generations of pain and persecution. The cycle of the Psalm types tends to repeat in the pits of real life.

Faith for the long haul must grow and gain seasoned maturity. Discipline in the Christian life over the centuries has sought in different ways to overcome the obstacles to the fulfillment of the gospel imperative to love God and one's neighbors. A common aspiration is the one uttered in the fourth-century prayer of Serapion of Thmuis: "Make us truly alive!" Discipline on the way to being truly alive is called *asceticism,* from the Greek *askēsis,* "discipline" or "training" (see the glossary). Instructions of Jesus in the Sermon on the Mount stress the need for self-effacement in order to acquire the things of the Spirit. Jesus said, "If any want to become my followers, let them deny themselves and take up their cross daily and follow me" (Luke 9:23). By the late third and early fourth centuries, many Christians combined these biblical instructions with a mistrust or even contempt for the body and went into solitary places to engage in severe forms of self-discipline. There is a rich spiritual literature from the lives of the Christian "desert fathers." A key example is *The Life of Anthony* by Saint Athanasius. By the fifth century, the individualism of the solitary ascetics gradually gave way to communal forms such as established monastic communities. Whether in highly disciplined communities or privately, the quest for self-mastery and knowledge of God remained. By the time of the Renaissance and the Protestant Reformation in the sixteenth century, there was a marked reaction against the perversions of such an ascetic ideal.

Martin Luther (1483–1546) objected to ascetical practices on the ground that they placed greater emphasis on works as necessary for salvation than on the gift of salvation made possible by the freely given grace of God. His famous *The Freedom of a Christian* (1520) makes clear that the Christian is justified by grace through faith alone and is completely free of any need to establish worthiness before God through ceremonial, legal, or moral works. In response to what God has freely given in Christ, Christians should discipline their bodies and serve their neighbors in love, without any expectation of reward or thought of self-justification. Virtue is to be found less in dramatic patterns of personal denial and more in the acceptance and affirmation of the loving and redeeming act of God on our behalf. After all, the body and soul are interdependent aspects of the integrated and whole Christian person. Unlike the ancient Greek, the Hebrew world of the Bible views people as good by creation, even if now fallen. To the Hebrew, a human being is a dynamic body-soul unit that is called to serve God passionately with the whole being and within the physical world. Rather than fleeing the world and demeaning the body, believers should find God in the midst of both—and rejoice in the divine goodness.

Unfortunately, Christian believers commonly indulge themselves in various ways rather than living disciplined lives of freedom and joy. So the Christian tradition brings the believer back to the sacrifice of Christ and to the crosses that still are to be carried for the sake of the world. Having considered in chapter 2 the Advent-Christmas-Epiphany cycle that opens the Christian year, we now turn to the second annual cycle.

The Church Year: Lent, Holy Week, Easter

Advent, Christmas, and Epiphany initiate the Christian year with the cycle-of-light celebrations of the birth of Jesus and the first illuminating appearances that accompanied his incarnation long ago. Now comes the second seasonal cycle, the cycle of life. Life is its theme because it recalls the death and resurrection of Jesus (John 15:18–25). It is a somber time of serious preparation, both of Jesus for his eventual cross and of his disciples for their sacrificial lives in every present time.

If Advent, Christmas, and Epiphany represent the innocence and excitement of the childhood of the faith, the season of Lent introduces the awkwardness of adolescence. Faith does not function in a vacuum, so we must face the harsh realities about ourselves and this world. Believers in Jesus are in a continuing battle with "principalities and powers" (Eph. 6:12; Col. 2:8) in their lives and in human history itself. Says John Westerhoff, "Feasting and fasting are at the heart of the Christian life. During Eastertide we feast, during Lent we fast. . . . Lent is the season to remember how easy it is for us to forget that we are dependent on God's grace for life."[15] Lent lasts forty days in keeping with the symbolic meaning of forty in the Bible. Moses spent forty years in the wilderness, and Jesus spent forty days in the desert. Central here is the idea of spiritual preparation for the demanding task that lies ahead (Matt. 4:1–11). We who believe prepare to accompany Jesus to his death, including observance of Holy Week when the final events leading to the crucifixion are recalled and applied to the current meaning of carrying one's own cross for Christ.

Originally, Easter (and every Sunday, the weekly Easter) was the only annual Christian celebration. The resurrection of Jesus was the event that had launched the faith and is the point on which the weekly and annual cycles of the Christian calendar turn. Every Sunday and every Easter celebrate the sacrifice (1 Cor. 5:7) and resurrection of Jesus. They anticipate the day when the same Lord will come again in glory to judge the living and the dead and finally establish God's universal reign. The hymn "For the Lord's Day" by Charles Wesley says it well:

Come, let us with our Lord arise,
Our Lord, who made both earth and skies;
Who died to save the world he made,
And rose triumphant from the dead;
He rose, the Prince of life and peace,
And stamped the day for ever his.

Then let us render him his own,
With solemn prayer approach the throne,
With meekness hear the gospel word,
With thanks his dying love record;
Our joyful hearts and voices raise,
And fill his courts with songs of praise.

There soon developed annual Christian celebrations in addition to Easter which eventually were joined to form a cyclic pattern of celebration we now call the Christian year. A sense of the sanctification of all time arose. Christ was known to be the center of the new age that had come, was coming, and yet would come in its fullness. All time should be seen in Easter light and redeemed by Easter power. Therefore, "in worship we sanctify present time by enacting the past event of Jesus in time which transforms the present and gives shape to the future."[16] The oldest evidence of a primitive church year is found in Paul's first letter to the Corinthian Christians in A.D. 57. Here Paul refers to "Christ our Passover lamb" and urges the people to "keep the Festival" (1 Cor. 5:7–8 NIV). Soon one way to keep the Easter festival was to baptize on that great day. New converts to the faith had themselves begun to be resurrected to new life in Christ. A time was set aside prior to Easter for them to study, reflect, and be disciplined. This time became the season of Lent. Eventually, it also came to be regarded as wise that each year at this time all believers remake their own baptismal preparations and vows. The Christian spiritual life is an ongoing journey for us all.

The weeks of Lent now form the time when any believer who would be a maturing disciple can be humbled and disciplined. Lent consists in doing something, not merely in doing without something (e.g., fasting). For forty days Moses had remained on Mount Sinai waiting for the word of the Lord. For forty days Jesus was in the wilderness sorting out the motives and means of his mission. Forty days of self-denial before Easter is therefore judged an appropriate annual discipline for believers. Lent is a time for cleansing, strengthening, clarifying, and refreshing the soul. It has to do with the self-sacrificing journey of Jesus to the cross—and of us sinful humans who are being saved by grace and wish to join that journey.

Israel had wandered in the wilderness for forty years, and Nineveh had been given forty days to repent. For Christians, a similar period in the winter season is set aside for the double focus of considering both our human condition, including sin and its deadly consequences for both individuals and society, and the new possibilities offered to us in Jesus Christ.[17] This difficult season opens with Ash Wednesday, a deliberate time of confrontation with the unwelcome reality of sin and death. The truth is, "By the sweat of your face you shall eat bread until you return to the ground, for out of it you were taken; you are dust, and to dust you shall return" (Gen. 3:19). Recall the distressing text of Joel 2:1–2 that speaks of trembling fear accompanied by fasting, weeping, and mourning, followed fortunately by the hopeful verse 13: "Return to the Lord, your God, for he is gracious and merciful, slow to anger, and abounding in steadfast love, and relents from punishing." The prominent themes are judgment and hope, the reality of sin and death, and the potential of new life by the grace of God. The journey of the Lenten season brings one to the foot of the cross of Christ, aware of the gravity of sin, the starkness of death, and the glorious nearness of forgiveness and new life.

For Christians, the inauguration of a new creation in Christ was seen as such a comprehensive reality that it produced an organizing principle for the calendar itself. The time of Christ was to be the time to organize all time. Not only were all years now thought of as B.C. (before Christ) and A.D. (*anno Domini*, "in the year of our Lord"), but every week now was to begin with the Lord's Day. This day celebrates the resurrection of Jesus in ways intended to do much more than merely remembering. The intent is for a worshipper to experience transforming resurrection power in the present and thereby begin to live in the ways of God's future when transformation will be complete. In the Christian's annual calendar, Easter has preeminence. It is the resurrection of Jesus that interprets his birth and the whole meaning of his person, life, and death. It is an adaptation of the Jewish fifty-day celebration of the spring harvest that began two days after Passover. For the Jews who first claimed Jesus as their long-awaited Messiah, the symbolism and symmetry were perfect. The church would annually celebrate the resurrection of Jesus for fifty days, starting two days after the offering up of Christ, the Paschal Lamb, on the cross and reaching ahead to the great Pentecost event. Jesus is the ultimate springtime of new life that keeps yielding the fruit of all fruit, the very presence and power of God's Spirit in the midst of the church.

The oldest of the Christian festivals, Easter proclaims the amazing power of the resurrection of Jesus. The strong note of the original Christian preaching was that Christ had arisen on the third day according to the Scriptures. Keynoted in this dramatic message are God's victory over the kingdom of evil, Christ's eternal lordship, the assurance of a life that no grave can finally cancel, and the power of an endless life for those who, themselves risen with Christ, "seek the things that are above" (Col. 3:1). Easter is the new beginning provided by God's amazing grace and awesome power. Accordingly, through the Easter story "we remember the dream come true, the vision become reality, the fullness of life made present. . . . Jesus, the Christ of God, confronts the principalities and powers that distort God's reign, and through the mystery of his passion and death he fulfills the hopes of humanity for *shalom*."[18]

Some doors can be opened only from the outside. Isaiah wrote of one such door. Israel was entering into a long night of Hellenistic dominance that attempted to force a repugnant foreign faith on the Jews. This darkness eventually would lead to a bloodbath in the Macabbean revolt. Chapters 24–27 of Isaiah are made up of visions of a better day and psalms of praise in the night. On such a Good Friday night, with Jesus dead and hope apparently gone, his first disciples suddenly experienced bright light and almost unbelievable good news that nerved them in the face of all opposition. Isaiah's cry of confidence that God would one day open the doors from the outside had become reality for them. Indeed, "O Lord, you are my God; I will exalt you, I will praise your name; for you have done wonderful things, plans formed of old, faithful and sure" (Isa. 25:1). According to the Easter festival, Jesus is no longer in the grave; now is the time to celebrate that we who know the entrapment of death will see this door opened for us by that same divine hand. Its opening allows us to live new lives in the present and with God always.

The historical fact of the resurrection of Jesus is crucial for Christian faith. From that first Easter morning until now, there have been many people seeking to debunk the story, with no real success. The stone had been moved, the tomb was empty, and the body was gone. Jesus' disciples feared for their lives while the Romans and Jews had everything to gain if someone, anyone, could produce the body. But they did not. Instead, the shocked and terrified disciples suddenly claimed to have seen Jesus alive and started proclaiming his resurrection in the streets of Jerusalem and soon in other nations. They were thrilled and fearless, utterly transformed people. Why? So far no credible answer has emerged—except for the one they all insisted on. Jesus was risen!

The Contemplative Tradition

If the Evangelical tradition of Christianity focuses on the coming of God and proclamation of the good news brought by that coming (see chapter 2), the contemplative tradition seeks to appropriate God's presence by pursuing intimacy with the now graciously available God in the light and power of the resurrected Jesus. He taught his disciples to pray, "Our Father in heaven, hallowed be your name. Your kingdom come. Your will be done, on earth [in and through us] as it is in heaven" (Matt. 6:9–10). By the grace and under the law of God, believers are to pursue daily intimacy with the God of all the saints in heaven. M. Basil Pennington calls on all Christians to cultivate a "contemplative dimension, just as Jesus prepared for his active days of ministry by going apart and spending forty days in the school of the Spirit."[19] Contemplation is not disengagement from Christian responsibility, but a distinctive kind of Christian prayerful life. It reaches out to God like this:

> By the grace You grant me
> of silence without loneliness,
> Give me the right to plead, to clamour
> for my brothers imprisoned
> in a loneliness without silence![20]

Celebrating and nurturing the presence of God should move to a deepening pattern of consciously participating in that presence. Spirituality can be defined as "the sense of the divine presence and living in the light of that presence."[21] If God's Spirit (*ruach*) is "the confronting event of the personal presence of God," then one important aspect of the meaning of this divine presence is breadth (*rewah*). God's active presence creates space and "leads out of narrow places into wide vistas, thus conferring life."[22]

Three classics of the Christian contemplative tradition are *Letters by a Modern Mystic* (1937) by Frank Laubach, *The Pursuit of God* (1948) by A. W. Tozer, and *New Seeds of Contemplation* (1962) by Thomas Merton. These three Christians, although different in many ways, nonetheless shared one common and overriding perspective. They thought that believers in Jesus Christ are to search the Scriptures for more than theological ideas. Christians must move through the words of revelation into vital and personal contact with the risen Christ who desires to live now as the eternal God in our souls. Beyond mere religion, even beyond being saved, there should be the active pursuit of intimate relationship with God. God has come so near to us; now we must draw near to God.

In the Christ event, God chose to become like us (full incarnation, except for sin) in order that we might be enabled to become like God. What an extraordinary claim and privilege! All Christians are called to give serious attention to the presence of God and to live so that an increasing union with God grows. This kind of mindfulness is especially prominent in the Eastern Christian tradition (Byzantine, Eastern Orthodox) where the resurrection of Jesus is viewed as divine victory over the evil powers, and *theosis,* or divinization, of believers is envisioned as the goal of salvation (the word *sanctification* is more common in the West).

Gregory of Nyssa (331–396) was one of the fathers of the early church who had great influence on the spirituality of the Eastern church. He believed that the main use of the Bible is as a resource for growth in Christian virtue. In his *The Life of Moses,* he offers guidance in making regular spiritual progress. Gregory sought to build a bridge between sophisticated Greeks and the Jewish Scriptures by developing an elaborate spiritualization of the Moses story.

While seeking a union with God is central to authentic Christian life, a key distinction must be made clearly. It begins by understanding the crucial difference between *pantheism* and *panentheism* (see the glossary). The first is the Greek for "everything is God." God and the creation are essentially identical. Sometimes Hinduism, Buddhism, New Age, and other spiritual faith traditions speak of God as the soul of the universe—while the universe is thought of as God's body. This view denies the biblical perspective of the true transcendence of God who was before the creation and will be when there is no more creation. Panentheism, on the other hand, seeks to recognize the biblical insistence on the deep involvement of God in the creation, but without in any way equating the two. God's being permeates all creation so that everything exists in God and God is close to all things; nonetheless, the creation is never equivalent to, nor does it ever exhaust, God's being or presence.

Important spiritual implications flow from this distinction. In church history there are two quite different understandings of the goal of prayer and the Christian life in general. They are mysticism and biblical personalism. Mysticism, following Plato and Plotinus, emphasizes the beatific vision of God and envisions the goal of the Christian life as near possession of and union with God. Assumed is the personal reality of God with whom an individual can enjoy an unmediated link by super-rational experiences.[23] Central is the notion of *theosis,* the deification of the dedicated believer who, by God's unmerited grace and the believer's faithfulness, comes by stages to "participate in the divine nature" (2 Pet. 1:4 NIV). Most of Eastern Orthodox Christianity is quite mystical.

Biblical personalism, on the other hand, focuses more on the sovereignty of God and stresses the importance of obedience to God's will rather than any excessive contemplation of and union with the divine being that violates God's singular and sovereign nature. John Wesley (1703–1791) is a classic example of a serious seeker who was influenced deeply by Christian mysticism.[24] Later, he would become critical of aspects of typical mysticism, although he and his theology were deeply enriched by some of it to the end of his life.[25]

Mysticism's influence is obvious in Wesley's concept of sanctification, which carries the same view of spiritual maturity as reflective of God's very nature now becoming visible in human life. At the same time, his mature doctrine of perfection, for instance, recognizes human depravity and the futility of any attempted ascent to God by means of self-purification. He combined a pessimism of fallen human nature with his optimism of divine grace to attain the mystical end of full communion with God in love. Wesley is one of the few major theologians of the West who exhibits significant affinities with Eastern Orthodox thought. These include an appreciation for mystery as opposed to a confident rationalism and for experiential adoration of God rather than extensive theological analysis that sometimes borders on human arrogance. He had sorted the dross from the gold of the mystics, finding the way to avoid rampant subjectivism without abandoning the vision of Christian faith leading to living communion with (even union with) God.[26]

It is possible to join mysticism and biblical personalism. We who truly believe are to be "in Christ"[27] in a way that fulfills and does not shift authority away from the Bible to the uncontrolled subjectivity of experience. Donald Bloesch cautions helpfully that the vision of God that Paul speaks of in 1 Corinthians 13:12 is "a full understanding of God's will and purpose and unhampered fellowship with him, not a perpetual ecstatic gazing upon the being of God." The biblical Christian "strives not for *deification* in the sense of transformation into God but *sanctification*, meaning an increasing conformity of the human will to the will of God. Our aim is to be elevated not to the level of deity but to the realm or state where there is perfect fellowship with deity."[28]

The goal is not to transcend creaturehood and become divine, but to be able to glorify God as reborn sinners who recognize their creatureliness and helplessness apart from the amazing grace of God and have entered into Christ where alone there is health, life, and hope.[29] Having noted that the original meaning of the word "theology" was "union with God in prayer," Henri Nouwen explores the real need of Christian leaders and concludes, "If there is any focus that the Christian leader of the future will need, it is the discipline of dwelling in the presence of the One who keeps asking us, 'Do you love me? Do you love me? Do you love me?' It is the discipline of contemplative prayer." Will the leaders of the future truly be men and women of God, "people with an ardent desire to dwell in God's presence, to listen to God's voice, to look at God's beauty, to touch God's incarnate Word, and to taste fully God's infinite goodness?"[30] Once cautioned about the dangers of unchecked mysticism that tends to lose biblical authority and historical relevancy, one is free to appreciate without misunderstanding the gospel record of Jesus being portrayed as the vine and the members of his church the branches (John 15:5). This is a graphic way indeed of describing the intended intimate union of the believer with God in Christ.

Few believers are called to monastic isolation, but all Christians are called to fan the flames of what should be their "first love" (Rev. 2:4 NIV). Few believers are called to the severe ascetic practices that sometimes have appeared in church history and often have been based on a false view that the physical world is inherently evil. Even so, while Matthew openly reports that the Son of Man (Jesus) came eating and drinking (11:19), he also reports Jesus' teaching that disciples have hard choices to make, choices that have associated costs. The spiritual formation demanded by Jesus involves a single-minded commitment, an either/or choice between "God and wealth" (Matt. 6:24). On occasion this commitment should have an ascetic dimension (Matt. 9:15; 26:29). Controlling bodily needs and desires (fasting, celibacy, etc.) are obvious examples.[31]

There is a human longing for the real presence of God. Christians should stand amazed at John's apocalyptic vision that constitutes much of the Book of Revelation. When John was exiled in what was supposed to be a miserable solitude on the island of Patmos, God used the solitude to fill John with wisdom and joy rarely known on the struggling human scene. Being "in the Spirit" (Rev. 4:2), John was blessed with profound insight into the ways and intentions of God. He practiced the divine presence and shared the fruit of the blessed relationship that resulted. It was clear to him that God is not a transcendent object available for comprehensive intellectual curiosity—an unfortunate inclination of too much of Western theology. Rather, as Eastern Orthodox Christianity teaches, true biblical theology is "experiential as well as intellectual. God is not merely a transcendent object of detached intellectual scrutiny. He is also an immanent Subject who . . . must be experienced directly. . . . For Orthodoxy, true theology involves not only intellectual erudition but a spiritual experience with the living God."[32] This more dynamic conception can correct Western models of theology that tend to be academic reflection on propositions.

God's great love for us and our answering love are prominent themes of John's New Testament writings. Divine love is at the heart of the Christian contemplative life (1 John 4:19). God is love, and those who abide in God intentionally abide in a reciprocal love relationship (1 John 4:16–18). It is by beholding the Lord that believers are changed from glory into glory and increasingly reflect God's likeness (2 Cor. 3:18). Since the wholly other God has chosen to create and now remains available to the creation by the Spirit, "let us worship and bow down, let us kneel before the LORD, our Maker!" (Ps. 95:6).

The New Testament's ideal for the Christian life is the human will in harmony with God's will as believers become new creations in Christ. True believers can enjoy real relationships with the living Christ through the indwelling of Christ's Spirit. There is a caution never to be forgotten, however. Any notion of spirituality as heightened religious experience sought as an end in itself is alien to biblical faith. Nonetheless, the essence of Christian spirituality does involve a vital sense of the divine presence. Jesus was God really with us. Among the final words of Jesus were these: "And remember, I am with you always, to the end of the age" (Matt. 28:20). In sending his disciples on mission, Jesus assured them of the Spirit's continuing presence: "What you are to say will be given to you at that time; for it is not you who speak, but the Spirit of your Father speaking through you" (Matt. 10:19–20). There are two necessarily related biblical imperatives. First, "Believe on the Lord Jesus, and you will be saved" (Acts 16:31). Second, "Live according to the Spirit" (Rom. 8:5). One is to be alive in Christ; the other is to be maturing in the Spirit.

The names E. Stanley Jones (1884–1973), Frank C. Laubach (1884–1970), Thomas Merton (1915–1968), Georgia Harkness (1891–1974), and Henri Nouwen (1932–1996) loom large as superb representatives of the contemplative tradition. The 1925 book *The Christ of the Indian Road* written by Methodist missionary E. Stanley Jones challenges Christian mission strategies with a daring multiculturalism ahead of its time, one that drank with appreciation from the fountains of Hindu spirituality without violating the essential priority of faith in Jesus Christ. He resisted the tendency to bring both Christ and the civilization of the West to India, arguing that Christ's attitude is to fulfill, not destroy.[33] Frank Laubach's *Letters by a Modern Mystic* (1937) includes hymn lines he sang as a boy:

Moment by moment I'm kept in His love;
Moment by moment I've life from above;
Looking to Jesus till glory doth shine;
Moment by moment, O Lord, I am thine.[34]

Here is his later reflection on these lines:

> It is exactly that "moment by moment," every waking moment, surrender, responsiveness, obedience, sensitiveness, pliability, "lost in His love," that I now have the mind-bent to explore with all my might. It means two burning passions: First, to be like Jesus. Second, to respond to God as a violin responds to the bow of the master.[35]

Thomas Merton was a Cistercian (Trappist) monk whose spiritual autobiography became a best-seller and who likely is the most widely read monk in all of Christian church history.[36] In his *New Seeds of Contemplation* (1961), he speaks as follows about the highest expression of the Christian life:

> Contemplation is the highest expression of man's intellectual and spiritual life. It is that life itself, fully awake, fully active, fully aware that it is alive. It is spiritual wonder. It is spontaneous awe at the sacredness of life, of being. It is gratitude for life, for awareness and for being. It is a vivid realization of the fact that life and being in us proceed from an invisible, transcendent and infinitely abundant Source. Contemplation is, above all, awareness of the reality of that Source. It *knows* the Source, obscurely, inexplicably, but with a certitude that goes both beyond reason and beyond simple faith.[37]

The psalmist says that "happy are those . . . [whose] delight is in the law of the LORD, and on his law they meditate day and night" (Ps. 1:1–2). The contemplative life is not something far from everyday reality, something practiced only by a few spiritually elite monks and nuns in mysteriously walled communities. It is to be the daily delight in God that is the heart of the Christian life.

Henri Nouwen was a beloved Roman Catholic priest who taught at Yale, Harvard, and Notre Dame and then spent his final years selflessly serving profoundly handicapped adults. In his *Making All Things New* (1981), he reflects a theme central to Eastern Orthodox Christianity and seen biblically in Psalm 82:6, John 10:34–35, and 2 Peter 1:4:

> Jesus sends the Spirit so that we may be led to the full truth of the divine life. *Truth* does not mean an idea, concept, or doctrine, but the true relationship. To be led into the truth is to be led into the same relationship that Jesus has with the Father. . . . Thus Pentecost is the completion of Jesus' mission. On Pentecost the fullness of Jesus' ministry becomes visible. When the Holy Spirit descends upon the disciples and dwells with them, their lives are transformed into Christ-like lives, lives shaped by the same love that exists between the Father and the Son. The spiritual life is indeed a life in which we are lifted up to become partakers of the divine life.[38]

Such glorious partaking, however, is hardly automatic. So, in the face of the hectic life being experienced by so many contemporary Christians, Nouwen adds that without solitude, it is virtually impossible to live a spiritual life. The discipline of solitude enables a coming in touch with the gracious presence of God in our lives and thus allows us to taste even now the beginnings of the joy and peace that belong to the new heaven and the new earth.

Georgia Harkness's *Mysticism: Its Meaning and Message* (1973) quotes 1 John 3:1–3 about disciples having the privilege of actually being the children of God, knowing that one day they will be "like him," and carrying this responsibility in the meantime: "And all who have this hope in him purify themselves, just as he is pure." Her conclusion is that "this love, this hope, and this self-purification through the Spirit have given vitality to Christian mysticism through the centuries."[39] She also concludes that when we have finished our theologizing, all mysteries will still not be known. "We are but human pilgrims following the pathways of knowledge, and to the end of the earthly way we shall still 'know in part.' Yet our faith in Jesus Christ our Lord can give us the *assurance* of things hoped for, the *conviction* of things not seen. And is not that, after all, the object of the quest?"[40]

The contemplative tradition highlights the prayer-filled life with the common images of purging fire and enveloping love. Prayer is that intimate communication with God that fans the flame of the Christian's "first love" (Rev. 2:4 NIV). The core message of the contemplative tradition is that believers should love God with all their hearts. The contemplative life "is always calling us back to our beginnings, always forcing us to the root, always reminding us of our foundation. It keeps saying to us, 'Fall in love with Jesus over and over and over again.'"[41]

In the contemplative tradition, we have highlighted the important personal journey involved in building a grace-enabled intimacy with God. It should not be an excessively isolated individualism. Nonetheless, an intense privacy of real relationship is essential for the health of public commitment and selfless service for Christ in the world. Believers are to follow Christ into the private closets of prayer and then into the crowded and often chaotic marketplaces of public life. Often a divine-human intimacy has been sought by Christians who left the usual walks of life to join a monastic community where pursuing intimacy with God is supported in every way possible. But the pursuit usually must be carried on in the middle of the bustle of everyday living where real-life witness is urgently needed. But whether inside or outside highly disciplined communities of faith, the spiritual quest must proceed. The contemplative tradition calls believers to perfection and union, a divine-human relationship of love that brings peace that passes understanding. It is an extravagant spiritual vision that is truly amazing and foundational. It is the intentional quest for the God known to be questing after us. After all, our human desire for God is only an echo of God's more passionate and prior desire for us. We seek because first we have been sought. We love only because God first loved us.

The Apostles' Creed

Believers who seek to maximize the reality of the divine-human relationship readily agree with this judgment: "The core of the Christian faith is a person [Jesus], not a set of abstract ideas or beliefs. We must resist the temptation to speak about Christianity as if it were some 'ism,' like Buddhism, Freudianism, or Marxism. These are essentially abstract systems that have become detached from the person of their founder and reduced to sets of ideas or doctrines."[42] Christian faith is to be a dynamic relationship with a living Lord.

A fish became the early symbol of Christian faith because the five letters of the Greek word for fish came to represent the slogan "Jesus Christ, Son of God, Savior." The longest section of the Apostles' Creed is an elaboration of the life and impact of Jesus Christ on the world. The claim being made is so significant that it is either the most important claim imaginable or it is sheer folly. Jesus is said to be God's "only Son, our Lord." He was "conceived by the Holy Spirit," and this is the most significant event since the creation itself.

What emerges is the conviction that Jesus was right. God is our Father, or as the Apostles' Creed puts it, "I believe in God the Father." Christians believe in more than the paternity of God (God as the originating cause of the whole creation). They believe in the fatherhood of God. God, in all of the unimagined divine immensity and mystery, is not aloof and detached, but deliberately intimate, loving, a seeker after real relationships, the *Abba* of Jesus—even in relation to a rebellious world (Mark 14:36; Rom. 8:15; Gal. 4:6). Here is no philosophic and passionless deity, but a God whose love is unbelievably personalized and whose tenacity in seeking is extraordinary (Luke 12:6; 15:1–10). The one who created now pursues in order to re-create.

Christianity is an Easter faith with the death and resurrection of Jesus on center stage. When one looks into the face of hopeless despair and death, it now is possible to say, "He is not here—nor need I be!" It is a prayerful faith that offers a real, transforming, and eternal relationship with the God who is truly Father to all made alive in Christ through the Spirit. To participate in this relationship is to escape the clutches of mere religion. All such escape, however, is based on a sturdy theological foundation, a clear understanding of the amazing identity of the risen Jesus. Exactly who was this Jesus? Sometimes Christians sing a song that begins, "Jesus, Jesus, Jesus, there's just something about that name." This is a reverent, meditative, appropriate song of Christian devotion. The only problem, often the problem characteristic of spiritual believers given to nontheological sentimentality, is that the song never gets around to identifying exactly what is so special about that name.

Here is the uniqueness, the amazing identification made in the New Testament and affirmed by orthodox Christians across the centuries. Paul makes clear in Colossians 2:9–10 that Jesus is the source of Christian truth, the divine good news from and about God. Jesus alone is the crown of God's self-revelation. In Jesus "the whole fullness of deity dwells bodily"

Jesus Christ Is Lord!

"Therefore," declares Paul, pacing his cell like a bear, "God has highly exalted him and bestowed on him the name which is above every name, that at the name of Jesus every knee should bow, in heaven and on earth and under the earth, and every tongue confess that Jesus Christ is Lord, to the glory of God the Father" (Phil. 2:9–11 RSV).

Jesus Christ Is Lord!

That is where the whole faith came together for those early Christians. They had their debates about other things, the way we do. But this was the one overwhelming fact of their lives, the transforming center of their total experience—that Jesus Christ is Lord. Let the churches debate the nature of the incarnation, let them discuss the Trinity, let them fuss about methods of baptism and serving the Lord's Supper, let them quarrel over which holy writings to canonize and how to set up their local administration. There was one undebatable proposition at the heart of everything they believed—that Jesus of Nazareth was somehow the Son of God and therefore the mighty Lord of their lives!

John Killinger, *You Are What You Believe*

(2:9). This fullness does not mean that Jesus merely reflects divine qualities to an unusual degree, but that he actually is the incarnate presentation of the divine essence, the earthly appearance of the very presence of God. In Jesus, God actually was with us, so much so that there is an intimate oneness of the being of God and the being of Jesus. The Son, a theological designation of Jesus in relation to God, is not only the servant or supreme earthly manifestation of God. The Son is God with us!

John 3:16 is the famous verse that speaks of Jesus as the "only Son" of the Father, willingly given for our salvation. The creed says that Jesus is God's "only Son, our Lord." The "only" is the Greek *monogenēs*. *Mono* means "one" and *genēs* has to do with genetic, gender, kind, or nature. *Monogenēs* means the only one of a particular kind. When applied to Jesus, the meaning is that Jesus alone is of the same essence as God. Stunning! He is God with us, God uniquely demonstrated in human form. The foundation of Christian spirituality is that Jesus Christ is the only Son of the Father. True spirituality begins when, with Thomas, one realizes the presence of the risen Christ and exclaims in amazed faith, "My Lord and my God!" (John 20:28). In response to the many people who try to reduce Jesus to an outstanding moral teacher, but no more, C. S. Lewis is direct about the real options before us:

> Any man who is merely a man and said the sort of things Jesus said would not be a great moral teacher. He would either be a lunatic on a level with the man who says he is a poached egg, or else he would be the devil of hell. You must make your choice. You can shut him up for a fool, you can spit on him and kill him as a demon, or you can fall at his feet and call him Lord and God. But let us not come with any patronizing nonsense about his being a great human teacher. He has not left that open to us, he did not intend to.[43]

Upward into Divine Intimacy

Now that key distinctions have been made so that false assumptions and conclusions can be avoided, the upward spiritual journey may safely proceed. As the resistance within us is overcome by the grace-empowered operations of faith, hope, and love, we begin moving upward into intimacy with God. This movement in turn empowers us for ministry to others so that the authentically upward move is necessarily the inevitable outward move. Illustrating this is one of the best-loved of all the books of Christian spirituality written in the twentieth century, the 1935 volume by Oswald Chambers titled *My Utmost for His Highest.* Here is the upward journey toward intimacy with the divine. Another superb resource is Richard Foster's *Prayer: Finding the Heart's True Home* (1992). He says that adoration is "the spontaneous yearning of the heart to worship, honor, magnify, and bless God."[44]

The quest for the fullness of life in the Spirit is a trail of amazement and an adventure in adoration. If adoration functions in the rarefied air of selfless devotion to God, then the prayer of adoration is our process of loving God for who God is and not for what God might do for us. Life becomes full of thanksgiving and praise. The Psalms often employ the language of praise and thanksgiving: "O give thanks to the Lord, for he is good; for his steadfast love endures forever" (Ps. 106:1); "I will give thanks to the Lord with my whole heart" (Ps. 9:1); "O Lord my God, I will give thanks to you forever" (Ps. 30:12). Luke closes his Gospel with the report that the early Christians "were continually in the temple blessing God" (Luke 24:53). It is safe to magnify the Lord and hard to exaggerate when it comes to God. To magnify something is to increase its appearance out of proportion to reality. But when we magnify God, we are on safe ground. We simply cannot say too much about God's goodness or love. The most seemingly exaggerated statements will still be far below what is actually the case. Amazing!

Biblical verses like 1 Peter 1:15 are nothing less than stunning. Christians are called to be holy because God is holy. How do people become holy as God intends? The Bible focuses in Isaiah 6 on a highpoint of its whole narrative. The place is in the temple in Jerusalem at the foot of God's throne. The young prophet wants a vision for God's people and gets it only by first getting a vision of the holy God. For us to really be about God's business, God must be known by us as "holy, holy, holy," the One other than us, beyond us, different from us and our world and usual church life. Rather than hyped ministry success stories, we need in the church today humble, broken Isaiahs of God. We do not need more great men and women of God, but men and women who really know a great God. We do not realize God's true reign by standing tall ourselves, but by the "woe is me" humility that comes when one is face-to-face with the holy God. We are to come into God's presence with awe and repentance. We become holy only by being filled with a radical amazement about God.

As Jesus said, we are holy when we pray "hallowed be your name" (Matt. 6:9–15) with our hearts and then live in a distinctive way that actually blesses God's name. We are to walk with a difference because we have encountered the different God. True faith comes from the amazement of an Easter-like encounter. Note these dramatic words of Charles Wesley in his hymn, "And Can It Be That I Should Gain?":

Long my imprisoned spirit lay
Fast bound in sin and nature's night;
Thine eye diffused a quick'ning ray,
I woke, the dungeon flamed with light;
My chains fell off, my heart was free,
I rose, went forth, and followed Thee.

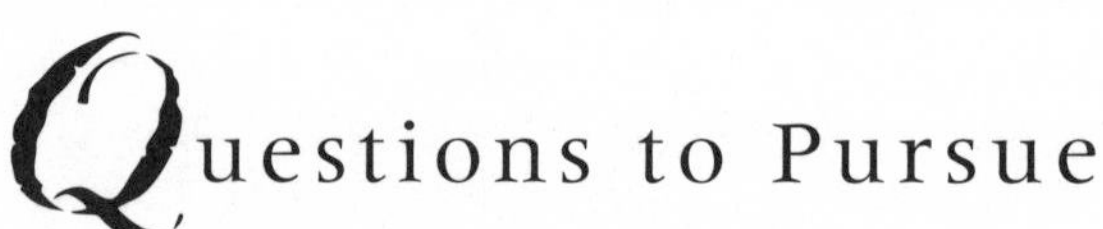

Questions to Pursue

1. How significant is the resurrection of Jesus for the Christian faith?
2. Is a sense of awe and amazement before the reality of a holy God compatible with a scientifically minded culture that is inclined to reason, manipulate, and gain profit from all possible things?
3. In what ways can it be said that the Spirit of God is extravagant?

4. Is pursuing intimacy with a graciously available God just so much doctrinally dangerous subjectivism, or is such a pursuit vital for Christian faith and life?
5. What is the significant meaning of *monogenēs* in relation to Jesus?
6. What are the meanings of *theosis* and *panentheism* (see the glossary) in relation to Christian spirituality?

4

Truly Belonging: The Spirit's Act

Blessed be the God and Father of our Lord Jesus Christ, who has blessed us in Christ with every spiritual blessing in the heavenly places, just as he chose us in Christ before the foundation of the world to be holy and blameless before him in love. He destined us for adoption as his children through Jesus Christ.

Ephesians 1:3–5

The church is the fountain of the living water that flows to us from the heart of Christ. Where the church is, there is the Spirit of God, and where the Spirit of God is, there is the church and all grace.

Irenaeus

The world is full of refugees, orphans, and other struggling persons. Even if they have homes and families, these people do not feel accepted, do not belong, and are disconnected, therefore experiencing life as aliens and strangers. Millions of modern people have entered the twenty-first century feeling cut off from much meaning in life. They function like the past has been unhooked from the present, and the future at best will probably be more of the same. People today often find themselves lonely, even in a crowd, and are unsatisfied in spite of indulging in fascinating and expensive things. Living is from day to day, from paycheck to paycheck, and often from fix to fix. Somehow daily existence has gotten largely orphaned from life itself.

Early in the story, the Bible reveals God calling a people, electing a nation, and giving a promised land to wanderers in the wilderness. The One who originally created is the same One who chooses to relate redemptively to restore family, to adopt back children who have become lost and orphaned. The love of God does not rest when relationships are broken. God comes to offer renewed belonging. Jesus did not come to condemn but to save (John 3:17). Unfortunately, the world—and sometimes even the church—does much condemning. Consider this moving testimony of R. Eugene Sterner given when he was a sixty-year veteran of outstanding Christian ministry:

> My early life was not a happy one. There was much humiliation and ridicule, a general atmosphere of negative, judgmental attitudes and very, very little expression of love. I felt so utterly alone, alienated, and unloved. . . . When I first heard evangelistic preaching, I was drawn to become a Christian. But the strong emphasis was on instantaneous "experience" where all of one's problems would be immediately solved. . . . The big trouble was that, for me, that was not true. . . . It has been a long pilgrimage from the negative mentality and guilt-ridden life, and I have not arrived, but the change has brought increasing victory, peace, and joy.[1]

Biblical revelation is not intended as more condemnation, but love extended and true family offered.

Peter writes to "God's elect, strangers in the world, . . . who have been chosen . . . and given . . . new birth . . . and . . . an inheritance that can never perish" (1 Pet. 1:1–4 NIV). Jesus promised a continuation of God's long-standing attitude—"I will not leave you as orphans" (John 14:18 NIV). The work of the Spirit of God is to activate true belonging. It is the continuing work of atonement or "at-one-ment" with God. It is the church emerging by grace as the family of God. It is a believer being enabled by grace to come home to the Father who waits with open arms (Luke 15:11–32). The action of the Spirit moves people of faith toward true belonging.

Conversation Partner, Community Builder

How far this tragic circumstance of being orphaned is from the original intent of God! God created in a way consistent with the divine nature as a loving and relating being. God is gracious and self-communicating. Creation is best understood as the fruit of the overflowing of God's love. The Spirit of God fosters conversation and communion between God and creation and among created persons. There is in creation the possibility of prayer and a yearning for community where love is shared and fulfilled. The Spirit encourages and enables prayer, fellowship, true belonging, and the bond of love.[2]

What is it in the nature and character of God that both summons and enables the human response of prayer? Because of who God is and how God chooses to relate to creation, the divine-human relationship is intended to function as a relationship of reciprocity, a true dialogue between God and humanity. God speaks, acts, and listens. People speak, act, and listen in response. In this amazing conversation, believers find their true home.[3] Clark Pinnock finds much significance in such reciprocity, including a reflection of the nature of God as "open and unbounded." With love as a reigning attribute, the sovereign God, truly transcendent, has chosen to make room for others and to seek real and mutually responsible relationships with them.[4] God is a covenant-making God.

In the difficult times of World War II, George Buttrick found bedrock meaning in Christian prayer. He announced that "if God is in some deep and eternal sense like Jesus, friendship with Him is our first concern, worthiest art, best resource, and sublimest joy." He spoke of his troubled generation as one "with pride shattered and body bruised," longing for "sanctuary, for fruitfulness, for an abiding Home." In his classic book titled *Prayer*, Buttrick proclaimed that "prayer is a rock staircase to an inviolable sanctuary, a courage to win fruitfulness from sand, and a home, even amid earth's changes, in the Eternity of God."[5] To be adopted as children of God is surely to be at home in the most profound sense. That home has many brothers and sisters. The Spirit works in this family (church) to bind all members together. Consider this spiritual wisdom:

> Christians who have not learned to experience God as the Spirit are still in a preliminary state of faith. They do not yet know the *confidence* of faith, for they lack the sense that God is truly with them at all times. They are little acquainted with the true *community* of faith, for they have not felt the spirit binding them together with others in the faith. . . . And they are missing the *power* of faith, for they have not experienced God moving in and through them to correct human situations, heal the sick, or improve the world.[6]

The confidence and power of faith are tied closely to the community of faith. Faith flowers best when it is at home in a faithful church.

Given the mass displacement of many people today, one timely metaphor for heaven is the end of homelessness. Jesus promised that he has gone to prepare a place (John 14:2–3), a place where one truly and eternally belongs, has identity, where relationships are whole, since all who are there are in fulfilling relationships with God and each other. But the challenge is here and now. What will be then should begin now. The church is to be a sign of grace to the world, a pre-heaven fellowship of acceptance and love. The Christ community should be a real home place for the lost and place-less. Christians, as pilgrim people in societies of listless wanderers, look forward to a place "whose architect and builder is God" (Heb. 11:10). However, they are to be faithful in the meantime, participating with God in making a place for others, even now.

Christian spirituality is a matter of friendship received and expressed. The primary relationship that Jesus came to offer is friendship with God. He said, "No longer do I call you servants, for the servant does not know what his master is doing; but I have called you friends, for all that I have heard from my Father I have made known to you" (John 15:15 RSV). True spirituality is not easy believism or another self-mastery technique. It is friendship where you really belong and participate. It is a move from legalism to grace, from being on the outside with slaves to the inside with family. God welcomes you home—and intends for the invitation to be passed on to others. You may have wasted much, lowered yourself far, and become the ugly opposite of all that God's family stands for. But, according to the parable of Jesus, the merciful Father is waiting with a ring and a big party (Luke 15:11–32). This is all a matter of grace. If you come, you qualify. If you are finally coming home, the big celebration is all for you.

The Wonderful Bible Word

A wonderful New Testament word, a belonging word, tells of a magnificent adoption into all that is good and fulfilling. This adoption involves divine parentage. By the loving work of the Spirit of God, we all can really belong again. The wonderful story is first told by Luke in the composite work Luke-Acts. There he recounts the work of the Spirit following the resurrection and ascension of Jesus. In so doing, Luke gives us his inspired vision of what the life of faith should involve for the people of God in all times. There is to be a real continuity between the life of Jesus and the life of his people. A new age has dawned. It is the age of the Spirit in which the grace of God is made available to all people. Believers belong to a new community of adoptees, the church. The new family relationship comes by virtue of the new birth in Christ that is our adoption by God so that we actually are daughters and sons of the most high.

Now let us look at the biblical word that speaks about the wonder of us mere humans actually being adopted by God after the empty lostness of our not being who we were created to be. The word is *huiothesia.* The basic noun *huio,* "son," is put into action when compounded by *thesia,* "placing,"

We're Orphaned without You! Mahatma Gandhi and Jesus

The great Christian missionary E. Stanley Jones, a close friend of Mahatma Gandhi, commented that after Gandhi's assassination, the radio constantly broadcasted programs that eulogized the father of that great land [India]. Mrs. Naidu, a well-known Hindu poet, spoke three days after the assassination, "O Bapu, O Little Father, come back. We're orphaned without you. We're lost without you. Come back and lead us."

Jones said he could sympathize with her plea, representing the cry of a stricken nation. But . . . he thought, "O God, I'm grateful I don't have to cry that cry for the leader of my soul: 'O Jesus, come back. Come back. We're orphaned and stricken without you.'" He knew that his Master had been received in glory to sit at the right hand of God the Father and that he *is* coming back to redeem the entire world. Gandhi was a great man. But Jesus is Savior of the world, "and will come again to judge the living and the dead."

John Killinger, *You Are What You Believe*

to generate the composite meaning of "placing as a son." We who were not now are. We who were nothing but slaves are granted by sheer divine grace the status of family members. What a wonderful word of life!

Here is a beautiful picture from the ancient Greek/Roman world. Sometimes a simple declaration in the marketplace turned a slave into a son. When there was no male heir in a wealthy household, an adopted son could immediately become heir to everything the family had. Adoption then and now involves an official transfer of position and privilege. For the Christian believer, we are talking about God taking an action, undeserved and by divine grace only, that makes all the difference for slaves to sin who become adopted and thus are liberated new sons and daughters of God. In God's case, however, the motive is not saving family pride or protecting the continuity of family property. There is no crisis in the heavenly family, no desperation on the Father's part. The adoption is a grand love act. And when this family's wealth is shared with new children, it is not diminished. The love keeps reaching for still others, and, no matter how many respond and are thus adopted, the family resources remain more than adequate.

This wonderful word of adoption appears biblically in three tenses. Divine adoption is viewed as past event, present process, and future prospect. We first consider the past because what we call to memory forms identity and character in the present and determines what we anticipate as future possibility. The sobering fact is that believers who are not consciously related to their biblical roots seldom do much more than reflect their own cultural contexts in the world. Christian spirituality is first of all a gift of God in line with biblical precedent.

People today face constant change. Companies downsize, jobs disappear, moving trucks arrive again, and names of local banks change for the fourth time in a decade. Today's technology alters the way we communicated, computed, and played just yesterday. Who and where we are as individuals, churches, communities, and even nations seems unstable. Where is the sure anchor—or is there one anymore? To this question the Judeo-Christian tradition has always said yes and given great prominence to memory. From the tradition's beginning, "the call and the commitment to remember make up the great antiphon of covenant intimacy between God and the people of Israel."[7] To remember in this case means to participate by grace in a loving relationship with God that understands the present and embraces the future in light of a known and defining past. To be adopted by God today is a current flash in the long and blazing glory of God's adoptive history.

Adoption as Past Event

Salvation, really belonging again to God, is not earned. It is a gift of God. Too often people try to live so God will love them, but in fact they should be living in a godly way because God loved them first and enables such living by the presence of divine mercy, love, and power. While no one can buy chosenness, we all have been chosen nonetheless. We were adopted by God as an act of divine love before any awareness or action on our part. In fact, God "has blessed us in Christ with every spiritual blessing in the heavenly places, just as he chose us in Christ before the foundation of the world to be holy and blameless before him in love. He destined us for adoption as his children through Jesus Christ" (Eph. 1:3–5). To understand this requires both memory and faith.

Biblically speaking, ancient Israel became the paradigm for the faithful of all times, a model of the way God's saving grace is experienced. The dramatic story is told in Exodus 14 and then repeated elsewhere in Scripture as a way of rooting the people of God in the gracious historical actions of the God who heard their cries and elected them to be a special people for him. They who were no people became God's people by a covenant of love and responsibility. The biblical record of this stunning adoption is clear and central. The whole message of salvation rests on this record and builds on it in the glorious and cumulative act of God in Jesus Christ. In fact, an excellent way to think of Christian worship is as an act of congregational remembering—remembering who God is, what he has done, and whose we now are by the adoptive act of God's redeeming love. The briefest of biblical reviews yields many insights about God's treasured possession (Exod. 19:4–5), the heart of God's true people (Jer. 24:6–7), belonging by adoption (Rom. 9:4), and being chosen as God's own people (1 Pet. 2:5, 9).

Obviously, Hebrew roots are crucial to authentic Christian faith. A particular and pivotal past provides a necessary framework for today's Christian faith. All Jews trace their ancestry to Abraham as father of the Hebrew nation. The Lord proclaimed through his prophet, "Look to the rock from which you were cut . . . look to Abraham, your father" (Isa. 51:1–2 NIV). The New Testament teaches that Gentile believers—those who are spiritual rather than lineal descendants of Abraham—also share in this Abrahamic kinship (cf. Gal. 3:8). Consequently,

> the authors of God's Word—virtually every one of them a Jew—have a profoundly Hebraic perspective on life and the world. If we are to interpret the Bible correctly, we must become attuned to this Hebraic setting in the ancient Near East. . . . The message of the New Testament is in the Hebrew tradition as against the Greek tradition. Our tutors to Christ are Moses and the Prophets, and not Plato and the Academies.[8]

Paul made plain that Gentiles are heirs with Israel of a common heritage and thus are one body (Eph. 3:6). For Christians, Israel's history is now their history. To forget this special history and to believe in a different framework is to lose one's spiritual identity as a Christian, to be a plant without a root, to hope for a future that is cut off from its foundation.

What is the Hebrew foundation? It is the ancient conviction of the Jews that, because God has graciously chosen and called, an obedient response brings belonging. James Muilenburg puts it clearly:

> Israel lives by the consciousness that she belongs to the historical invisible King who reigns. When she is faithful to her vows, she is not stranded on the shoals of time, but lives in a relationship to the ultimate Lord. She lives by her belongingness.[9]

Truly belonging to the family of God and becoming the person and faith community in whom the fullness of God can dwell is not a goal to be accomplished on one's own. Only with all the saints are believers enabled to move toward realizing for themselves and others the knowledge of God's love in Jesus Christ. The saints, the true friends of God, are joint travelers on the journey of faith. Being longer on the way and farther into the process, they can be welcome guides who surround the church today. The believer should seek the company of the friends of God, including those of previous generations through the many spiritual diaries, autobiographies, and biographies now available. To become what is intended in Christ involves an intentional belonging to the lives of other believers.

Those who have gone before are a cloud of witnesses and cheerleaders (Heb. 12:1) for those believers who yet struggle in this world and cry out to God in their pain and with their questions. The message from the gallery of the saints of yesterday is that current disciples should believe that God still hears, chooses, adopts, redeems, and shares a wonderful destiny. Even more, those who have taken the journey of faith in earlier times have left a legacy of wisdom that now is a rich resource for today's faithful. We are urged to remember the foundations and realize the potential fruit of being adopted by God.

Adoption as Present Process

When the time was right, God acted in Jesus Christ "in order to redeem those who were under the law, so that we might receive adoption as children. . . . So you are no longer a slave but a child, and if a child then also an heir, through God" (Gal. 4:5, 7). This is the core of the gospel story. John reports that Jesus came into the world, the very world that had come into being through him, and he was not even recognized. However, "to all who received him, who believed in his name, he gave power to become children of God, who were born, not of blood or of the will of the flesh or of the will of man, but of God" (John 1:12–13). We who repent and are adopted by divine grace are now granted full rights as God's children, but we have not yet received the full realities of our rich inheritance. We are on a journey, still very much in progress.

The journey metaphor is central to a biblical view of the Christian life.[10] A primary model is Jesus himself. The important central section of the Gospel of Mark is constructed as a journey of Jesus from Caesarea Philippi to Jerusalem. It is a journey of revelation and spiritual encounter that includes three passion predictions, each accompanied by the phrase "on the way." To follow Jesus means journeying with him to a coming cross and then on to an empty grave. The Christian way is both costly and full of glorious new life. Christian spirituality as depicted by Luke in Luke-Acts is journey spirituality. The revelation of the risen Lord comes to two disciples on the road to Emmaus (Luke 24:13–35), the Ethiopian eunuch was converted on the road from Jerusalem to Gaza (Acts 8:26–39), and the revelation of the risen Lord to Saul happened dramatically on the road to Damascus (Acts 9:1–9).

In fact, the Christian life itself is designated as "the Way" (Acts 9:2). Jesus leads and guides along the path of faith (Acts 5:31; Heb. 2:10; 12:2). Luke fosters a strong sense of the life of faith as a journey, with the Lord Jesus making known and possible along the way "the qualities of character he requires of his followers."[11] When Peter suggested building cabins for long-term spiritual residence on the Mount of Transfiguration, Jesus said no (Luke 9:28–36). Being with Jesus requires moving from glorious revelation to assisting people in need and joining in the burden of the cross. Holiness is serving on the move. It is "a geyser of spiritual energy, transforming people into the image of the Holy One, and advancing his rule on earth."[12] The creator God did not merely once create, but continues to create. Creation, well beyond a past event, is a present relationship of reclaiming and re-creating love. Since God is personal and love, the divine intention is real and reciprocal relationship.

The phrase *going on* is characteristic of John Wesley's concept of the gospel's involvement in the believer's life. Christian life is a process toward perfection, attainable in significant part by serious believers within time and history. The Wesleyan order of salvation is a carefully outlined way to the realization of the reign of God in all of life. Every spiritual experience, whether gradual or instantaneous, is an invitation and command to move on to a higher level of spiritual reality. The Christian is one who is going on in the might of the Lord, from faith to faith, from grace to grace, until at length one realizes "the fullness of God" (Eph. 3:19). There is little tolerance for any spiritual status quo, any resting on past laurels, regardless of the degree of spiritual maturity attained.

The spiritual goal for Wesley was nothing less than Christian perfection, leading to his conclusion that "how much soever any man has attained, or how high a degree soever he is perfect, he has still need to grow in grace and daily advance in the knowledge and love of God his Savior." Wesley's exhortation was simply this: "Whereunto we have already attained, we hold fast, while we press on to what is yet before, to the highest blessings in Christ Jesus."[13] Sanctifying grace, like grace generally, is unearned and unearnable. Nonetheless, believers are to press on. Richard Foster is right: "Holiness *is* a 'striving to enter in,' as Jesus tells us. *Effort* is not the opposite of grace, *works* is."[14]

To be holy is to really belong, to be in the process of being formed by the Christlike vision, practices, beliefs, and mission of the historic people of God. To be sanctified is to intentionally be on the way with Christ and in the midst of Christ's people, on the way to allowing the Spirit of God to re-form the image of Christ in individual hearts and the community of believers. It is to be grateful and obedient resident aliens in this world.[15] To facilitate this reformation and make possible this alien status, we must remember that prayer should be the primary language of the Christian community. Prayer directs the church to the God who forms it. Henri Nouwen is right: "Praying is not one of the many things the community does. Rather, it is its very being."[16]

Adoption as Future Prospect

That which was, and increasingly is, yet will be in greater fullness. The community of Christian faith stands with one foot rooted in the long tradition of God's gracious adoption and the other foot planted in the still arriving future of God's final redemption, judgment, and gathering home. As Paul put it when writing to the Romans, "We ourselves, who have the first fruits of the Spirit, groan inwardly while we wait for adoption, the redemption of our bodies" (8:23).

The future, like the past, is an arena of God's presence and action. God's people are to live toward this future, anticipating the eventual fulfillment of his desire and intent for love, justice, and wholeness. When believers are in touch with God's past and thus know who they can be in the present, the result should not be a smug resting in any identity attained to date. To the contrary, being God's people means to be on a hazardous and costly mission as alternative communities in the world, faith communities that question cultural norms in light of covenant standards. Living out of God's past and toward his future makes today a dynamic, meaningful, and demanding enterprise. All is possible because it is empowered by the God who calls, adopts, and provides.

The Rich Christian Tradition

Spiritual adoption means belonging. It is a family affair. The individualistic assumptions many Christians now bring to their spirituality did not apply in the first century. As Judaism developed a congregational form of worship in the synagogues of the Diaspora, so Christians, the first of whom were all Jews, assumed that public, communal worship was basic to the spiritual life of faith. Most of the basic elements of Christian worship were inherited from the synagogue—prayer, psalms, Scripture reading, sermons, and singing.[17] The church makes a serious error when it abandons the corporate dimension of its Jewish roots in favor of the rugged individualism of a Christianity that has lost its biblical sense of accountability to each other in the community of faith. God chose a people (Deut. 7:7). Jesus taught his disciples to pray, beginning with "*Our* Father" (Matt. 6:9). Like Israel of old, the church came to be called "the people of God" (1 Pet. 2:10 NIV) and is expected to function with communal self-awareness.[18] In many ancient and modern synagogues, when the congregation completes the reading of one of the books of Moses, the entire congregation exclaims loudly together, *"Hazaq, hazaq, ve-nithazeq!"* ("Be strong, be strong, and let us strengthen one another!"). The intense corporateness of this Hebrew heritage is a vital root system of the rich Christian tradition.

Being adopted by God necessarily implies becoming part of God's family. The Christian faith is not an individual affair. Christian spirituality in large part is Spirit-assisted life in the community of faith. Stanley Hauerwas reports that he is an "evangelical catholic," a way of highlighting his United Methodist affiliation that rejoices in the transforming good news in Jesus Christ and has deep roots in the broad traditions of Christianity. The phrase "evangelical catholic" points to a believer's privilege of belonging to the whole church and to the wisdom of rediscovering holiness not as an individual achievement, but as the work of the Holy Spirit who builds up the body of Christ. To be the built-up church is to return to John Wesley's understanding of the church as a disciplined community of faith within which "perfection is but another name for submission."[19] To be spiritually whole is to belong to the whole body of Christ.

Protestants struggle with how to submit to a disciplined community without, on the one hand, getting lost in the frequent mediocrity of community legalisms or, on the other hand, rebelling altogether and joining the ranks of individualism and consumerism—two common idols of contemporary societies and churches.[20] Even so, the whole church should play an important role in biblical interpretation and discipleship guidance. The prejudice against church tradition typical of Protestants goes too far. There is great value in the accumulated wisdom of past generations of Christians who have engaged the Bible with Spirit-led seriousness. The Spirit of God has been interpreting the meaning of Jesus in the church for a long time. The resulting heritage is an obvious resource for today's church. Note this:

> While it is true that Christians are people of the Book, it is also true that the Bible is a book of the people. It was the Spirit's gift to them collectively. The canon was determined by the churches as they listened to the Spirit. If this is so, and if we respect the wisdom of tradition in giving us the canon, ought we not to respect it in other ways too—for example, in matters of interpretation? The guidance needed to secure the text of the canon is also needed in areas of interpretation, which is never final and which continues within the community in a never-ending conversation.[21]

Biblically understood, the church is a charismatic community. The word *charismatic* derives from the Greek *charisma,* meaning "grace gift." This is the heart of the Christian gospel. Salvation is by divine grace, a reality flowing from God's self-giving. Such gracious mercy is the foundation of the very life of the Christian community. The church is charismatic in at least two senses. First, it is called into being and constituted by God's gracious work of redemption by the Spirit through faith in Jesus Christ. Second, God's Spirit continues to work graciously in the church to build it up and equip it with needed spiritual gifts for its ministry.[22] It is crucial that such gifts, given sovereignly by God, be received gratefully and allowed to operate as intended. The inspiration and manifestations of God's Spirit in power, revelation, work, and service all are necessary. Without them church life soon deteriorates into human status, gift becomes fixed office, ministry becomes bogged in bureaucracy, the body of Christ becomes a mere religious institution, and Christian fellowship is reduced to times of distraction, amusement, and occasional kindness together.[23]

The dynamic of Pentecost, where the church first began, calls for and provides so much more than the usual human imitations. This Pentecost potential remains central for the integrity of the church's ongoing spiritual life. Approaching the annual Christian celebration of Pentecost should be characterized by a humility defined this way by the fourteenth-century Flemish mystic John Ruusbroec: "an interior bowing of the heart and mind before the transcendent majesty of God." We should pray that God's grace will allow us to be supple in this necessary posture of reverence. It was the way and instruction of Jesus (Matt. 11:29). It is the way of the Spirit and the real life of the church that was born by the Spirit at Pentecost.[24]

The Church Year: Pentecost I

The Easter season of fifty days is an extended celebration of the launching event of Christian faith, the dramatic resurrection of Jesus. This season culminates a focusing on the centrality of the resurrection by celebrating an immediate consequence of resurrection faith, the formation and growth of the church. The day of Pentecost (the fiftieth day) closes the annual Easter festival by highlighting the Holy Spirit as the agent who makes the risen Christ always present to the church. Easter and Pentecost are much closer together in meaning than is often recognized. It was the illuminating power of the Spirit that allowed Jesus to finally be understood properly as God's Christ, and it was in understanding Jesus Christ that the life-giving power of the Spirit was experienced among the disciples. One might say that "the grace of the Holy Spirit was presented in the subjective appropriation of the salvation objectively brought about by Christ."[25]

Theologically, there should be no separation of Christ and the Spirit. The Spirit is none other than the Spirit of Christ. The Spirit recalls and declares all that Jesus said (John 14:26). Only by the Spirit can one confess "Jesus is Lord" (1 Cor. 12:3). The purpose of the giving of the Spirit is to transform believers into the likeness of their Lord (2 Cor. 3:18; Gal. 5:5–6, 13–25). No New Testament passage so fully shows the nature of the church in the power of the Spirit as does Acts 2:1–42. Laurence Stookey summarizes:

> The Day of Pentecost is about the formation of the church out of a frightened band of followers; that tight-lipped crowd, which had huddled timidly behind closed doors, is thrust by the Spirit into the streets of Jerusalem to proclaim the gospel in terms everyone can understand. How are we to account for this change? Only by recognizing that the Spirit is the One who forms the church by making the Risen Christ manifest in power.[26]

Those early followers of Jesus were mostly Jews. They were used to celebrating in the springtime the key events that had made them God's covenant people. Passover was an agricultural feast rooted in the original rescuing of Israel from Egyptian bondage. Following that ancient exodus had come the giving of the law at Sinai, the completion of the initial covenant relation of the liberating redeemer to the newly constituted people. For Christians, Pentecost completes the cross-resurrection event by the coming of the Spirit who also would interpret, guide, and empower the people (the Christian Mount Sinai of the Spirit).

The Christian celebration of Pentecost involves a dramatic juxtaposition of Genesis 11 and Acts 2. The first passage is the story of the Tower of Babel, where human pride and presumption led to chaos and a divided humanity. The second is the glorious reversal, the Spirit's arrival to relocate a people from many places so they can become God's united community in which there is understanding and humility. The church is the place of reconnectedness (1 Cor. 12:4–31) that reverses the curse of Babel. Rather than thinking of the church as a voluntary organization of individuals who gather for the sake of personal enrichment and ministry effectiveness, the church in fact is the community called together by the risen Christ. Rather than choosing to associate together for reasons of convenience and preference, believers are to gather because they are summoned—the Greek word for church (*ekklēsia*) means "those who have been called forth," like a summons to appear in court. The church is God's choice and intent, not something optional for compatible believers. To be in Christ is to be part of Christ's body, the church.

We who believe are called together by the court of heaven to be God's servant people on earth. Pentecost celebrates this calling, recounts its first dramatic occurrence, and encourages belief that the Spirit still calls, gathers, equips, and sends. The primary place of the Spirit and the intended home of the Christian is the church, the body of Christ that is alive in Christ's Spirit. The goal of Christian life is not merely to get one safely into heaven, but to get heaven actually into present life so that through such

Christlike life the world might be changed. The goal of any Christian congregation should not first be concerned about being relevant, growing, or successful. The central goal is to be alive in God's Spirit. Such life is the root reality of all the church is to be and the dynamic that allows it to act in the power of the Spirit. No wonder Clark Pinnock begins one of his major books with this:

> As we begin, let us say: Welcome, Holy Spirit, come and set us free! Let each one catch the living flame and be ravished by your love! Let our souls glow with your fire. Help us overcome our forgetfulness of the Spirit.[27]

While he says "each one," note the corporate focus of the "we" and "us."

When the church is faithful to the Spirit's ministry, it becomes set apart for God's purposes and purified in Christlikeness. New believers mature into saints by God's sanctifying grace. The Epistle of James highlights the formation of Christian moral character by focusing on the heart of virtue, the source of action. There is a spiritual reality that can produce a different kind of person. Reflecting Jesus' teaching in the Sermon on the Mount, James

> shows us a person who can face trials of all kinds with rock-solid joy, a person who is plugged into a divine wisdom that sees "bitter jealousy" and "selfish ambition" for the impostors they truly are, a person who instinctively relates to all peoples on the basis of the "royal law" of love, a person who out of divine resources is able to "tame the tongue," a person who eschews "fightings and wars" because the inner wellspring of life is so purified that from it naturally flows blessing and not cursing.[28]

This inner wellspring is the heart of the Holiness tradition (see chapter 5) and is not to be dismissed as mere legalism, perfectionism, or otherworldliness, dangers this tradition sometimes faces. It is the vision of life that works as it was intended by God. The vision is fulfilled by

> sustained attention to the heart, the source of all action. It concerns itself with the core of the personality, the well-spring of behavior, the quintessence of the soul. It focuses upon the formation and transformation of this center. . . . Holiness is loving unity with God. It is an ever-expanding openness to the divine Center. It is a growing, maturing, freely given conformity to the will and ways of God. Holiness gives us our truest, fullest humanity. In holiness we become the persons we were created to be.[29]

Although many Protestants have reacted negatively to the Roman Catholic practice of naming and honoring saints, the reaction deserves some reconsideration. Without question, a significant way the Lord remains present to his disciples in every generation is through the faithful lives and compelling testimonies of those who have matured in Christ and thus have become especially effective agents of the Spirit. Not only do Christians make Christ present to the world by preaching the good news, they also make him present by embodying Christ in real life, individually and together as the church of the Spirit. There is a significant ministry for testimonies, for believers telling their stories of the experienced goodness of God. In addition, a great cloud of witnesses, those sainted ones who have gone, have left behind their rich witnesses of the graciousness of God. Pentecost is the Christian season that encourages emphasis on lives being changed by the Spirit. When such change occurs, a community of the Spirit arises, nurtured by the remembering and sharing of the testimonies of those once in and those now in the earthly fellowship of the redeemed.

The church, to be at her best, always should be on the path to holiness and celebrating the lives of the saints of God. Effective ways must be found to keep visible before the church the worthy lives of Christian pioneers and mentors. Particularly the young need regular reminders that the transformative power of Christ is still present and at work in this troubled world—including in the lives of some people actually known by them. Beyond sound theology, people need stories, reports, demonstrations, and witnesses. One idea is to use the children's time in worship services for the celebration of Christian biography.[30] Some church communities schedule an "All Saints Day." One way to highlight such a sacred remembrance is to honor all of the local saints who have died in the previous year. The point is to rejoice in what God has done for others and thus be strengthened in one's own resolve to live a life worthy of imitation because we have opened ourselves to the sanctifying power of God. As poet-theologian Daniel S. Warner put it:

> How sweet this bond of perfectness, The wondrous love of Jesus!
> A pure foretaste of heaven's bliss, O fellowship so precious!
> Beloved, how this perfect love, Unites us all in Jesus!
> One heart, and soul, and mind we prove,
> The union heaven gave us.[31]

Those who share life in the Spirit find themselves in real community with each other—the key to authentic Christian unity. A. W. Tozer once observed that one hundred pianos all tuned to the same fork are automatically tuned to each other. They are of one accord because they are set by a common standard. Similarly, "social religion is perfected when private religion is purified. The body becomes stronger as its members become healthier."[32] The common tuning fork for Christians is Jesus Christ. Charles E. Brown said it well:

> The church can only regain her lost visible unity by rallying around our Lord Jesus Christ. In the past there have been cries to rally around this doctrine or that creed, or to rally to this or that battle-cry. Now the call is to come alone to Jesus Christ. . . . Doctrine is very important; but more important it is to get back to the supreme Person, who is the source of all true doctrine.[33]

Rallying around doctrine, creed, or limited battle cries can easily degenerate into mere religion and even destructive division. Rallying around the person of Jesus Christ, however, centers and unifies.

Celebrating the saints in an alive community of the Spirit pulls together many of the themes of the whole Christian year. These themes include "the work of resurrection grace in all of God's people; the devotion and discipline needed in the life obedient to God; the divinization of our humanity by the incarnation of divinity, accomplished by the power of the Spirit; the connectedness of all believers; the hope of life beyond death."[34]

The Charismatic Tradition

If the Evangelical tradition focuses on proclaiming the good news of the God who has come in Jesus Christ (see chapter 2) and the contemplative tradition focuses on an active pursuing of spiritual intimacy with this now graciously available God (see chapter 3), the charismatic tradition celebrates the transforming and enabling that is provided by the divine presence with the church. This tradition is essentially about Christian life being immersed in and empowered by the Spirit of God. Exploring it is essential because it is only through the transforming presence of the Spirit that believers are enabled to do God's work, evidence God's life, and really be God's church together. There is a deep yearning among God's people to actually experience the immediate presence of God. The charismatic tradition addresses this need directly by focusing on the centrality of the fruit and gifts of the Spirit in Christian life—individually and corporately as the church.

If the facts of the Christ event are the historical foundations of Christian life, the continuing presence of Christ's Spirit is its energy. The apostle Paul instructed believers to be "filled with the Spirit" (Eph. 5:18). This filling should be evidenced by the fruit of the Spirit, which includes "love, joy, peace, patience, kindness, generosity, faithfulness, gentleness, and self-control" (Gal. 5:22). These virtues are not the products of human cultivation (mere religion), but the gracious results of the indwelling presence of God's Spirit. Christians do not live by their own wits and wisdom. Authentic Christian life is life in and through God's Spirit. The Spirit is none other than the sovereign God, the breath of the divine that blows where and how God wills (John 3:8). A key aspect of the ministry of the Spirit is to empower and gift believers for building the church, witnessing, and serving in the world. The Spirit will not be domesticated to improper goals. We believers too easily are distracted by the process of institutionalizing the faith. We become satisfied with little more than the pious comforts of religious talk and routines. But the charismatic tradition insists that "the kingdom of God depends not on talk but on power" (1 Cor. 4:20).

The charismatic stream is illustrated biblically in clear ways by the life and writings of the apostle Paul. Reports Richard Foster:

> [Paul] had a well-nigh amazing balance between the rational, objective apprehension of the gospel and the ecstatic, subjective charisms of the Spirit. . . . He gives us both the most carefully reasoned theological treatise in the New Testament—Romans—and the finest practical teaching on exercising the spiritual gifts—First Corinthians.[35]

The charismatic witness of Paul begins early in his ministry with the speaking of the Holy Spirit to the church leaders at Antioch. The issue was the Spirit's choosing, calling, and sending of Barnabas and Paul on missionary service (Acts 13: 2, 4). Soon Paul, "filled with the Holy Spirit," overcame opposition to the gospel of Christ (Acts 13:9–11). Guided in his journeys by the Holy Spirit (Acts 16:6–10), he ministered in Ephesus on his third missionary journey by teaching some converts. When he laid hands on them, "the Holy Spirit came upon them, and they spoke in tongues and prophesied" (Acts 19:6). It is the life, energy, wisdom, and transforming power of God's Spirit that carried the church forward in its first dramatic generations.

Problems in the church arose early, however. The Corinthian congregation is a distressing example. The *Didache* from the early second century already reflects a trend toward structuring the church's life away from the charismatic spontaneity of its earliest years. The followers of Montanus emerged in the mid-second century with a new prophecy that expected the return of Christ very soon and allegedly even identified Montanus as the counselor promised by Jesus. Whatever the real truth (records may not be dependable), the Montanists finally were judged to be heretics, a judgment that added to the growing disfavor of charismatic phenomena. Spirit-gifts were replaced by established church offices. Good order and an increasingly institutionalized apostolic succession became the norm. The energy of the Spirit was channeled, ordered, and regularized.

Another round of church institutionalization troubled the generations following the flood of renewal in the Protestant Reformation of the sixteenth century. Dynamic spiritual insights had become fixed into inflexible and mandatory creedal traditions. The faith of the heart migrated to a relatively sterile religion of the head. Soon fresh voices arose calling for new and less controlled life in the Spirit. These voices launched the efforts of Anabaptists[36] and then Calvinistic Puritans and Lutheran Pietists who were determined to complete the Reformation through allowing the Spirit to reform their lives as well as their doctrines. The Puritans attempted to form congregations of visible saints who were both doctrinally orthodox and spiritually alive. The goal of their spirituality was a live orthodoxy that exhibited the power of godliness.

The eighteenth-century Wesleyan revival in England focused strongly on the actual transformation of life by the power of God's Spirit ("perfect love"). Spreading to the English colonies in North America, this Wesleyan impulse helped give rise to Pentecostal spirituality.[37] In the opening years of the twentieth century, Montanus-like events again took place. The fresh Spirit events were initiated in part through the ministry of William J. Seymour (1870–1922). An African-American born in the post-Civil War period in Louisiana, he found his way to Cincinnati, Ohio, joined the Evening Light Saints (later the Church of God, Anderson), and through this holiness reform body was impressed with an antidenominational stance and a broad-mindedness on issues of racial and gender equality. He acquired a strong commitment to radical holiness ideas like the immediacy of the Spirit and the inclusiveness of the church. Beginning in 1906 when ministering in Los Angeles apart from the Church of God movement, he received the gift of tongues and helped launch the Azusa Street Revival and the twentieth-century Pentecostal movement.

This charismatic renewal is now a major worldwide phenomenon in Christianity. It crosses all denominational lines. There is much to be said about it on both positive and negative sides. J. I. Packer, seeking to assess this renewal biblically, announces twelve positives and ten negatives. The positives include joyfulness, Spirit-empowered living, and missionary zeal. The negatives include emotionalism, anti-intellectualism, sectarianism, and spiritual elitism.[38] The problems are obvious, but the biblical rootage is equally obvious. To be spiritual as a Christian is to be Spirit-centered. The church or body of Christ is a charismatic reality.[39] It is constituted by the Spirit, gifted by the Spirit, and thus should be governed by the Spirit. Clark Pinnock took a courageous step beginning in the early 1970s by publishing a trilogy of articles in *Christianity Today* in which he argued that Bible-believing evangelicals would have to find a way to get over their rigid rationalism and inordinate fear of emotional excess in order to avoid a quenching of the Spirit. He had no personal case to make for any divisive spiritual elitism or any insistence that a divine gift like speaking in tongues is for every believer as a necessary sign of the reception of the Spirit. It was just that he appreciated charismatics as "those evangelicals with a little more spiritual voltage." He was one with them, at least in their claims for the "heart dimension" of the faith.[40]

Current postmodern thought emphasizes that the process of knowing and identity formation is shaped significantly by the community in which one participates. Believers are called to participate in a community of faith that shares a common biblical story about encounter with God historically in Jesus and now in the Spirit of the Christ. This story is to be newly embodied. Centered on a proposal by Stanley Hauerwas about the sanctified body, the essays comprising the book *Embodied Holiness* (1999) insist that any genuine Christian holiness must be vitally related to our physical and social bodies (including the body of Christ, the church).[41] The Easter truth of new life with Christ should be understood by the Pentecost truth of the empowerment of the Christ community, the church.

The Apostles' Creed

Article 3 of the Apostles' Creed affirms plainly the core belief in the Holy Spirit. In fact, this belief is assumed to be so central that all that is affirmed in the whole creed about the church and the Christian life, present and future, comes under the dominant reality of God's Spirit:

> I believe in the Holy Spirit;
> The holy catholic church;
> The communion of saints;
> The forgiveness of sins;
> The resurrection of the body;
> And the life everlasting.

A crucial transition occurs in the Apostles' Creed when historic memory moves to contemporary meaning. Having affirmed as sacred memory that Jesus was conceived, born, suffered, crucified, died, buried, descended, risen, and ascended, the creed dramatically shifts to meaning in the present tense. This same Jesus now is "seated at the right hand of God" (Col. 3:1). This being "seated" is the time of the church's life, bracketed by the past events of Christ on earth and the anticipation of Christ's coming again "to judge the living and the dead." Between formative past and culminating future is the present of the Spirit, the reigning and ruling, enlivening and gifting of the Spirit of Christ.

In the Apostles' Creed, the Spirit of God is not encountered primarily in the sphere of the inward and personal, but in a social community identified as the "holy catholic church" and the "communion of saints." Belief in the Holy Spirit involves sturdy belief in the reign of God already present in the church. One might say that the church is—or ought to be—the corporate presence of the Spirit of Jesus in the world. Those who have been adopted and set free from self-preoccupation and self-interest receive a

Discrimination Should Die at the Cross

As an orthodox Jew, Paul knew that human society traditionally has been broken down and segregated. Each morning he, along with other orthodox male Jews, would recite a prayer in which he thanked God that he was not a Gentile, that he was not a slave, and that he was not a woman. . . . It gives real meaning to what Paul taught in Galatians: "In Christ there is neither Jew nor Gentile, bond nor free, male nor female, but we are all one in Christ Jesus." He was taking aim at socio-economic and political alienation, bond and free. He was taking aim at sexual alienation, male and female. And he was saying all those things are fundamentally wrong, and they are resolved at the Cross. For at the Cross male and female, bond and free, Jew and Gentile find their oneness; they realize that they're all the same and move into the church of Jesus Christ.

Stuart Briscoe, *The Apostles' Creed: Beliefs That Matter*

new life that is based on love and is open to others, particularly others in the household of faith. To be a maturing Christian believer is to be a Spirit-assisted participant in the believing community.

The prophetic Christian voice of Dietrich Bonhoeffer announced that the experience of divine revelation, while personal, comes through the church which is "Christ existing as community."[42] The essential nature of Christian experience is communal. Becoming a Christian makes one part of the church, a family member with all other believers. The Spirit constitutes the body of Christ without racial, gender, or economic consideration. Here is one human community being enabled to abolish as wholly inappropriate the usual human barriers to true fellowship (Gal. 3:28; Col. 3:11).

First, the Jewish Passover celebrated the historic exodus, God's miraculous deliverance of the people from Egypt (see Exod. 12–13). Then Jesus transformed this joyous remembrance into the Lord's Supper, the communion of his grateful disciples. Most dimensions of Christian spirituality are highlighted graphically as a congregation of believers gathers at the table of the Lord. The very gathering is a sign of Christian unity. According to Paul, "Because there is one bread, we who are many are one body, for we all partake of the one bread" (1 Cor. 10:17). The command of Jesus is for the community of believers to eat and drink with awareness of the significance of his life poured out and his willing participation in the already inaugurated and still coming reign of God (Matt. 26:26–29). The church is to be a partaking community that remembers in the rich Hebrew sense of being truly present for the past events of God's acting and newly present to the immediate significance of these events. To participate properly in the Lord's Supper is to belong to God's redeemed people and to be freed (a new exodus) for the journey of intimacy with God in God's Spirit and with God's people.

While the second article of the Apostles' Creed recounts the crucial historical facts of the Christ event as the basis of salvation, the third article teaches that salvation happens in the community of the saints. To speak rightly about the Spirit of God is to recognize God at work in the world, in me, and especially in the church, the community of faith. God remains present as the Spirit of Christ for the purpose of transforming the world into Christlikeness. The church is the concrete and visible, although obviously provisional and partial, presence of the new creation promised by the Hebrew prophets and launched through the life, death, and resurrection of Jesus.[43] The final reign of God is not yet, but already—even if ambiguously—it is being made visible in the world through the reality of the faithful church of the Spirit.

Alone in Community

A well-known book by David Riesman is titled *The Lonely Crowd*. It is a study of the changing American character that loves superficial togetherness and still remains disturbingly alone. In this regard, we can gain much wisdom from the example of the great redwood trees of California. Their width and height and age are awe-inspiring. What massiveness and endurance! Surely they must have huge and deep roots to allow them to stand so high for so long. But they do not. I am told that their roots are relatively shallow. The secret is that they grow in groves, and the roots of the trees intertwine beneath the soil. In this way, they stand together with a massive root base. For a huge wind to take one down, it would have to take a whole cluster of them down together. Christians are supposed to be like that. The spiritual journey through the sometimes great difficulties of this life is not to be a solitary affair. The church is a called-out community, a grove of believers assisting each other in the face of life's violent winds.

The second-century manual of Christian church life is commonly known as the *Didache*. It offers this instruction: "Meet together frequently in your search for what is good for your souls." Crucial indeed for healthy Christian life is the close fellowship of the body of believers. The spiritual growth of individual believers is mysteriously intertwined with the lives of all others in the community of faith.[44] Much of Western Christianity in recent centuries has been troubled by the tendency to individualism and a relatively weak doctrine of the church, especially in branches of Protestantism.

The typical Protestant distinction between the visible and invisible church is not appropriate. Real love is visible in word and deed. Much too often, what the church shows to the world are structures of division and programs of only pious decoration. The one, holy, catholic, and apostolic church of God is both gift and task. Its very possibility is a miracle of God's Spirit, and wherever it becomes actual, disciples faithfully use their gifts from God to make visible the current reign of God in the body of Christ. Jesus promised that he would always be with his faithful disciples. Note, however, that this promise was in connection with their carrying forward his mission. The mission of the church is to be an expression of the healing and saving power of the Spirit of Christ. Said Jesus, "Go therefore and make disciples of all nations, baptizing them in the name of the Father and of the Son and of the Holy Spirit, and teaching them to obey everything that I have commanded you" (Matt. 28:19–20). In this process of mission faithfulness, he promises, "I am with you always, to the end of the age." Those participating in the church that is pouring itself out in redemptive life will never be alone.

The Christian spiritual life is to be a life-in-relation existence patterned after and enabled by the Triune God. This life takes shape in the community of faith that has been initiated by Jesus in the coming and power of Christ's Spirit at Pentecost. Note this from Simon Chan:

> The purpose of Christian formation is not developing a better self-image, achieving self-fulfillment or finding self-affirmation; nor is it the development of individualistic qualities that make singularly outstanding saints. Rather, it is developing certain qualities that enable us to live responsibly within the community that we have been baptized into.[45]

Community and solitude are not to be separated. Believers are nurtured in silence, while accountability arises in the active life of the church. The person who never learns to be alone before God will be swallowed up by the fellowship, functioning only as a parasite on or a pawn of the large community. It is self-defeating to attempt to live for others without first deepening one's own self-understanding, freedom, integrity, and capacity to love out of the experienced richness of God's love. One first must "be" before being able to effectively "be for others."

Even so, as much of monasticism has shown over the centuries, an excessive aloneness easily breeds unhealthy isolation, loss of community values, fresh heresies (my own voice is surely the voice of God), and mission irresponsibility. Christian spirituality is new life in God, shaped and lived in the church for the sake of the world. The genius of early Methodist spirituality lay in its plan of guidance for believers that led them into a maturing discipleship empowered by grace, shaped by the doctrines and ordinances of the church, and disciplined for good works (see chapter 8). John Wesley accomplished this with a connectional church polity that remains a viable paradigm for Christian spiritual formation—although it is not an attractive paradigm in our social context of extreme individualism.[46]

Because of the work of the Spirit of God across the ages, those who are lost can be found, those who are empty can be filled, those cut off can be connected again, and those willing to be witnesses can be gifted for the task. Those who have become detached from meaning, joy, and relationship with God can be newly secured in their true home so that they really belong and are heirs by adoption of all the divine riches. God has chosen us! We can be family with the heart of the universe and the ages. While we were yet sinners, Christ died for us. We love him because he first loved us and chose, called, and gifted us to be God's children, the people of God doing God's work in this world. We truly belong.

Questions to Pursue

1. What is the proper relationship between condemning sin and adopting sinners? Did Jesus come to condemn? Does the church you know best have the right attitude about this?
2. Explain the meaning of a relationship of reciprocity in relation to salvation and prayer.
3. Detail the meaning of the three tenses of *huiothesia* (being placed as a child of God).
4. What is the relationship between Easter and Pentecost, and how are the events of the first Pentecost celebrated in the charismatic spiritual tradition?
5. Think about how the Apostles' Creed places its teachings on the church, salvation, and the future under the present ministry of the Spirit. Do you understand and agree with this prioritizing?
6. How can a Christian be alone in a community? Why should this not ever be?

5

Truly Knowing: The Spirit's Eyes

> Jesus said, "And this is eternal life, that they may know you, the only true God, and Jesus Christ whom you have sent" (John 17:3). Is anything obstructing our knowing this Jesus—who is the perfect angle of vision for knowing God?

> Revelation consists essentially not in the transmission of propositions but in personal address by the living God, which involves the communication of information, yet only in the context of mystical participation in the spiritual reality that the propositions seek to express. . . . There can never be an identity between human statements of faith and divine revelation, but there can be a correspondence through the illumination of the Spirit.[1]

The comments above suggest that truly knowing about spiritual things requires the right angle of vision and the right relationship with God. Faith is required. Knowing is difficult and even impossible apart from Spirit-relatedness. You may be able to read, but surely not in every language. In Shakespeare's classic *Julius Caesar*, the character Cicero speaks in Greek to avoid any passersby understanding him. Said Casca, "Those that understood him smiled at one another and shook their heads; but for mine own part, it was Greek to me." This comment about Greek has entered the English language as a reference to anything that is foreign and not understandable. The apocalyptic images of the Book of Revelation communicated well to persecuted Jewish Christians of the second century, but were religious-language nonsense to uninitiated outsiders (in some ways including us).

Without proper preparation, nearly anything can be mystifying. For instance, do you know that most of planet Earth has never been seen by human eyes? The hidden deep-sea environment that covers 71 percent of the planet's surface dwarfs all other earthly habitats combined. Entering this vast black abyss presents the challenges of deep darkness, intense cold, and crushing pressure.[2] Not knowing the environment hampers accurate understanding. It seems much the same with a pursuit of the knowledge of God. The vastness of the divine can be overwhelming and chilling, crushing hope that somehow we can penetrate and truly know. Whatever we manage to learn, it is hardly even a beginning.

The traditional language about God sounds foreign to many people today. To typical ears of the early twenty-first century, the theological vocabulary of the church rarely connects with what they know and where they live. Nonetheless, we read the following from a spiritual master of the twentieth century:

> One of the indubitable facts about the world is the fact that a great many people, including large numbers of those generally accounted the best and wisest of mankind, have reported what is known as religious experience. They have asserted both confidently and humbly that their minds have been aware . . . of that which they interpret as divine. . . . It is maintained that the finite knower has been conscious of contact with that which is supremely real yet neither human nor physical.[3]

For some people there is the experience of an actual relationship with God in which meaningful if only partial knowledge of God is received as a gift. The biblical affirmation is that the humble seeker after God's truth is enabled by grace to actively apprehend (never fully comprehend). God intends to be known as the Holy One, who loves and reaches for renewed relationships. In fact, the available truth of God is best apprehended in the context of renewed relationship with him. Seeking divine truth while avoiding or neglecting intimate spirituality is a dead-end effort. Note this from Kallistos Ware:

> As a Christian of the Orthodox Church, I wish particularly to underline this need for *living experience*. To many in the twentieth-century West, the Orthodox Church seems chiefly remarkable for its air of antiquity and conservatism. . . . For the Orthodox themselves, however, loyalty to Tradition means not primarily the acceptance of formulae or customs from past generations, but rather the ever-new, personal, and direct experience of the Holy Spirit *in the present*, here and now.[4]

To be in Christ through the present life and guidance of the Spirit is to be set free and on the path of Christian knowing.

Knowledge of the Holy

The world today is filled with people whose physical eyes function perfectly and yet who are virtually blind in a crucial sense. They are unable to see into the depths of life. The "eyes" of their hearts fail to be aware of much of the meaning not immediately available to the physical senses. Many brilliant people are blind to spiritual truth. They regularly analyze, categorize, synthesize, and compute facts, but they eliminate consideration of the most basic reality of human existence—God is. Henry David Thoreau once made this comment in his journal: "The question is not what you look at, but what you see."[5] How do we really come to know when the issues are ultimate? What senses are required for spiritual knowing? We all have experienced meeting someone who is vaguely familiar. The memory is searched while one tries to avoid embarrassment. We look hard at that face with our eyes. We see, but we are not yet really seeing. Suddenly comes the "Oh, yes!" We have managed to recall the context and the name. Looking only with the eyes is quickly transformed into really seeing—finally knowing.

Context is crucial. The knower is always conditioned by time, place, and the community within which the work of interpretation proceeds. Here, then, is an important assumption. Christians gain knowledge of God primarily through past revelation in Jesus Christ as conveyed in the Bible (the particular historical context of faith). In contrast to much of contemporary theology, spiritual knowledge for Christians is not essentially an experience-based phenomenon. It is a gift of God's revelation. Even so, in order to think biblically in reference to spiritual truth, authentic insight is a byproduct of the Holy Spirit living and working within a believer and the believing community. After necessary study, discipline, and prayer, understanding the biggest truths is a matter of revelation. Revelation, however, not only has the necessary historical roots but also requires current illumination by the Spirit. In other words, spiritual things are "spiritually discerned." William Barclay once quoted this wisdom from Anselm:

> He who has not believed will not experience; and he who has not experienced will not understand; for just as experiencing a thing is better than hearing about it, so knowledge that stems from experience outweighs knowledge derived through hearsay.[6]

Howard Thurman reports in his autobiography that the recurrent challenge of his life was

> how to honor my feelings without vitiating my power of reflective thought, how to escape the aura of sentimentality typical of the religious quest, as well

A Generous Orthodoxy of the Spirit

In the process of contending for orthodoxy, evangelicals dare not forget to qualify the noun by its proper adjective. If it is not prefaced by the word "generous," "orthodoxy" risks being modified by qualifiers like "dead," "narrow," or "uncharitable." Therefore . . . harbingers of the new center must orient themselves around the grand consensus of the church throughout the ages and take care that they avoid dogmatizing points of doctrine beyond this consensus. . . . The "generous" side of the renewal of orthodoxy arises from an understanding of the crucial difference between the truths of the Christian faith and the doctrinal formulations in which any one set of these truths comes to expression at any given point in history. . . . Theological reflection that seeks to articulate and maintain right doctrine is also the servant of the Spirit's work in the new birth and the transformed life.

Stanley J. Grenz, *Renewing the Center*

> as the prejudgment of emotionality with which black people are associated [Thurman was African-American], while giving full rein to that which I feel. It is a misreading of the role of feelings to separate them from the function of mind at work! . . . After all, it may be true that what is called "thought" is a function of feeling, reduced to slow motion.[7]

In a time like today when the quest to be spiritual is publicly popular and seems to many conservative Christians little more than subjective and self-serving chaos, leaders like David Wells call for a fresh commitment to understanding truth as objective and certain knowledge derived directly from divine revelation.[8] This call, while understandable and appropriate to a point, must be cautioned by the need to recognize that theology is a second-order language, a language needing a more spirituality-based than creed-based identity for believers.[9] For the ancient Hebrews, "truth was not so much an idea to be contemplated as an experience to be lived, a deed to be done."[10] Truly knowing spiritually, therefore, cannot be separated from experiencing and being obedient. Nor can such knowing be fully captured in polished logic and be the assured fruit of hardheaded reasoning. The Hebrew verb *yada* ("to know") means to encounter, experience, or share relationship in an intimate way. To really know requires being rightly related. Seeing means looking through the eyes of the Spirit who personalizes and contextualizes the truth of revelation.

Spiritual knowledge involves the whole human personality—a joining of the cognitive and affective. It is not merely the process of intellectualizing religious information. The Hebrews had a way of saying things paradoxically. For instance, the Book of Exodus says both that Pharaoh hardened his heart and that God hardened it (Exod. 8:15; cf. 7:3). The prophets taught that God both judges and forgives, is at once holy, righteous, and loving, formed light and created darkness, and in the midst of wrath always remembers mercy (Isa. 45:7; Hab. 3:2). Themes of predestination and freedom stand side by side with no seeming sense of contradiction. The Jews were more practical than systematic theologians. They knew they did not have all the answers for the ultimate questions and refused to force a rational harmonization on the enduring enigmas concerning God's truth. They finally had to walk by faith and let mysteries stand. In fact, faith begins in awe, not in intellectual formulas and logic. "When mind and soul agree," Abraham Heschel said, "belief is born. But first our hearts must know the shudder of adoration." Faith is "a blush in the presence of God."[11]

There is mystery attached to Christian faith; all things spiritual do not have to be fully rationalized (a Western preoccupation). When they could not understand, the Hebrews were called to accept the paradox and trust God in the process. Note this: "The Semites of Bible times did not simply *think* truth—they *experienced* truth. . . . Truth is as much encounter as it is propositions. . . . To the Jew, the deed was always more important than the creed. . . . Neither did he feel compelled to reconcile what seemed irreconcilable."[12] Beginning toward the end of the twelfth century, however, much Christian theology in the West increasingly took on a scientific form. Theology concentrated on a critical understanding of the faith's doctrinal content. This minimized the affective and personal dimensions of the Christian gospel. In an extensive analysis, William Abraham rightly laments this shift.[13]

People can at least approach knowing God in ways similar to how they often know other persons and things within the field of their experience. Note these biblical references to the knowledge of God. "O taste and see that the Lord is good . . ." (Ps. 34:8). God's "robes are all fragrant with myrrh and aloes and cassia" (Ps. 45:8). Jesus said, "My sheep hear my voice" (John 10:27). He also said, "Blessed are the pure in heart, for they will see God" (Matt. 5:8). Taste, see, smell, and hear are only figures of speech, of course, when it comes to knowing the divine. What they suggest is that knowledge of God involves direct experience with the divine. This is in contrast to the Pharisees who are pictured in the New Testament as so busy finessing the formulas of religion that they lose track of the reality the formulas signified. A moving witness to authentic faith comes from Brennan Manning who was converted after twenty-two years of "living by secondhand faith." On that wonderful day of grace and new life, he finally knew

God's love and power "with a knowledge greater than our knowledge because it is beyond the capacity of mere human knowledge."[14] He understood much better when he was rightly related.

A certain detached rationalism characterizes many Christians and causes them to be cautious about giving much room for the illumination of the Holy Spirit. The fear is that human subjectivity will replace biblical authority. Conservatives regularly resist the liberal tendency to view divine revelation in terms of human experience and current human wisdom. However, another tendency is also a real danger. It is the tendency toward a mechanical view of revelation that grants legitimacy only to timeless propositional content. Such a fixed verbal approach to Christian truth leaves limited room for contextual and historical factors and risks placing a fence around the written Word of God in a way that easily excludes the work of the Spirit in textual interpretation. Having inspired the text of the Bible and guided the church in knowing what texts are truly inspired by God (canon), the Spirit should be permitted to continue to open the Bible's meaning to believers. Explains Clark Pinnock:

> The Spirit, at work in the contexts of our lives, helps us to grasp the divine intent of Scripture for our time. What is given is not the communication of new information, but a deeper understanding of the truth that is there. . . . Because Scripture is spiritual, it has to be spiritually appraised (cf. 1 Cor. 2:13).[15]

A basic thesis of Robert Mulholland is surely correct. The flawed identity of the human ego-self is developed and protected today by the informational, functional, and doing modes of being that prevail in secular culture. A key task of Christian spiritual formation is to break this deadening crust.[16] To break through the rational and pragmatic crust requires more than systematic Bible reading or the mastery and use of critical skills of scholarly biblical interpretation. The Bible needs to be approached in a relational mode (prayerfully, obediently, in conversation with the church, in openness to the Spirit). The Bible can only be understood through the illumination of the Spirit who first inspired it. Readers open to the Spirit's involvement become participants in an ongoing process of biblical inspiration (the work of the Spirit when the Bible was written and the work of the same Spirit when it now is read and needs to be understood in different settings and times). My plea echoes that of Dwight Grubbs who insists that

> mysticism, asceticism, spiritual theology, grace gifts, theocratic leadership, and experiential faith be given their rightful places in the belief system and the practices of the church. What I am praying for is a great surge of empha-

> sis upon spiritual formation that will enable us to move beyond defending doctrinal positions, or debating theological formulations, beyond a mainly intellectual approach to the Christian faith, all the way to that place where persons experience a dynamic, personal relationship with a living God.[17]

To "know" in the realm of faith is intimately related to knowing the knower (God) in the context of the believing community—the church.[18] Spiritual knowledge is much more than just a collection of correct religious information. Beyond information is spiritual formation. Beyond ideas is the God in whose vast mystery lies real understanding. It is important to think of God inspiring both the biblical text and the current reader of the text. The first secures the bounds of Scripture while the second empowers the insight of the reader, especially when the reader is open to the wisdom of Christ's Spirit and body, the church. The Christian encounter with God is transformative. To know God is to be changed by God. Being changed allows yet greater knowledge. To speak objectively about knowing God is as unrealistic as a lover claiming to speak dispassionately about the one loved. For Christians, to know the truth is first to be known by the truth. Christian theology has no obvious subject matter since God is not an object of human knowledge and is not scientifically accessible as most physical objects are. Faith and relationship are essential for spiritual knowing. Seeking for truths about God is not to precede or overshadow actually knowing God.

There are several theories of how believers come to "know" and what is meant by religious knowledge. In recent centuries, a preferred theory has centered on the assumption that a clear, certain, and exclusive norm acts as the base for all knowledge. William Abraham calls this theory "foundationalist epistemology" and announces that now it has fallen on hard times.[19] This approach is nearly exhausted theologically and spiritually. The exhaustion calls for a return to the fuller heritage of the early church that grounds and defines spiritual knowledge by an ecclesial canon that is essentially "a means of grace: that is, materials, persons, and practices intended to initiate one into the divine life."[20]

Sinners need transformation, not merely information and justification. The goal of the Christian knowing process is to participate in the very life of God. It is a mistake to view Christianity as a theory of knowledge, a collection of sacred books, or a highly structured and authoritative community of believers. Such views tend to mean mere religion. Early Christianity was first and foremost a response to a series of acts of God that arose in and around Jesus Christ and were made clear and present through the working of the Holy Spirit. Christianity "was first a pneumatological event which disrupted the way of death and opened up a radically different way of life for those who were initiated into new life in Christ."[21] The Holiness movement's call for people to "let go and let God," "lay all on the altar," and be "clay in the potter's hand" was a direct challenge to the pretension that humans are self-grounded subjects capable of dominating rationally over an objectified world.[22] We really know only as we become children of God and look at God through Jesus with the eyes of the Spirit.

What should be the focus and goal of spiritual knowledge for the Christian? The dual answer is simple: (1) gaining transforming knowledge of the holy and (2) actually participating in that holiness as it seeks to renew all of creation. What is the eternal life that Jesus promises? It is "that they may know you, the only true God, and Jesus Christ whom you have sent" (John 17:3). Here is what God said long ago through the prophet Jeremiah: "Do not let the wise boast in their wisdom, do not let the mighty boast in their might, do not let the wealthy boast in their wealth; but let those who boast boast in this, that they understand and know me, that I am the LORD; I act with steadfast love, justice, and righteousness in the earth, for in these things I delight, says the LORD" (9:23–24).[23] This calls for much more than mere religion. What gives God the most pleasure? God desires "steadfast love and not sacrifice, the knowledge of God rather than burnt offerings" (Hos. 6:6). There is a great distance between knowing God with the intellect and loving God with all that one is. Loving releases real knowing.

What conditions of the human spirit tend to prepare one for gaining knowledge of the living God? The Quaker philosopher David Elton Trueblood once listed the five following conditions: reverence, a childlike spirit, quietness, moral obedience, and a combination of aloneness and togetherness. Being humble before mystery, being unashamed of searching, being prepared to implement what one comes to know, and staying quiet long enough with oneself and fellow searchers are attitudes and practices that lead to spiritual knowledge. We are instructed by the psalmist to be still and know (Ps. 37:7; 46:10). We also are told that the pure in heart come to know God (Matt. 5:8), and the one prepared to do God's will is most likely to know what that will is.

The pattern of Jesus is clear. He was intentional both in engagement with the public, willingly facing all of its needs and foibles, and in disengagement for serious prayer and reflection. Christian believers are to retreat into their closets, walk and worship with fellow believers, and serve in the practical realities of God's world. Insight comes in the mutually supportive contexts of retreating, walking, worshipping, and serving. Careful attention to the five conditions identified by Trueblood does not guarantee unusual spiritual wisdom, of course. These conditions in themselves are hardly sufficient for knowing God; but they are necessary conditions without which seeing and knowing God are unlikely at best.[24] A dependable and satisfying vision of God finally is a gift, an act of divine grace. Right relationship is followed by divine revelation.

The Wonderful Bible Word

There is a wonderful biblical word for spiritual discernment. The word is *epiginōskō*. The basic verb *ginōskō*, "to know," is intensified in meaning by addition of the prefix *epi*. Now more than just knowing superficially, we are talking about really knowing, knowing in depth, truly perceiving, intimately, beyond the normal range of human awareness. In 2 Corinthians 3:14–16, Paul speaks of the inability of the rabbi in the synagogue to understand his own Scriptures until his heart and mind are turned to the Lord Jesus. Failing to experience the power of God is to fall short of really knowing God. Let us follow our biblical word through the New Testament and learn about really knowing as aided by relationship to God through the Holy Spirit.

Dependable Knowledge

Spiritual knowledge is much more than possessing some quantity of religious information. Even so, Christian faith is based on the revelation of God in actual historical events. Accurate information about these events is crucial. Luke wrote his Gospel out of a concern that Theophilus might "know the truth concerning the things about which" he had been instructed (Luke 1:4). This Christian physician had been enabled by God's grace to research and write an account about Jesus that was a reliable guide for future generations who would consider this information and decide questions of faith based on it. Biblical inspiration means the right story has been told in the right way.

To be a Christian is both to know the biblical story and to respond to it by participating in its transforming potential. Both the story and the participation are seen in two hymns that emerge from the Church of God (Anderson) tradition. One is "Back to the Blessed Old Bible" by D. Otis Teasley and the other is "I Am the Lord's, I Know" by Teasley and Charles W. Naylor. The first points to the source of dependable perspective, and the second celebrates personal involvement in the good news, an involvement that yields insight, joy, and assurance. Kallistos Ware is right: "There is only one means of discovering the true nature of Christianity. We must step out upon this path, commit ourselves to this way of life, and then we shall begin to see for ourselves."[25]

According to Genesis 4:1, Adam "knew" his wife Eve, and she gave birth to Cain. That knowing obviously was more than recognizing her name and face. It was direct involvement, intimate relationship, a profound knowing that involved the intentional relating that allowed conception and finally made birth possible. Likewise, true wisdom lies in relating intimately and properly to the great mystery of Christ and his cross. St. Paul maintains that living fully and faithfully in the mystery of Christ will prepare the Colossians and now us to see through the deceptions spun by specious or plausible arguments (Col. 2:4). The wisdom Paul learned in Christ is the wisdom of the cross, which unveils the folly of human wisdom and guides humans to real understanding grounded in love (Eph. 3:17–20).

George Fox (1624–1691), founder of the Society of Friends (Quakers), was an unschooled apprentice to an English shoemaker. He went in search of enlightenment and came to rely on the "inner light of the living Christ." In 1649 he was jailed for interrupting a church service with an impassioned appeal from the Bible on behalf of the Holy Spirit as the authority and guide for Christian believers. The next year he was imprisoned as a blasphemer, and the judge nicknamed his followers "Quakers" because Fox had exhorted the magistrates to "tremble at the word of the Lord." According to Elton Trueblood, the genius of Fox lay in his core idea that "Christian experience could be couched in the present tense." Fox aroused men and women in a remarkable way by use of this direct question: "What canst *thou* say?" He had rediscovered the power of moving from speculation to experience, thereby providing verification of the reality of spiritual experience by the only evidence which is convincing, "the evidence of changed lives."[26] To gain confidence in one's awareness of the faith, one must be a committed disciple. Doing and being are critical for knowing.

Full Recognition

Real understanding is much more than seeing with the eyes and hearing with the ears. Could a baby born into poverty in a distant place long ago be God among us? He came to his own people, and they knew him only as the baby from Bethlehem, a boy from Nazareth, and a troubler of Jerusalem. He was hardly the Messiah from God (John 1:10–11). To affirm messiahship takes revelation and faith. Could ordinary humans with all their sin become God's people on earth? To say yes requires more than most people see possible on the surface of things. One can know and still not know. Paul explained to the Romans that people suppress the truth despite knowing about the revelation of God in creation—a false knowing that does not translate into proper practice (Rom. 1:32).

Following the resurrection of Jesus, the bold public testifying of Peter and John was successful and annoyed a range of Jewish religious leaders. An arrest followed. When those in authority saw the boldness of these disciples, they were amazed and more fully recognized them as committed companions of Jesus (Acts 4:13). On another occasion, Peter engaged a crippled beggar and pronounced healing in the name of Jesus (Acts 3:1–10).

People are inclined to look and not see, observe and not really understand. But when they saw this man standing, walking, even jumping as he praised God, "they recognized him as the one who used to sit and ask for alms at the Beautiful Gate of the temple; and they were filled with wonder and amazement at what had happened to him" (Acts 3:8–10). Their mere looking had become real recognition and understanding.

After the resurrection of Jesus, two men walked and talked with him on the way to Emmaus, but it was only over a meal at their home that "their eyes were opened, and they recognized him" (Luke 24:31). Later, Peter was delivered from prison and hurried to the house of Mary where many disciples were gathered in fear and prayer. Being completely unexpected, he knocked repeatedly. A maid was overjoyed "on recognizing Peter's voice" (Acts 12:14), but she had trouble convincing the others that it actually was Peter. Their ears were open, but their understanding remained closed. Still later, Paul wrote to the Colossians to express gratitude for more than that the gospel had come to them. His thanks was for the wonderful fact that the coming of the word of truth was obviously bearing fruit and spreading and had been doing so "from the day you heard it and truly comprehended the grace of God" (Col. 1:6).[27] One Christian tradition speaks of "seeing the church." Beyond the all-too-visible institutions and human failings of much that carries the name of Christ, the eyes of faith can be enabled to actually see the shining body of Christ, the family of God. The seeing comes only from first being. Being rightly related to brothers and sisters in love initiates a bond bigger than human divisions.[28]

Discerning Truth

Most Christians claim belief in the central authority of the Bible in the church's life. Among these Christians, however, there is much disagreement about what the Bible teaches on a range of subjects. So it appears obvious that, beyond the issue of claimed authority, there is the complex issue of biblical interpretation. We all see the words on the page. But what do they really mean? One ministry of the Spirit of God is to assist communities of Christian faith to discern the truth in what they read. There is a "divine reading" in which the mind descends into the heart, and both are enveloped by the love and goodness of God. The Spirit enables the Word to be exposed in the words as the spiritually open reader moves beyond information to formation.

A prayerful reading of the biblical text is the path to a profound discerning of truth. A gracious interweaving of prayer and Scripture opens the door for God to clothe us in love, wonder, and wisdom. Even if one is technically deficient and informationally deprived, a prayerful openness to the divine presence is a spiritually fruitful posture. God's heart is set on us with the intention of comforting and nourishing (Isa. 49:15). Prayer is the believer's continuing work of setting the human heart on God. The Bible is an essential guide. We can "pray the Bible" by reading in expectant reverence and experiencing this testimony of Jeremiah, who addressed God: "Your words were found, and I ate them, and your words became to me a joy and the delight of my heart" (Jer. 15:16). We are to "taste and see that the LORD is good" (Ps. 34:8). We must remove the obstructions between head and heart so that reading the Bible can lead to the kind of understanding that is life transforming.[29]

One Christian leader has reflected on the dilemma he faced in his transition from formal theological education to active pastoral duties:

> Whatever else I learned in seminary, it was clear that, as a pastor, I would be expected to deal with spirituality. Of course, no one told me exactly what spirituality was. Nor did I realize how vital it was to work on my own spiritual needs.[30]

In this regard, Helmut Thielicke once observed that the souls of many theological students are in grave danger. They find themselves immersed in a maze of theories, specialized language, and analytical preoccupations. Thus, "Under a considerable display of the apparatus of exegetical science and surrounded by the air of the initiated, [the student] produces paralyzing and unhappy trivialities, and the inner muscular strength of a lively young Christian is horribly squeezed to death in a formal armor of abstract ideas."[31] Let us be clear. The need is not to forfeit the theological and analytical, but to keep it properly connected to the spiritual.

The key issue is seen in the story of the man born blind, told in John 9. From beginning to end, a deep irony is in this story: the people who should have been able to see turn out to be blind, while the one who was obviously blind comes to full sight. When writing about the moral and spiritual chaos at Crete, Paul identified himself as one who had been enabled to discern true godliness: "Paul, a servant of God and an apostle of Jesus Christ, for the sake of the faith of God's elect and the knowledge of the truth that is in accordance with godliness" (Titus 1:1). He instructed Timothy on how to discipline straying saints in the task of discernment: "God may perhaps grant that they will repent and come to know the truth, and that they may escape from the snare of the devil" (2 Tim. 2:25–26).

Even though we who believe know only in part, when we are enlightened by the Spirit and remain on journey with the Spirit, our knowledge will continue to increase. Explained Paul to the Corinthians, "For now we see in a mirror, dimly, but then we will see face to face. Now I know only in part; then I will know fully, even as I have been fully known" (1 Cor. 13:12). Donald Bloesch has wisely said, "I affirm a hermeneutics of love in which the fuller understanding of the [biblical] text remains hidden until Christians learn to live in unity and love with one another."[32] The prayer of a Christian naturally is:

Open my eyes, that I may see
Glimpses of truth Thou hast for me;
Place in my hands the wonderful key,
That shall unclasp and set me free.[33]

The capacity to recognize truth in the ordinary affairs of life increases the more closely a believer faithfully lives with God in the world. Discernment and obedience function together.

In Jesus' world, the pursuit of truth was not the highest ambition so much as was the doing of truth. Truth was a given in the self-disclosure of the Holy One. The chief task of the Jewish sage was to interpret rightly this divine revelation preserved in Holy Scripture and teach disciples by word and example how to obey the divine will. Likewise, the way to the truth that fully liberates, saves, and enlivens is found on the path of faithful discipleship to Jesus. "If you continue in my word," said Jesus, "you are truly my disciples; and you will know the truth, and the truth will make you free" (John 8:31–32). Albert Schweitzer once made this classic observation about the true identity of Jesus and how one comes to know it:

> He [Jesus] comes to us as One unknown, without a name, as of old, by the lakeside. . . . And to those who obey Him, whether they be wise or simple, He will reveal Himself in the toils, the conflicts, the sufferings which they shall pass through in His fellowship, and as an ineffable mystery, they shall learn in their own experience who He is.[34]

Disciples also learn as they immerse themselves in the biblical text and in the community of Bible believers. When combining such immersion with vibrant belief in the illuminating ministry of God's Spirit, one is blessed with Scripture once spoken and now speaking. Discernment comes from the biblical text as read through the eyes of the Spirit in the context of the church community (present and past). It is one thing to claim that the Bible is the written Word of God. It is an important other thing to recognize that the voice of God is alive and free as the sovereign God is free. Therefore, "it is the spirit that gives life; the flesh is useless. The words that I [Jesus] have spoken to you are spirit and life" (John 6:63).

Dealing with Doubts

In the vocabulary of religion, the word *doubt* has had bad press. Faith is said to be the victory that overcomes the world, but doubt is identified as faith's chief enemy. Yet, all of us know our own times of doubt. Even though it might be inappropriate to dwell in public on our stray feelings and even occasionally our frightening misgivings, we all have a stake in the ancient prayer, "I believe; help my unbelief!" (Mark 9:24). A real advancement in the life of faith is awaiting Christians who finally develop a more realistic and wholesome attitude toward the doubts they occasionally feel and tend to repress. Christians must move beyond feeling guilty for merely doubting the faith or questioning God. Indeed, there may be more genuine faith in honest doubt than in a blind acceptance of some conventional creed. Faith involves risk, a calculated risk that always leaves room for mystery and some uncertainty. If there is never any doubt, it is questionable if there is ever any faith. There are some amazing passages in the Hebrew Scriptures where sincere Jewish believers confront God with very candid questions indeed (e.g., Job and Habakkuk).

I recall the wonderful sermon by Harry Emerson Fosdick titled "The Importance of Doubting Our Doubts." Spiritual maturity involves doubting one's believing and believing in the midst of one's doubting. Says Fosdick:

> The older I grow the more I ponder Judas Iscariot. He came so near to *not* betraying Jesus. He was a loyal disciple. It took courage to join that little band, and Judas had it. Then doubts began. What kind of Messiah was this who refused violent revolution and talked about loving one's enemies? Was not this idealistic Jesus letting them down? So the doubts grew, until in an explosive hour . . . Judas sold his Lord. He came so near *not* doing it that when he saw what he had done he hanged himself in shame. Ah, Judas, if you had only doubted your doubts enough to wait until Easter, until Pentecost, until Paul came, you would not be the supreme traitor of the centuries.[35]

In contrast to the Gospel of Matthew, where one finds an emphasis on the presence of God and the abiding presence of Jesus, the Gospel of Mark seems to feature the hiddenness of God and, at the end, even the mysterious absence of Jesus himself. God is gracious, but the truly sovereign God sometimes is experienced as almost unfathomable mystery. At the death of Jesus, Mark records a sense of God's abandonment—even of his own Son (15:34)! Mark presents a side of the Jesus story particularly relevant to suffering believers who need reassurance that, although Satan's opposition is strong, it is in its terminal stage (cf. 1:24). Since doubt and anxiety have the potential of paralyzing faith, any Christian spirituality that fails to address such a potential has limited value for the church.

The early twenty-first century is not the only time when the uncertainty of the faithful has been common. In the sixteenth century, John Calvin declared that he had been born in a most unhappy age. It groaned under the weight of calamities similar in gravity to those associated with the collapse of the Roman Empire centuries earlier. Augustine had stepped into that gap with his great faith document *City of God* (c. 413–427, after the sack of Rome in 410). The Protestant Reformation led by Calvin, Martin Luther, and others spoke and acted prophetically to a church plagued by anxiety about its own future and that of civilization in general. Faith should include letting oneself fall into the arms of God regardless of surrounding circumstances. A central characteristic of Reformation spirituality was its insistence on a transformative encounter between the believer and the risen Christ. The essential is faith. And what is faith? It is "not merely, nor even primarily, an act of understanding. It is an act of will. It is a decision to trust in the person and promises of God, despite the intellectual doubts and difficulties that may arise. It is a deliberate decision to commit oneself to God."[36]

Deliberate decisions to trust necessarily mix faith into life's knowing and not knowing. Note how the inspired hymn writer acknowledges the many things not known for sure and also affirms the central thing that, once grasped by faith, brackets all else with hope:

> *I know not why God's wondrous grace To me He hath made known,*
> *Nor why, unworthy, Christ in love Redeemed me for His own . . .*
>
> *I know not how this saving faith To me He did impart,*
> *Nor how believing in His word Wrought peace within my heart . . .*
>
> *I know not how the Spirit moves, Convincing men of sin . . .*
> *I know not when my Lord may come, At night or noonday fair,*
> *Nor if I'll walk the vale with Him, Or "meet Him in the air."*
>
> *But "I know whom I have believed, and am persuaded that He is able*
> *To keep that which I've committed Unto Him against that day."*[37]

Such radical commitment on the basis of knowing and not knowing is seen clearly when one recalls the Pentecost season and the Holiness tradition of the Christian church.

The Rich Christian Tradition

The landmark passage Jeremiah 31:31–34 gives the promise of God that Pentecost fulfilled. With the words "the Holy Spirit also testifies to us," the Letter to the Hebrews introduces an extended quotation from this passage (Heb. 10:15–17). Discovered in Jesus Christ is the freedom that comes when the law is not an outer restraint but an inner assent. Early Christian believers remembered this assurance: "I [God] will put my law within them, and I will write it on their hearts" (Jer. 31:33). Nothing is so irksome as an imposed discipline; nothing is so liberating as a discipline espoused freely. Paul declared, "Not that we are competent of ourselves to claim anything as coming from us; our competence is from God, who has made us competent to be ministers of a new covenant, not of letter but of spirit; for the letter kills, but the Spirit gives life" (2 Cor. 3:5–6).

The Church Year: Pentecost II

In the previous chapter, we spoke initially of Pentecost, focusing on its celebration as a post-Easter event that reversed the human tragedy told in the Tower of Babel story. We spoke of the historic Christian practice of identifying and honoring saints in the church's life—both the value of and the concerns about such a practice. Now we turn to the central intent of the Pentecost reality. Thinking of this reality in terms of a gift, the crucial consideration is the giver rather than particular gifts. As Jürgen Moltmann observes, "But when Christian theologians talk about 'the Holy Spirit,' they always mean God himself, never merely one of his gifts. The Spirit is the giver in what he gives."[38]

There must be movement forward in Christian spiritual life. Hope exists for life after death (Easter). There also is hope of new being in Christ after we are granted a forgiven status before God. In other words, being forgiven of the guilt of sin is one thing, one very important and beginning thing; but being truly renewed through character reformation by the Spirit's ministry is another thing—or at least an additional dimension of the first thing. We who believe are called to cry out for God to search and know us, know our hearts, and root out every wicked way in us (Ps. 139:23). Jesus sent his first disciples on mission to the world. First, however, he instructed them to wait until they received the transforming presence and power of the Spirit of God (Acts 1:4–5). A vital community of Christian faith, then and now, is one in which spiritual transformation is held in higher priority than congregational tradition, structure, staff, or programs. A wide-eyed waiting on God should precede all ministry action. Such waiting is not group passivity, but a people's pointed intention to become God's church, living out God's life, toward whatever ends God chooses—all in God's time and way.

Pentecost is about distinctive Christian possibilities. Prominent and intended possibilities are said by Jesus to be "the promise of the Father," a potential baptism "with the Holy Spirit" (Acts 1:4–5). The Christian life is not a static or unaided process. Sin no longer needs to dominate. Believers can walk in newness of life by being "conformed to the image of [God's] Son" (Rom. 8:29; 6:12–14). Says one Christian theologian, "The indwelling of the Spirit brings the divine energies of life in Jesus to rapturous and overflowing fullness."[39] John 3:34 describes this endowment with the Spirit as being "without measure."

Pentecost is the completion of the Easter season, the bringing to fullness of resurrection life. Holiness people speak of "going on to perfection." The Christian life is a spiritual pilgrimage never satisfied anywhere short of the promised land. John of the Cross (1515–1582) compared the human soul to a smudgy window through which a pure ray of light is trying to pass (the revealing presence of God). The cleaner the window, the more light can get through. If completely clean, it would become one with the sun's rays. The Pentecost prayer is for cleansing so that the believer can be holy as God is holy, for the sake of the lost world. We now give attention to the Holiness tradition of the church.

The Holiness Tradition

Previous chapters have highlighted the Evangelical, Contemplative, and Charismatic spiritual traditions of Christian faith. Consideration now is given to the Holiness tradition that gathers up the others and seeks to "go on to perfection." Here was Isaiah's prophetic vision: "A highway shall be there, and it shall be called the Holy Way; the unclean shall not travel on it, but it shall be for God's people; no traveler, not even fools, shall go astray" (Isa. 35:8).

Martin Luther was committed to what became a typical teaching of the Protestant Reformation. The continuing existence of sin is in the Christian believer, although this sin does not negate the believer's status as a true Christian because of what Christ has done. Alister McGrath explains:

> In justification we are given the status of righteousness while we work with God toward attaining the nature of righteousness. . . . The justification of sinners rests upon no delusions, no legal fictions, and no pretense of holiness. God accepts us for what we are while he works within us that which he wants us to be.[40]

Many Christians have questioned the adequacy of this way of dealing with sin in the believer.[41] The Holiness tradition highlights this questioning and urges consideration of a better, more helpful answer. The better answer that is put forward centers in defining sin as voluntary transgression of God's known will. At least at the conscious and volitional levels, a new creation in Christ can and clearly should, by God's grace, attain to a holiness that involves having the mind of Christ, with love reigning as the habitual state of the soul because of humble openness to the abiding presence of the Holy Spirit. In this state, sometimes called sanctification or perfect love, there is at least freedom from knowingly and willingly functioning outside God's will. What gets perfected is not performance, but the divine-human relationship.

This better answer has a long history in Roman Catholicism, Eastern Orthodoxy,[42] and Anglicanism and gained particular prominence among some Protestants through the work of John Wesley in the eighteenth century. By Wesley's own account, it was while he was a student at Oxford that he sought a more disciplined spiritual life. He followed the advice given by Bishop Jeremy Taylor in his 1650 book *The Rule and Exercise of Holy Living and Holy Dying*. Records Wesley, "I began to take a more exact Account than I had done before, of the manner wherein I spent my Time, writing down how I had employed every Hour."[43] He was "exceedingly affected" by that part of Taylor's book which related to "purity of intention." Therefore, "instantly I resolved to dedicate all my life to God, all my thoughts, and words, and actions, being thoroughly convinced, there was no medium; but that every part of my life (not some only) must either be a sacrifice to God or myself, that, in effect, to the devil."[44] The essential nature of the resulting Methodist spirituality is a combination of the Anglican holiness of intent and the Puritan inward assurance, as lived out in accountable discipleship.

Paul appeals to believers "to present your bodies as a living sacrifice, holy and acceptable to God, which is your spiritual worship" (Rom. 12:1). The goal of the Christian spiritual pilgrimage is gaining and living in the mind that was in Christ Jesus (Phil. 2:1–11). The claim of the Holiness tradition is that a genuine holiness of heart and life is available to every believer, even in this present life, by way of the sanctifying grace of God. Paul said long ago to the Galatians that he felt like he was in childbirth for them "until Christ is formed in you" (Gal. 4:19). The center of "perfect love" is Christ; the path to perfection lies in obedience to Christ and in constant trust in Christ's forgiveness and reconciliation. Say some contemporary authors:

> Every Christian generation has produced two kinds of Christians: the common, ordinary garden variety, and those who have discovered the deeper

> life. Some call this deeper life entire sanctification. Others call it the baptism with the Spirit, Christian perfection, perfect love, or holiness of heart and life. Whatever the label, it reflects a deeper experience of Christlikeness. . . . [Such spiritual formation is] the whole person in relationship with God, within the community of believers, growing in Christlikeness, reflected in a Spirit-directed, disciplined lifestyle, and demonstrated in redemptive action in our world.[45]

The taproot of early Methodist spiritual formation lay in the dialectic of salvation by divine grace and disciplined growth in the spiritual life through faithful participation in the "means of grace" (see chapter 8). Wesley's pastoral theology centered in his encouraging believers to discipline their lives methodically ("methodists") by practicing designated habits designed to enable spiritual growth. Of course, such practices can become mere religion if believers get caught up in the mechanics and are distracted from focusing on the real presence of Christ. But they also can be vital means of divine grace that are necessary for the well-being if not the being of the church and its Christian pilgrims. The outward practice is never the bringer of salvation, but it does signify and is able to nourish that salvation and become an instrument in the hands of the Spirit.

In the North American setting of the nineteenth century, a Holiness movement of significant proportions emerged. Gaining momentum in the quarter-century prior to the Civil War, this movement was rooted deeply in the same biblical orientation as that of the earlier Pietists in Europe and the Wesleyan revival in England. It shared John Bunyan's Bedford jail dreams of a Christian existence on the borders of heaven, a spiritual plateau beyond the "Valley of the Shadow," out of the reach of the "Giant Despair," and not even within sight of "Doubting Castle."[46] Advocates of this revival claimed biblical authority and experiential authentication for what they believed was John Wesley's own teaching on Christian perfection. They preached a necessary second-crisis experience of evangelical faith for every Christian.[47] This "second blessing," subsequent to conversion, involved an utter consecration of oneself to God through Jesus Christ. It was believed that God would then free the believer from the inner disposition toward willful sin and fill the heart with divine love.

This was a charismatic revival that generated considerable controversy and resulted in much spiritual renewal.[48] A parade of prominent Christian personalities like Orange Scott, Phoebe Palmer, Asa Mahan, Charles Finney, Daniel Steele, J. A. Wood, and Hannah Whitall Smith provided leadership.[49] In evidence of the renewal's popularity, Wood's 1861 book *Perfect Love* sold more than 60,000 copies in his lifetime. Steele gives a moving testimony regarding his personal renewal:

> My early religious experience was variable and for the most part consisted in "sorrows and sins and doubts and fears, a howling wilderness." The personality of the Holy Spirit was rather an article of faith than a joyful realization. He had breathed life into me, but not the more abundant life. In a sense, I was free, but not "free indeed." I was free from the guilt and dominion of sin, but not from the strong inward tendencies to yield to it, which seemed to be a part of my nature. . . . The study of the promised Paraclete led me to see that He signified far more than I had realized in the new birth and that a personal Pentecost was awaiting me. . . . November 17, 1870, [was] my most memorable day. I now for the first time realized "the unsearchable riches of Christ." Reputation, friends, family, property, everything disappeared, eclipsed by the brightness of His manifestation. . . . The sphere of this wonderful phenomenon was the affections. It can be best described as "the love of God shed abroad in the heart by the Holy Ghost."[50]

Steele had found his way beyond mere religion. It was a move from an article of faith to a personal Pentecost.

On the nineteenth-century North American scene, holiness revivalists regularly preached the immediacy of the sanctifying work of God's Spirit in the lives of converted and seeking believers. Some varied slightly in the presumed how of attaining this immediate result. Especially influential was Phoebe Palmer (1807–1874) who authored the classic book *The Way of Holiness* (1843). For many years she led in her New York City home the "Tuesday Meeting for the Promotion of Holiness." She taught that God is serious when commanding believers to be holy (Matt. 5:48). Sanctification can be a distinct and instantaneous work of God's cleansing grace. Because "the altar sanctifies the gift," she taught, and Jesus Christ is the altar, a person is sanctified when all of oneself is laid on the altar. Since God's promises are true, one can then claim sanctification regardless of feelings. Palmer's influence was extensive. Her shorter-way approach to sanctification was controversial among holiness teachers, but her basic concern was not. Leaders said with one voice that the holiness of believers is the intent and provision of God. Palmer's hymn "The Cleansing Stream" is one of the great praise and testimony songs of holiness hymnody.

Oh, now I see the cleansing wave!
The fountain deep and wide;
Jesus, my Lord, mighty to save,
Points to His wounded side.

Refrain:
The cleansing stream I see! I see!
I plunge, and oh, it cleanseth me!

Oh, praise the Lord! it cleanseth me!
It cleanseth me—yes, cleanseth me.

I see the new creation rise;
I hear the speaking blood.
It speaks! Polluted nature dies!
Sinks 'neath the cleansing flood.

Amazing grace! 'tis heav'n below
To feel the blood applied,
And Jesus, only Jesus know,
My Jesus crucified.

The nineteenth-century holiness revival in North America found its way back to the England revived by the Wesley brothers generations before. A key figure in this return was another American woman, Hannah Whitall Smith (1832–1911). A Philadelphia Quaker, Smith was introduced to holiness teaching by Methodists. Her 1870 book *The Christian's Secret of a Happy Life* became widely read and influential. She and her husband, Robert Pearsall Smith, became leaders in England's "higher life" or Keswick movement that is still active in the twenty-first century. The Smiths assumed that real holiness is possible, is God's work of grace once a believer entirely surrenders, results in victory over sin, and is not a static place but a dynamic day-to-day walk. Jesus came to save us now from the power and dominion of sin. Our natural spiritual heritage is "life hid with Christ in God." The blessed life, Hannah Whitall Smith wrote, "must not be looked upon in any sense as an attainment, but as an obtainment."[51] Holiness is God's gift to us in Jesus Christ. The sanctified soul finds itself becoming one in character with God.

An English woman was deeply influenced by the ministry of Americans Phoebe and Walter Palmer because of their time of English ministry during the American Civil War. Catherine Booth (1829–1890) joined Phoebe Palmer in defending the right of women to preach and in seeing the centrality of the experience of entire sanctification. Like a modern Deborah, Catherine Booth was a fulfillment of Moses' prophetic prayer that the day would come when "all the Lord's people" (women and men) would be prophets and "the Lord would put his Spirit upon them." In 1865 Catherine and William Booth founded the Salvation Army. A dramatic 36,000 people attended Catherine's funeral in 1890, a tribute to her unusually effective Christian ministry. By the 1880s holiness teachings set to secular tunes were played in the streets by brass bands. "Invasions" of these Christian soldiers of the Salvation Army flooded into the United States, and, by

Catherine's death, there were some nine hundred corps, with nearly one-third of them outside Great Britain. The ministry was practical holiness in the streets with the most needy people. Homes were created for endangered girls, released prisoners, and the homeless. Soup kitchens, leper colonies, and home industries in India aided the disenfranchised. These and many other programs of social action multiplied in the name of Christ's perfect and practical love.

To be holy includes a heart change and a radical change of life on behalf of the most needy of God's children. It rests on strong belief in the transforming potential of intense relationship with the Spirit of God. Such belief is affirmed by the Apostles' Creed.

The Apostles' Creed

The Apostles' Creed and many others begin with "I believe." Everyone believes in something (overtly or by default). The creed focuses Christian belief on God. It declares belief in one God, belief *in* rather than merely belief *that*. It is possible to believe someone or something exists, but with this belief having no practical effect on one's life. Christians are to believe in God as a person, not just as an abstract theory or principle. One sure way to know God is to enter into the divine mystery through a relationship of mutual love. The believing involved goes well beyond intellectual affirmation. It is intended to include committing one's whole life to a particular view of reality.

By its trinitarian structure, the creed says that God is known best in Jesus and is related to us humans through life in God's Spirit. The second article of the creed gives a brief summary of the historical life of Jesus, intentionally highlighting the distinctive nature of Christian faith and knowing. Knowledge is based on certain historical events as opposed to being merely a religious philosophy of life. God is said to have acted in human history in specific, revealing, and redeeming ways. To know is to recall the acts of God and participate in their present meanings. Such participation is the path to holiness.

Often free-church Christians insist on not going beyond the stance of "no creed but Christ." While much more complex statements of faith than the Apostles' Creed have seemed unavoidable in Christian church history, there is wisdom in the call to the simple and personal. Christianity is less a highly refined system of religious ideas and more a particular attitude toward a certain historical person. Maybe that is why the earliest Christian creed likely was the plain statement, "Jesus is Lord!" Such a simple but life-changing statement must be spiritually discerned since, according to Paul,

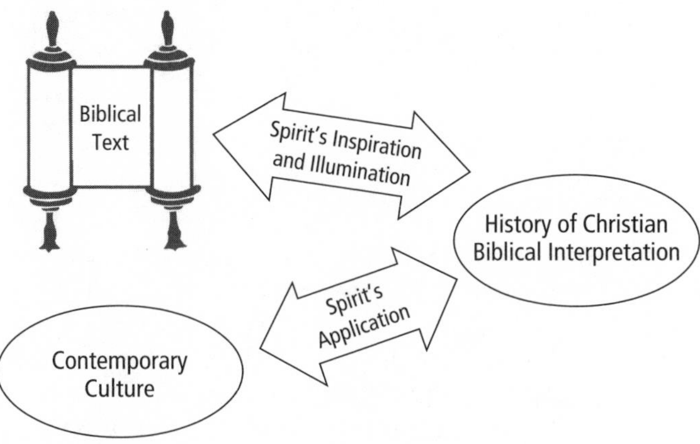

Figure 5.1 Three-Way Conversation with the Biblical Text

"no one can say 'Jesus is Lord' except by the Holy Spirit" (1 Cor. 12:3). To really know requires being instructed by the one who is to be known.

British theologian Alan Richardson rightly says that "the acceptance of Christianity as our own personal religion is not a mere assent to an intellectual proposition, but the living response of our whole personality to the fact of Jesus."[52] To believe in God is to trust in God and allow God to transform—so that good theology and good spirituality are not to be separated. A classic illustration is John Wesley's recording of his own spiritual awakening:

> On May 24, 1738, I went very unwillingly to a society in Aldersgate Street [London], where one was reading Luther's preface to the Epistle to the Romans. About a quarter before nine, while he was thus describing the changes which God works in the heart through faith in Christ, I felt my heart strangely warmed; I felt I did trust in Christ, Christ alone for salvation; and an assurance was given me that he had taken away my sins, even mine, and saved me from the law of sin and death.[53]

This is biblical true belief. God is; God comes in Christ; God comes to save; salvation impacts the whole being of the believer; assurance comes that life has been moved from the world of death to the world of life. Really knowing such wonderful things is no easy, individual, or merely intellectual exercise. To know is to engage in a three-way conversation involving the biblical text, the long tradition of the church's interpretation of this text, and the current relevance of the text to the world of today that God so loves. Reading the text, engaging the interpretive tradition, and relating the burden of the text to current mission all depend heavily on being sensitive to the work of God's Spirit—both in the past and in the present.

Knowing through Focusing

The early twenty-first century is dominated far too much by the sophisticated and spiritually blind worlds of technology and marketing. We are constantly encouraged to look at people and see profit potential or sexual objects, not persons of individuality, integrity, and infinite value. We look at lovely wooded hillsides and flowing streams and want, if possible, to start a new housing development to attract wealthy buyers. We seem willing to pollute almost anything in the name of progress. It is easy to get discouraged by the pettiness of some people in the church who see little but problems. The trivial dominates our attention.

We too often are like the ancient Israelites in the wilderness on their way to the promised land. They were the elect of God who were wanting to go back to slavery because they saw only the present problems and not the future promise. Their focus became their reality—and their near destruction. People come to know as presumably true that to which they give regular attention. If only the spiritually hungry could share the following witness of the psalmist to the faithfulness of the gracious God: "My soul is satisfied as with a rich feast, and my mouth praises you with joyful lips when I think of you on my bed, and meditate on you in the watches of the night; for you have been my help, and in the shadow of your wings I sing for joy" (Ps. 63:5–7). Knowledge came to this psalmist through being still, thinking, remembering, meditating on the meaning of the memories, and coming to see the lovely pattern of the big picture among the thousands of little threads. If you want to truly know, I ask: Are you prepared to share this prayer of A. W. Tozer?

> O God, I have tasted Thy goodness, and it has both satisfied me and made me thirsty for more. I am painfully conscious of my need of further grace. I am ashamed of my lack of desire. O God, the Triune God, I want to want Thee; I long to be filled with longing; I thirst to be made more thirsty still. Show me thy glory, I pray Thee, so that I may know Thee indeed.[54]

Questions to Pursue

1. Does adequate knowledge of God necessarily include living experience? How does spiritual experience relate to divine revelation?
2. What does it mean to approach the Bible in a relational mode? How does responsible biblical interpretation involve the Spirit's illumination?
3. The Bible word highlighted in this chapter means "really knowing." In the Christian's spiritual life, is there an important difference between knowing and really knowing, between information and formation?
4. How would you summarize what the holiness spiritual tradition has meant by "going on to perfection"? In what sense is perfection a practical goal in this life?
5. Look again at the personal testimony of Daniel Steele. Have you known someone personally with a testimony like this? Have you had a similar experience?
6. Are we what we choose to focus on? Is the early twenty-first century too focused on technology and marketing?
7. If a large storehouse burns down, the owner for the first time might have an unobstructed view of the shining moon that was hidden behind it. Often insight comes only after a crisis. Do your possessions blind against some higher truth? What is our spiritual angle of vision, and how much truth does it allow us to see? Might something need to burn down in our lives before our eyes are really opened? What are we storing that is obstructing the most important of life's needs?

6

Truly Living: The Spirit's Way

And it is no longer I who live, but it is Christ who lives in me.

Galatians 2:20

Unfree men are horrified by the suggestion of accepting a daily discipline. Confusing inner control with external tyranny, they prefer caprice to self-restraint. They would rather have ideals than norms . . . faith than forms. But the goal and the way cannot long endure in separation. . . . Unless the outer life expresses the inner world, piety stagnates and intention decays.

Abraham Heschel

Christian spirituality is particularly concerned with the conjunction of theology and the practical life of faith in the church and world. The concern is not to live our way, but the Spirit's way. In the early twenty-first century, the stakes are high. Cultures and religious communities are interacting all over the world as never before. For the sake of the future of the human community, these increasing interactions must be creative encounters, true dialogues. The common quest is for the wisdom on which true human community can be based in our mobile and fractured world. The real challenge of today's global community is a spiritual one—a spiritual one with large political, economic, and even military implications. How, then, shall we live?

Only One True Spirituality

There is one spirituality in the church of the Lord Jesus: paschal spirituality. Essentially it is our daily death to sin, selfishness, dishonesty, and degraded love in order to rise to newness of life. Paul says, "It is no longer I who live, but Christ lives in me" (Galatians 2:20 NASB). Each time we deal a mortal blow to the ego, the pasch of Jesus is traced in our flesh. Each time we choose to walk the extra mile, to turn the other cheek, to embrace and not reject, to be compassionate and not competitive, to kiss and not to bite, to forgive and not massage the latest bruise to our wounded ego, we are breaking through from death to life.

Brennan Manning, *The Signature of Jesus*

Contemporary people in the fast-paced information age are immersed in the assumption that they have a right to do almost anything they want in the pursuit of happiness—usually defined as self-fulfillment and material well-being. This often frantic pursuit of position, status, and possessions is thought of as the good life. No wonder it seems almost incomprehensible when the New Testament calls for a person to forsake all (Luke 14:26) and find real life only by losing it (Mark 8:35–36). There is a good way to live. It is not living as we wish, but our choice to have Christ living in us as God wishes (Gal. 2:20). While many people fear death, others are rightly disturbed by an even more profound anxiety—that they might die without having really begun to live. What is true living? For the Christian, the answer centers in the ways of the Spirit, including what Brennan Manning calls "paschal" spirituality.

The Witness of Being

Progress toward happiness by the route of self-sacrifice does not compute for many people. This is nothing new. The Hebrew prophets warned God's chosen people when their religious rituals deteriorated into outward performances. Such rituals attempt to control God, improve personal circumstances, and gain merit with God through calculated actions rather than self-denial. Paul warned that even giving everything to the poor and denying oneself in dramatic and public ways may be worthless religion. One must get beyond mere religious practice to the key issue of real love (1 Cor. 13:3).

The world is full of persons whose lives are not attractive to others. Some of them are very religious. Unfortunately, it is their passion for particular religious claims and practices that makes them unattractive, intimidating, and sometimes even dangerous. Some of these unattractive people are publicly identified with the Christian faith. They are rude, crude, thoughtless, artless, hypocritical, selfish, aloof, withdrawn, ultra-faddish, or—to be less critical—they just appear to be antiquated, irrelevant, and restricted religious types who are afraid to have fun and seem more bound than liberated. I once saw a seminar advertised with the title, "Going Fishing without Leaving Town: How to Share Your Faith without Being Obnoxious!" Those who cannot share their faith with joy and graciousness are poor models of the new creation that is supposed to be in Christ.

Such bland, humorless, even offensive Christians are tragically disconnected from their Jewish roots. The Hebraic disposition has been living the life of faith as dynamic, feeling, celebrating, and fully human people. The drive is toward incarnational and down-to-earth humanness. Hebrew worship as seen biblically was hardly limited to dreary prayer and the endless study of old books. It included dancing with the tambourine (Ps. 149:3; 150:4), the blowing of trumpets (Ps. 150:3), hand clapping (Ps. 47:1), and even shouting (Ps. 47:1). Exuberant praise was the natural response of a grateful people who were chosen by the God who had created all things and would surely save, liberate, and re-create the chosen people. To be alive in this God is to be truly alive indeed!

The root meaning of the Hebrew word for *save* is "room, space, or width." The idea of salvation (being saved), then, is that people are freed up, given new space, liberated from being narrowly bound, given opportunity to expand to a new dimension. We are released into the wonderfully large arena of forgiveness and new life. Salvation is not the currently popular search to be freed "to be me" but the divine intention to set us loose to be all that God created us to be. How wrong and sad is the common perception that salvation is a restricting and cramping thing. To the contrary, those who witness to being in Christ report with joy what Charles Wesley pictured in his great hymn "And Can It Be That I Should Gain?":

Long my imprisoned spirit lay
Fast bound in sin and nature's night;
Thine eye diffused a quick'ning ray,
I woke, the dungeon flamed with light;
My chains fell off, my heart was free,
I rose, went forth, and followed Thee.

The good news is there are many superb Christian models being lived out in the world. Christians are supposed to be bearers of Christ's saving ministry and wonderful examples of good news. Believers are to be evangelistic, meaning in part that we are to live the best, most infectious lives possible by the grace of the Holy Spirit. We are to be the Christ-liberated "real thing" in a gentle and winsome way that lures the lost, lonely, hurting, and frustrated to something they recognize as truly wonderful. Our lives can and must make our words credible and inviting. Consider the life of J. Horace Germany. A Southern white man educated in the North, Germany returned to Mississippi before the gains of the civil rights movement of the 1960s. His burden was to begin an educational ministry that would give rural black Christians a chance to become trained church leaders in their own cultural settings. In this, Germany was one with his Lord, but socially ahead of his time. Finally, with apparent permission from the highest level of state government, a KKK group tried to beat him to death and scatter the school. But he survived, kept the faith, and moved the school to Texas where it still functions. Many people of both races now call this visionary and humble Christian man blessed.[1]

A central characteristic of the work of John Wesley was his insistence on the empirical character of Christian convictions. For him, Christianity is about changed lives. To truly live the Christian faith, one has to be on a journey with God, a journey of spiritual change that develops and newly tells the blessed story of the grace of God at work. To really believe in Jesus Christ necessarily becomes the ability to trace the present activity of the goodness of God and to witness by word and deed to what God is doing. However, we live in a world that no longer assumes that a religious, or in particular, a Christian account of life is necessary for decent and upright living. So the vital question has become: What difference, if any, does it make to be a Christian? If a genuine difference is not clear, then real witness is hardly possible.

The truth of the faith is not merely a set of accurate theological statements. The truth that is contagious and compellingly authentic is the actual presence in a broken world of a community of faith that has become united in love and is living in loving and healing ways. The existence of such a community is hard for the general public to explain—unless, of course, God really does exist and is making a difference in the lives of believers. It is like the resurrection of Jesus. The bare facts of the event are baffling—unless, of course, the power of God was at work. Christians should be transformed people who "have been sent out into a world of war to challenge the necessity of war, armed only with the weapons of love."[2] Jesus' people are to be different people in the same way that Jesus was different.

Most Jews and many others look at Jesus and do not see what Christians affirm gratefully by faith. Rather, they ask a difficult and proper question: If Jesus is the Redeemer, why, after two millennia, doesn't the world look more redeemed? There must be a meaningful answer for this question. A key part of the answer is that followers of Jesus are to make a real difference in the world by who they become in Jesus Christ and how they live their lives by the aid of Christ's Spirit. We are to be the answer!

The Wonderful Bible Word

A wonderful biblical word about authentic faith points to faith being made evident in Christlike living. The word is *kosmeō,* meaning "to adorn or make more attractive" (transferred to English as "cosmetic"). Having been summoned, adopted, and inspired by the Spirit, obedient Christian believers and the church itself are to be effective, infectious, winsome, and honorable representatives of the King of kings and Lord of lords. To be adorned by Christ in a way that leads to credible evangelism on behalf of Christ requires that believers be properly prepared, dressed, and active. Christians are to go into the world with their own lives in working order, in proper dress, in the line of duty, and with hospitality and humor.

In Working Order

Often the word *kosmeō* appeared in secular literature to describe an army in disciplined formation, a glittering and impressive array of polished might ready for battle. Being ready requires preparation that slowly but steadily evolves the potential of the ordered and beautiful. Good order and true beauty are related. Effectiveness requires that each link in the chain be strong and ready.

A famous musician was walking down a prominent big-city street with his valuable violin in hand. Someone stopped him and asked how to get to Carnegie Hall. The reply? "Practice, practice, practice!" The point of Matthew 25 is similar. The parable of the wise and foolish virgins teaches that wisdom involves having one's lamps trimmed and always in working order. Christ may return at any time; his servants should not be caught unprepared. It often is said that the call to preach is also the call to prepare to preach. Likewise, whatever one's function in church life, being a mature child of God requires discipline, focus, and spiritual maintenance. When it is time to work, be ready. When time runs out and no more work can be done, be ready for that too!

All aspects of life are to work properly and for the right purposes. Sexuality, for instance, should be an avenue to joy and beauty, an intimacy that becomes the roadway to a fulfilling ecstasy within a marital setting that is spiritually strong. But in our social environment, which is soaked in sexual perversion, constructively linking sexuality to Christian spirituality is difficult indeed (see "Gnosticism" in the glossary). Keeping our bodies and relationships in proper working order is as important as it is challenging. Our bodies are to be living sacrifices of spiritual worship (Rom. 12:1–2), used as they were intended to the glory of God.

In Proper Dress

When the Christian life is in working order and functioning as it should, its authenticity and relevance will be reflected in its visible appearance and impact on others. While avoiding the appearance of evil, Christians are to intentionally capitalize on the appearance of the good. What appears should provide public credibility to the witness being made. There obviously is nothing attractive about a professed believer who, instead of standing consistently and courageously on the promises of God, just sits idly and selfishly on the premises, language, and traditions of the church. The spiritual challenge is always to model the Master, imitate Christ,[3] and carefully distinguish between gospel essentials and cultural incidentals of the outer life of faith.

Concerning the dress of women, Paul instructed: "Women should dress themselves modestly and decently in suitable clothing, not with their hair braided, or with gold, pearls, or expensive clothes, but with good works, as is proper for women who profess reverence for God" (1 Tim. 2:9–10). Wives were not to build their reputations by the outward adornments of their bodies, but by the lovely perfume of their beings, "the inner self with the lasting beauty of a gentle and quiet spirit, which is very precious in God's sight" (1 Pet. 3:4). The gospel essentials and cultural incidentals need to be distinguished here, of course. To focus attention especially on women and to name particular adornment practices and articles of clothing are surely incidental and are to be reviewed with care in our very different cultural settings today. However, to speak of decency, modesty, and inner beauty in the context of expressing reverence for God is a gospel essential. What about those who would be leaders of the church? Paul says each should be above reproach, show obvious respect for the sanctity of marriage, and be "temperate, sensible, respectable, hospitable, an apt teacher, not a drunkard, not violent but gentle, not quarrelsome, and not a lover of money" (1 Tim. 3:2–3). These characteristics appear appropriate in any cultural setting because they are more closely related to the fruit of the Spirit than to passing cultural particulars.

Clothing is often used to advertise a club, company, or sports team. Choices are made to reveal what is important to the wearer. Special wedding clothes, a military uniform, the colors of one's school or team convey identity and pride. How significant that the apostle Paul employed the vivid imagery of believers being clothed in Christ as a way of expressing the radical change involved in setting out on the Christian way (Gal. 3:27; Col. 3:9–10).[4] Soon those believers who were newly baptized put on white robes and wore them for as much as a week after baptism, symbolizing the inner washing they had experienced. Now reborn and publicly declared, believers soon were instructed to remove the sign of initiation and prepare for mission in the world. Therefore, one must put on new clothes, "the whole armor of God" (Eph. 6:13–17). Coming out of the early Pentecostal revival in Los Angeles, here is a good list of the spiritual clothes that a true Christian fellowship should wear:

> Divine love to all, especially to the church, the body of Christ, of which every justified soul is a member. Humility . . . [so that] we humble ourselves under the mighty hand of God and constantly search the scriptures to know His whole will and plan. . . . Living holy lives, separate from the world, the flesh and the devil, and rescuing other souls to a life of purity and holiness. There is [to be] a Holy Ghost shine on the faces of the workers.[5]

In the Line of Duty

The spirituality of the Protestant reformers of the sixteenth century (Luther, Calvin, etc.) was oriented toward life in the everyday world. It sought to enable Christians to involve themselves firmly in the secular order, while bringing to public life something new and special. In a sense, the home replaced the monastery as the primary arena within which Christian spirituality was to be focused and applied. The home and church are to nourish believers so they can go out into the world and glorify, serve, and proclaim God. To withdraw from the world is to deny God the opportunity to work through dedicated and publicly involved believers. Salt preserves only as it permeates.

Christian believers find themselves citizens of many political establishments around the world. In the line of their public duty, they find it necessary to seek an understanding of what belongs to the public treasury and what must be reserved only for God (Matt. 22:15–22). Christian slaves soon after the earthly life of Jesus were instructed to do their duty in the prevailing social scheme so that their witness would be attractive, "an ornament to the doctrine of God our Savior" (Titus 2:9–10). Many Quaker Christians engaged in civil disobedience against the U.S. Fugitive Slave Law of 1793 which made it illegal to help runaway slaves. They were committed to a higher law than the unjust law of a human government. Much later, Martin Luther King Jr. did a similar thing in the name of Jesus, standing with courage in the face of social evil and doing so with a dignity that showed obvious respect for the principle of public law in general. Authentic Christian spirituality requires a believer to do one's civic duty, but without ever selling one's soul in the process. Remaining true to the faith in the public arena can bring anything from a little social awkwardness to violent martyrdom. Regardless, loyalty finally must be with the primary culture of the believer, the reign of Jesus Christ.

Jesus made clear that true disciples of his are to be the light of the world, shining with the kind of life that brings glory to God (Matt. 5:14–16). A gospel chorus by Albert W. T. Orsborn expresses this well:

Let the beauty of Jesus be seen in me—
All His wonderful passion and purity!
O Thou Spirit divine, All my nature refine,
Till the beauty of Jesus be seen in me.

With Hospitality and Humor

A distinctive aspect of Christian spirituality as emphasized in the Gospel of Luke is joy. The inauguration in Jesus of the new age of the Spirit prompts a response of profound gratitude to God and optimism for the future. This response is seen in Luke's reporting of numerous outbursts of rejoicing. It started with the birth story of John the Baptist (Luke 1:14) and came again when Mary's spirit rejoiced (1:47). It was good news of great joy for all people (2:10). Jesus rejoiced in the Holy Spirit (10:21) and emphasized the festive joy that accompanies the return of a penitent prodigal (15:11–32). After Jesus was taken up into heaven, his disciples returned to Jerusalem "with great joy" and constantly blessing God (24:52–53). To be retained in the life of a believer, joy must be shared. This requires exercising the Christian grace of hospitality in a fractured world full of grasping and empty of real belonging.

Society today seems increasingly full of marketers and manipulators of all kinds. A stranger could well be an enemy ready to take advantage and do harm. Even so, a characteristic of Christian spirituality is "the movement by which our hostilities can be converted into hospitality."[6] Hospitality is a way of life fundamental to Christian identity, "a framework [that] provides a bridge which connects our theology with daily life and concerns."[7] It also connects Christians to their Hebrew heritage generally and to Jesus particularly. God as generous and gracious host is an image found throughout the Bible. An overarching theme of Israel's history is the divine-human covenant relationship. Israel had been a stranger, an alien, a people with no home, and God had elected them when they were wholly undeserving, invited them in, and gave them identity and a home. Once in their own land, they still were to view themselves as aliens because God owned the land and they were only stewards. Knowing by experience what it meant to be powerless sojourners in a foreign land (Deut. 10:19), how was Israel to treat the strangers in its own midst? According to Exodus 23:9, "You shall not oppress a resident alien; you know the heart of an alien, for you were aliens in the land of Egypt." In the name of the great host who is God, God's people should risk keeping its welcome mat to the world visible and well-used.

For Christians, nothing is more central than this: In Jesus Christ, God willingly tasted the precarious existence of a stranger (Matt. 8:20). Then the God who endured rejection by his own creation became the loving and inclusive host who invites all, privileged and despised, to the divine banquet (Luke 14:16–24). Such gracious inclusion is to set the pace for Christian living. Says Paul, "Welcome one another, therefore, just as Christ has welcomed you, for the glory of God" (Rom. 15:7). Jesus holds hospitality high on the ladder of importance. For instance, he tells the story of the coming great judgment. To the sheep on his right hand, the king will say:

> "Come, you that are blessed by my Father, inherit the kingdom prepared for you from the foundation of the world; for I was hungry and you gave me food, I was thirsty and you gave me something to drink, I was a stranger and you welcomed me, I was naked and you gave me clothing, I was sick and you took care of me, I was in prison and you visited me." . . . [When did we do these things for you?] . . . "Truly I tell you, just as you did it to one of the least of these who are members of my family, you did it to me." (Matt. 25: 34–40)

To be truly hospitable is to express the good news of Christ to the poor and others judged unacceptable by a society. Howard Thurman's classic book *Jesus and the Disinherited* (1949) insists rightly that the religion of Jesus provides real hope for dispossessed and desperate people. Religion—including Christianity—is used much too often to justify inequitable relationships between the powerful and weak of a society. Thurman calls this exactly what it is, a profound moral and spiritual issue for Christian people. The deepest impulse of the way of Jesus is sharing and fellowship regardless of social status. Love is the ability and the will to view and treat every person as a potential neighbor. Jesus related freely, even scandalously, with tax collectors and sinners, drawing considerable criticism from the Pharisees and scribes (Luke 15:1–2). Following Jesus is to engage in "an ethic of open, boundary-crossing hospitality"[8] that will bring unpleasant reactions from those who are guarding the boundaries of social preference and practice (Luke 7:36–50).

For example, consider a dramatic incident when sincere holiness people began worship by following the prevailing law that insisted on strict racial segregation and finally were forced by the gospel of Christ to do the opposite:

> At the 1897 Alabama State Camp Meeting [of the Church of God, Anderson], Lena Shoffner rose to preach the sermon of the hour. She looked out on a congregation of people divided by a rope—black people on one side, white people on the other. Her text, in part, was Ephesians 2:14: "For he . . . hath broken down the middle wall of partition between us." Someone in the crowd could not bear the contradiction between those words and the taut rope dividing Christians in that tent. The rope fell slack, and blacks and whites mingled around an altar of prayer. Almost immediately some local citizens heard what had happened, and that night a mob went to the campground. Rocks were thrown; buildings were dynamited. Most of the preachers fled into the night.[9]

To hear and practice the gospel of Christ is to remove restrictive ropes and discriminatory walls and accept the risks involved.

An enduring keynote of Christian spirituality lies in the words, "I was a stranger and you welcomed me." In a time like today when so many alienated people are longing for someone to welcome them, Christians must recover their long tradition of hospitality. The very word *hospitality* shares a linguistic history with *hospital,* suggesting that practicing it brings healing to guest and host. Indeed, "because hospitality demonstrates a radically transformed human posture of receptivity to God and generosity toward God's creatures, it is a primary sign of the new creation, God's reigning in our midst."[10] This sign of hospitality has been expressed so well since the sixth century in the *Rule of Saint Benedict,* named for the saintly man often called the "Patriarch of Western Monasticism." Lest one assume that such a life of balance and openness, centered in prayer and love, has no contemporary relevance outside monastic walls, note should be taken of the life and writings of the British laywoman Esther de Waal who has taught and lived the way of Benedict while being an active wife, mother, and professor.[11]

The open heart and door of hospitality should be accompanied by a light heart of joy—even an occasional burst of laughter to relieve any overly somber spirituality. Frederick Buechner opens many dimensions of faith-related humor as he retraces the biblical story and does cameo treatments of various biblical figures caught in their more amusing moments. Here is a sample from a Genesis story with a serious point and a hilarious tone:

> Sarah was never going to see ninety again, and Abraham had already hit one hundred, and when the angel told them that the stork was on his way at last,

> they both of them almost collapsed. Abraham laughed "till he fell on his face" (Gen. 17:17), and Sarah stood cackling behind the tent door so the angel wouldn't think she was being rude as the tears streamed down her cheeks. When the baby finally came, they even called him "Laughter"—which is what "Isaac" means in Hebrew—because obviously no other name would do.[12]

The joy of righteous laughter burst forth when God first laid the cornerstone of the earth (Job 38:7). Israel recalled often that "when the Lord restored the fortunes of Zion, . . . then our mouth was filled with laughter" (Ps. 126:1–2).

A chapter titled "Laughing with the Gospel" seems unlikely in a serious book on Christian preaching, but David Buttrick writes exactly that. His reference is particularly to a pattern of proclamation in African-American congregations that "contrasts the foolish, delusional pretensions of the world—often a well-off white world—with the special insight granted to God's people, specifically to God's oppressed people."[13] What is this insight? It has to do with knowing what God is doing in the world for and through faithful if powerless people, a knowledge that the presumably powerful just do not have. It is bemusement over those who have a pretense of power without knowing that, in fact, they have no ultimate power at all. It is the improbable paradox of the cross where the murder of an apparently foolish and impotent Christ turns out to be the unconquerable power of God's love.

Sometimes the unexpected ways of God can tickle the funny bone of any perceptive person. The holy and the hilarious are not opposites after all. Laughter erupts from those who know the meaning and end of God's story. The eventual triumph of Christ and all those who are his is a sure thing. Puffed-up pretenders are in for the shock of their lives. The amusement over this irony is not gloating or vindictive since all people are sinners needing God's grace. Even church people are known to yield to the evil in the world, including "the bone-headed Galatians (3:1–5; 4:8–10) or the cowed Colossians (2:8–23) who end up overscheduled by 'new moons and sabbaths.'"[14] But beyond these ridiculous wrong turns, believers are encouraged to be fools for Christ. After all:

> God chose what is foolish in the world to shame the wise; God chose what is weak in the world to shame the strong; God chose what is low and despised in the world, things that are not, to reduce to nothing things that are, so that no one might boast in the presence of God. He is the source of your life in Christ Jesus, who became for us wisdom from God. (1 Cor. 1:27–30)

Christ-fools are blessed with what Paul calls *hilarotēs*, an abiding cheerfulness (Rom. 12:8).[15]

A comparison of Jesus and the Pharisees is an obvious example. Bigotry is peculiarly vulnerable to ridicule. Jesus saw bigotry and hypocrisy and lathered it with loaded ironies. Did no one laugh when Jesus reported to the crowd that the elite and self-absorbed Pharisees made their phylacteries broad and their fringes long (Matt. 23:5)? He added a humorous twist to his report that the Pharisees were great at philanthropy, including being sure that everyone knew that they were being so generous. Then came the twist. He said that they wanted to be praised by others and that "they have received their reward" (Matt. 6:2). In other words, be careful about what you want because you just may get it—even if it is so little and so silly as the programmed applause of a fickle and captive audience.

Jesus was inclined to use vivid imagery and shocking hyperbole to get attention and make important points. Remember when he used the image of the dead undertaker to emphasize his expected commitment of disciples (Luke 9:60)? Then there was that mixture of realism and sheer absurdity when he openly characterized the ritualistic legalism of the religious establishment with the image of a Pharisee unthinkingly swallowing a camel (Matt. 23:24). They carefully polish their cups on the outside and forget to check for all the dirt on the inside. They are so careful to police for a speck of defilement that might be located in the eye of a struggling shepherd, all the while maintaining the stately traditions in the temple with whole trees hanging out of their own eyes (Luke 6:41). Mere religion can be very funny—and tragic. How the crowds loved this stinging satire! Their numbers increased at Jesus' preaching sessions until the growing thousands on the shore forced him to get into a boat and speak to them from some distance—the politicians' dream of a grassroots revolution. But Jesus was not impressed with mere numbers, once commenting—surely with a twinkle in his eye and an ironic premonition of the future—"Wherever the corpse is, there the vultures will gather" (Matt. 24:28).[16]

The Christian spiritual tradition has too often featured an excessive asceticism that functions as a debasement of life. Enjoyment of the physical side of life is rejected in favor of a mortification of the flesh. Physical pleasures are thought to be a dangerous hindrance to the spiritual life. The attitude "Do not taste! Do not touch!" (Col. 2:21), however, is a stark departure from the norm of the Jewish tradition. The Hebrew Bible is a worldly book where everything is viewed as coming from the hand of God (Isa. 44:24). Jesus said a hearty yes to the material world, actively involving himself in weddings, holidays, eating, drinking, and celebrating. There is no gnosticism here. Paul said "all things are yours" (1 Cor. 3:21), implying that God's children are to participate fully and responsibly in this world of flesh and blood. Pleasure is not to be pursued as an end in itself, of course. Hedonism (belief that pleasure and happiness are the chief goals of life) is a plague in today's self-indulgent society. Nonetheless, for the committed

Christian to enjoy God's good creation is a blessing to the Creator, so that Paul instructs that "whether you eat or drink, or whatever you do, do everything for the glory of God" (1 Cor. 10:31).

When life in Christ is being lived as God intends, light appears, necessary risks are willingly taken, hearts and doors are open, laughter is heard, and the following little song-prayer becomes the witness of life:

> *I then shall live as one who's been forgiven,*
> *I'll walk with joy to know my debts are paid. . . .*
> *I then shall live as one who's learned compassion;*
> *I've been so loved that I'll risk loving, too.*
> *Your [God's] kingdom come around and through and in me,*
> *Your power and glory, let them shine through me.*[17]

The Rich Christian Tradition

Christian spirituality cannot be properly understood apart from its Hebrew roots. If one wishes to understand the biblical intent of the Hebrew word *ruach*, for instance, it probably is best to rethink the common Christian decision to use the English word *spirit*. Usually defined by a Western culture, Christians commonly assume that *spirit* implies something immaterial, disembodied, beyond the present realities of earthly life. But the Hebrew thought of Yahweh's *ruach* features this: "God is a tempest, a storm, a force in body and soul, humanity and nature."[18] God breathes life and love into the full reality of a needy creation. Those people who are open to this powerful divine breath are to become willing instruments of the rushing wind of God which seeks to rearrange how things are in this fallen world.

What things are to be rearranged or totally renewed? All things! The Hebrew Bible makes no distinction between the sacred and secular areas of life. All life is a unity, and it is all God's domain. Therefore, it is understandable that in the popular musical *Fiddler on the Roof* the rabbi is asked, "Is there a blessing for the Tsar?" and "Is there a blessing for a sewing machine?" The Jews in this Russian village are reflecting the ancient Hebraic belief that everything is theological. Spirituality is to envelop the whole person, community, and world. Christians can hardly grasp Paul's admonition to "pray without ceasing" (1 Thess. 5:17) except in the Hebrew context of the pervasiveness of Jewish prayer in relation to all of life. One might refer to this inclusive attitude as an authentic biblical humanism.

Having highlighted the Christian seasons of Advent, Easter, and Pentecost, we now move to a season that, while less dramatic and defined, is no less crucial. Once the great events have established the faith, it is left for the faith to be lived out in the mundane of everyday life.

The Church Year: Ordinary Time

For the New Testament, all time between Easter and the second coming of Jesus is the church's time, the time when the power of the Spirit is to rise to new life and rule in hearts and lives. The season of Kingdomtide ("Ordinary Time") is the portion of the Christian year that focuses on the ongoing celebration of the arriving of the reign of God in the full range of human life. The Spirit is working in all of our days—and thus this annual season is an extension of Pentecost as the Spirit keeps coming and working to make Christ known and to realize his reign. For those who read the Bible systematically with the guidance of a lectionary and in the flow of the Christian year, they now find themselves reading through the teaching portions of the Gospels of Matthew, Mark, and Luke. Here Jesus' instruction about the implications of the reign of God is clearly central.

The Sundays of the months following the celebration of Pentecost compose the ordinary time of the church's life and mission in the world. This season concludes with the arrival again of Advent and thus the beginning of the recycling of the whole Christian year. The "ordinary" designation of this large section of the year comes from the simple meaning of ordinal numbers (first Sunday of, second Sunday of, etc.). The meaning, however, should not be taken to suggest the merely mundane or routine. Given what has been made known in Christ and the presence of the Spirit, Christians are to view all time as now sanctified and brought into the orbit of resurrection life. Existence is to be under the reign of God through the ministry of the Spirit in everyday affairs. Everything Christian in a sense is to be after Pentecost and in light of Pentecost. Thus, Kingdomtide, or the flow of God's reign in the "ordinary," is to be experienced in the midst of our love, anxiety, grief, doubts, daily occupations, and growing faith. These months are the time to focus on the many issues of actual Christian living by finding and making contemporary applications of the Pentecost reality. John Westerhoff has said it well:

> Ordinary time may lack the drama of Jesus' life, death, and resurrection, but it more than makes up for it in the drama of his teachings about how our lives are to be lived faithfully. . . .
>
> . . . Stewardship . . . is nothing less than a complete lifestyle, a total accountability and responsibility before God. Stewardship is what we do after we say we believe. . . .[19]

Life under the reign of God is grounded in the life of Jesus and enabled by the ministry of the Spirit of Jesus who is with the church. To be spiritual is to grow up as citizens of God's reign, with the risen Christ being formed within (Gal. 4:19). It is also to be a willing agent of the Spirit who gives gifts for ministry in the church and world. The Christian life on mission in this world will have some suffering at its center. The Gospel of Mark emphasizes the suffering of Jesus who "came not to be served but to serve, and to give his life a ransom for many" (10:45). Christian life involves losing instead of saving one's life (9:33–37; 10:35–45). Those who would be faithful disciples of Jesus will have to experience personal denial and a cross (8:34–35).

There again must be a celebration of discipline, a new engaging in the spiritual disciplines that move believers to inner transformation, healing, and joy as they enter into deeper relationships with God. The curse of our times is superficiality. The need is not for more productive, intelligent, or gifted people, but for more genuinely changed people. The needed change comes only by divine grace, but God honors the way of disciplined grace. Richard Foster explores the corporate, inward, and outward disciplines of Christian spirituality. The outward includes simplicity, solitude, submission, and service. Through these come integrity and compassion in Christian relationships that bless others without being manipulative or seeking control. The discipline of simplicity frees us from the tyranny of greed and possessiveness. Solitude prepares us to be attentive and responsive with others. Submission trusts in God and liberates us to love others unconditionally.[20]

Such renewed attention to the disciplined spiritual life has a long and rich history. One classic book of Christian spirituality was originally written in Latin and first transcribed about 1418. In the intervening centuries, it has remained in print, been translated into numerous languages, and become what some say is the most read Christian book of all time except the Bible itself. Attributed to Thomas à Kempis and titled *The Imitation of Christ*, it emerged from the life of a European renewal movement called the Brethren of the Common Life. These reformers sought to renew the church from within through a call to penitence and faith and a consecrated walk with God in all aspects of ordinary life. The call was to prayer, reading of the Scriptures, surrender to the will of God, self-discipline, humility, the guidance of the Spirit, love, practical judgment, and cross-bearing.

The simple but profound writing of Thomas à Kempis captures the spirit of this movement of the fourteenth and fifteenth centuries in Germany and the Netherlands. The movement's leader, Gerhard De Groote (1340–1384), taught about the inner life of the soul and the necessity of imitating the life of Christ by loving one's neighbor as oneself. À Kempis wrote, "I would rather feel compunction of heart for my sins than merely know the definition of compunction." Again, "Man proposes, but God disposes." Spiritual freedom is gained through a purified forsaking of ourselves and our own will in favor of being submerged into God's will. This has implication for all life in the ordinary time when God is to be reigning. It leads to appreciation for the incarnational tradition of Christian spirituality.

The Incarnational Tradition

The fifth of the six Christian spiritual traditions seeks to translate new being in Christ into visible and concrete expressions in the world. People have an urgent need to see the reality of God made visible in the midst of everyday life. Believers face the challenge of realizing that everywhere is holy ground, and all of life is sanctified by the presence of God. The secret of sanctity, the heart of hope, the calling of the spiritual life for the Christian is to stand with the gracious God of creative love and see all people and things with the eyes of the artist-lover of creation. According to Evelyn Underhill:

> If we do not acquire this habit of looking at the complex natural world, including our natural selves, with eyes cleansed by prayer and brought into focus by humility—if we attempt to judge it from our own point of view, without a loving movement of the mind towards the Creator of all this splendour, this intricate web of life—then how easy it is to get lost in it, and lose all sense of its mysterious beauty; because we mistake our small self-interested conclusions, our vulgar utilitarianism, for the truth.[21]

There should be a vital link between the Christian's spiritual life and life in general. Spirit and flesh are to be delicately intertwined. Here is the keynote of the Christian faith: "And the Word became flesh and lived among us" (John 1:14). God is not an abstract concept or a mere philosophy for elite intellectuals. God is present, has become involved with us humans, visibly, understandably, in the actual person Jesus (Col. 1:15). Christianity is a "worldly" faith centered around God's grand choice to be enfleshed (incarnate) in Jesus. This world is God's good creation and, despite its desperate condition, God still chooses to be in its midst.

For the ancient Jew, the daily life of faith was seen as a journey. It was not a pie-in-the-sky escape from this troubled world on the way to heaven. Rather, it was the active quest for the good life, which was defined as acting justly, loving mercy, and walking humbly with one's God (Mic. 6:8). The essence of real religion lies in quality relationships with God and with all that God has created. It involves walking with God in the path of God's wisdom and in service to others who are in need. Georgia Harkness is a good example. Probably the first recognized female Christian theologian and said to be the most widely read of all theologians in the middle decades of the twentieth century, Harkness released her first book in 1921. At that time, she was a woman from a small town in upstate New York who was taking her first plunge into the urban world and encountering the massive social issues related to the large European immigrant community in New York City. She insisted that the church's ministry on behalf of racial progress "must aim to minister to every side of the immigrant's nature." Giving material aid is crucial, but so is developing "the higher spiritual values." Our ultimate goal, wrote Harkness, "must be the more abundant life which Christ came to bring to man. We must minister to the souls of men. We must seek to make them, not simply members of one church nor citizens of America, but members of the Church Universal and citizens of the Kingdom of God."[22]

The following assertions are basic for the life of Christian faith in the world: God created the material world and chooses to manifest himself through material means; the world is intended to enhance human life; what is physical should be infused with the spiritual; a key function of matter is to mediate the presence of God to those who seek. In fact, the high point of Christian faith is God's enfleshment (incarnation) in Jesus. The coming of the Messiah as a baby in poverty circumstances was the dramatic act of God, revealing on the human scene and in human terms the divine heart and plan. We best approach knowing the unknowable God by observing the attitudes and actions of one particular and real human being. In fact, "Where Jesus was, God was. What Jesus did was God in action. What happened to Jesus happened to God. In Jesus, the Kingdom of God had arrived, as Jesus had said all along. Jesus and his Father in heaven functioned as one and somehow actually were one!"[23] It is the preoccupation of the incarnational tradition of Christian spirituality to understand how the prayer-filled and Spirit-empowered life should function in ordinary human life and how ordinary things can convey the presence and grace of God to others. Jesus was the perfect model; we now are to be in him, sharing in God's ongoing incarnational activity. Brennan Manning points to the symbol of appropriate church life:

> The signature of Jesus, the Cross, is the ultimate expression of God's love for the world. The Church is the Church of the crucified, risen Christ only when it is stamped with his signature, only when it faces outward and moves with him along the way of the Cross. Turned inward upon itself in bickering and theological hair-splitting, it loses its identity and its mission.[24]

Medieval Catholicism recognized a fundamental distinction between the spiritual estate (the clergy) and the temporal estate (everyone else). As part

Finding by Sinking

There are those who seek to penetrate the immensities and to see God. One ought rather to sink into the depths and seek to find God among the suffering, erring, and the downtrodden. Then the heart is free from pride and able to see God.

Martin Luther

of the Protestant Reformation, Martin Luther declared this distinction null and void and set out to reclaim the biblical concept of the laity as the people of God.[25] Spirituality is a resource to be placed at the disposal of the whole church for the sake of the world—as opposed to reserving it for the clergy. He insisted that all Christians are truly of the spiritual estate (the only differences being function).[26] The church is to nourish believers so they can go out in the world with true Christian identity and effectively share the good news and serve human need. Wrote Luther, "I will therefore give myself as a Christ to my neighbor, just as Christ offered himself to me; I will do nothing in this life except what I see is necessary, profitable, and salutary to my neighbor, since through faith I have an abundance of all good things in Christ."[27] In a similar spirit, John Calvin actively rejected any division between the personal and public dimensions of Christian existence. His quest was for a spirituality that achieves a legitimate synthesis of Christian existence in the church and world.

A more recent Lutheran, Dietrich Bonhoeffer (1906–1945), wrote in the tragic circumstances of Nazi Germany. He took the world seriously, called for a sacrificial "existence for others," insisting that "the church is the church only when it exists for others."[28] By paying with his life, he left an authentic witness behind. The Christian life is not to be reduced to a series of respectful religious acts and associations, but is to be a real participation in the sufferings of God in the midst of secular life. In fact, a reformation stream even more radical than Luther or Calvin, represented today by the numerous Brethren, Mennonite, Baptist, and similar groups, sees holiness as more than what Christians believe or experience. It also has to do with how they live, especially how they live together as the church in the midst of the world.[29] Alan Kreider is one contemporary representative of this "radical" or Anabaptist stream who attempts to show what it means today to be a people of faith living according to the biblical way of holiness. The meaning is an incarnational commitment to "the church as the body of

Christ, simplicity of lifestyle and economic sharing, nonviolence and enemy love, and Jesus as the heart of God's revelation of an appropriate lifestyle for God's people."[30]

Christians are to be salt and light that truly impact the world. How can believers know if they are being appropriately salty and lighted? Insists Kreider, "Not by measuring their influence on the world, but by monitoring their similarity to their Master and their faithfulness to his teaching."[31] Since Jesus is Lord, no area of life should be conceded to the rule of Satan. Philip Yancey says of Henri Nouwen (1932–1996), "A better symbol of the Incarnation I can hardly imagine." Nouwen was an admirable model of "holy inefficiency."[32] A highly trained psychologist and theologian who taught on prestigious campuses like Notre Dame, Yale, and Harvard, he chose to become a priest in residence at a home for the seriously disabled in Toronto, Ontario. This dedicated disciple of Jesus had become deeply convinced that "the Christian leader of the future is called to be completely irrelevant and to stand in this world with nothing to offer but his or her own vulnerable self. That is the way Jesus came to reveal God's love. [This way] allows him or her to enter into a deep solidarity with the anguish underlying all the glitter of success and to bring the light of Jesus there."[33]

Susanna Wesley, mother of John and Charles, is a compelling model of incarnational Christianity. The details of her everyday living were the arena for her interaction with God and the place where she built a history with God. She home-schooled her children, launched a congregation in her kitchen, stood firm in the face of family tragedies, and tutored her son John in practical divinity throughout his tenure at Oxford. Late in life she prayed:

> Help me, Lord, to remember that religion is not to be confined to the church, or closet, nor exercised only in prayer and meditation, but that everywhere I am in Thy presence. So may my every word and action have a moral content. . . . May all the happenings of my life prove useful and beneficial to me. May all things instruct me and afford me an opportunity of exercising some virtue and daily learning and growing toward Thy likeness. . . . Amen.[34]

So, to be truly spiritual, Christians need to reflect the likeness of Christ in all that they are and do in the real world. To make this possible, it is crucial that they be spiritually nourished themselves. To reflect Christ requires being formed by Christ. This should happen in large part as one engages regularly in worship of God. In this regard, two incarnational words need to be clarified and then their meanings freshly embraced.

One key word is *liturgy* and the other is *sacrament* (see the glossary). Liturgy—*liturgia*—means "the people's work." And what is this work for Christians? It is to glorify God and be transformed by God through the process of worship and for the purpose of witness in the world. The reality of God is to shine in worship through physical forms, whether these be hymns, sermons, religious art, candles, group silence, holy dances, whatever is done in reverence and openness to God's presence. There are among Christians the formal liturgies of the high church and the much more spontaneous liturgies of the low church. Liturgies vary widely, but there are no nonliturgical churches.

Somehow people must pattern their approaches to God and receive through their patterns the sustaining, instructing, and maturing grace that they need. There are the icons of Eastern Orthodoxy, the footwashing observances of the Brethren, the weekly Lord's Supper celebrations of the Disciples, the times of group silence and waiting of the Quakers, the lectionary Bible readings of numerous denominations, among others. Believers see, touch, taste, and hear as God is made manifest through worship patterns and material means. The Anglican tradition of England has focused on formalized spiritual guidance for individuals and congregations, especially with its *Book of Common Prayer*. The Eastern Orthodox tradition has not suffered extensively from a separation of theology from spirituality or mysticism. True theologians are assumed to be those who experience the content of their theology. All Christians are to enflesh in the world the healing fruit of their spiritual experiences.

In addition to the word *liturgy* is the word *sacrament*. Many Protestants shy away from this word, thinking of it as a magical medieval practice of misled and overinstitutionalized Christians. Instead, it merely refers to practices consecrated by Christ himself that especially demonstrate God's use of matter to make present and visible the invisible realm of the Spirit (visible means of invisible grace). Two such practices recognized almost universally among Christians are baptism and the Lord's Supper. Richard Foster speaks of sacraments as "concrete actions by which we are marked and fed in such a way that the reality of God becomes embedded in our body, our mind, our spirit." The Holy Spirit grafts us into the divine life by burying and raising us in baptism and then continually feeds us "by enacting the death and resurrection of Christ in the Communion service, or Eucharist."[35] Is there a danger of making idols out of these and other institutionalized church practices, of confusing the means for the end? Yes, of course. But this must not deter believers from grateful participation.

Protestant complaints about the Christian sacraments often grow out of justified concerns. The medieval church did tend to quantify divine grace and control its transmission by those in privileged positions in the church. Now, however, we seem to face a different problem. The present danger is less that we will try to manipulate God and more that we will regard God as distant, impersonal, not present and accessible. Thus, Laurence Stookey observes that the Lord's Supper "shows forth the One who feeds us daily and enters into the feasting with us in order that we may thereby recognize how fully divine love pervades the whole of creation."[36] We are reminded that God's invisibility does not mean God's absence or inactivity. Likewise, the church is to be reminded that she also is to be visible and sacrificially active in the world. Baptism, the Lord's Supper, footwashing, and other activities, while not the means for accomplishing initial or final salvation, nonetheless are significant to the health and fruitfulness of salvation. They are means of graphic remembrance, public witness, corporate identity building, and ongoing personal sanctification that leads to human service.

Martin Luther King Jr. (1929–1968) insisted that God's mediated grace provides the "strength to love."[37] Creation is governed by a loving, personal God who is the companion of those who struggle for justice. In the life, death, and resurrection of Jesus, we see that unearned suffering is redemptive. Evil can be overcome with good. How should a spiritual life nurtured by the Spirit of Jesus become actively incarnational in our unjust world of racism, hatred, and violence? With Mahatma Gandhi, King combined the method of nonviolent resistance and the Christian doctrine of love to evolve a potent force in the struggle for human freedom. He led the civil rights movement in the United States from the mid–1950s until his assassination in 1968. Said King:

> If we are arrested every day, if we are exploited every day, if we are trampled over every day, don't ever let anyone pull you so low as to hate them. We must use the weapon of love. We must have compassion and understanding for those who hate us. We must realize so many people are taught to hate us that they are not totally responsible for their hate. But we stand in life at midnight; we are always on the threshold of a new dawn.[38]

Dorothy Day (1897–1980) wanted her Christian faith to be whole and relevant in its spiritual depth and practical love for humanity (Matt. 25:31–46). She was prepared to move against the social grain and even go to jail on behalf of the poor. Co-founding the Catholic Worker movement during the depth of the Great Depression of the 1930s, Day offered hospitality to the poor.[39] For almost a half century, she chose to live with the urban poor. She was not the kind of reformer who would live in one world while trying to change another. The full reign of God is not yet, but followers of Jesus must break their silence, lock their loving arms together, and find the strength to love in practical ways. There is a price to be paid when love is put into action and made incarnate; but the price should be paid willingly if Christian life is to be lived obediently. Beyond the cross is the resurrection!

The Apostles' Creed

The first article of the Apostles' Creed affirms, "I believe in God the Father Almighty, maker of heaven and earth." Since the Bible and early Christians assumed the existence of God, this creedal affirmation should be seen as less a denial of atheism and more a statement about the kind of God in whom Christians believe. Some people in the early years of the church called Gnostics believed that physical existence itself is evil and God would not be lowered into the disgrace of dealing with it directly. But the creed declares otherwise. The God of creation and of redemption are the same God. God created and said that it was good. The creation was not abandoned by God even when it chose evil. God still comes, touches, loves, suffers, and redeems. The God known to the ancient Hebrews is the same God who is the Father of Jesus Christ.

Some early Christians (e.g., Marcion) suggested there were two gods, an inferior one who brought the world into being and the superior one who manifested himself lovingly in Jesus Christ. It is true that some attitudes and actions attributed to God in the Hebrew Scriptures are not easily reconciled with those of Jesus, but suggesting that there are two gods is the wrong solution. There is one biblical God, known most fully in Jesus Christ. It is crucial to recognize that "if we accept the view that God's revelation of himself occurs in the context of human understanding, we have a viable way out."[40] For biblical Christians, there is to be no escape into a spiritual world, no retreat for mystical contemplation except as a way of better preparing for ministry in the world (as Jesus often did). The creed insists that the God of redemption is the God of creation.

What God did originally in creation was good; what God does now involves providential care of the same world that he wishes to redeem. The ongoing work of God recalls the original goodness of all creation and intends to send believers on mission with a "worldly holiness."[41] It is the holy one who in Christ overcame the principalities and powers of this world. We now are to be signs to the world of God's gracious overcoming. The God who made all things expects loyal disciples to be the vanguard of those who intend to stop unmaking all things. Theodore Jennings Jr. views the Apostles' Creed as a Christian pledge of allegiance to the practical demands of Christian faith. Specifically:

> I claim the earth itself, all creatures, for [God's] love; for it is the power that brings forth life not only for me, but for all that breathes.
>
> To this love I will be loyal, rejecting the temptation to return to bondage, rejecting the allure of force and division, rejecting rapacity toward my fellow

> creatures and seeking to show myself to be in truth the adopted heir of this love.
>
> I will be loyal to the way of Jesus, the way that leads to the reign of this love in all creation.
>
> I acknowledge [Jesus] as my only leader and swear to continue his mission until the world is transformed.
>
> I renounce all other gods, I will bow down before no power, however awesome or seductive, pledging my fealty only to the one whose will is inscribed in history by the mission of Jesus. He is animated by the divine spirit to announce the overthrow of division and domination and death and calls me to be of the same spirit.[42]

Adorning the Doctrine

A Christian is called to be a credit to the cause of Christ by adorning Christian teaching with one's life, being "an ornament to the doctrine of God our Savior" (Titus 2:10). From the early tradition of the Church of God (Anderson) movement comes a wonderful song that asks the right question. Are Christians "adorning the doctrine"?

> *Are you adorning the doctrine, The glorious doctrine of God,*
> *Walking so holy before Him, Following where He has trod,*
> *So when the world looks upon you, Nothing but Christ is in view?*
> *So when the world looks upon you, Nothing but Christ is in view?*
>
> *Are you adorning the doctrine, And making attractive the way,*
> *Honoring Christ by your actions, And by the words that you say?*
> *Are you, my brother and sister, Proving the Bible is true?*
> *Are you, my brother and sister, Proving the Bible is true?*[43]

What doctrine is to be adorned? The New Testament does not present a unified dogmatic system of theology, but in various ways it does tell and reflect on a unified story. The story centers in the actions of God, especially in Israel and then in Jesus, to create a community of witnesses to the good news of God's redeeming love (the church). Empowered by the Spirit of God, the church is called to receive and reenact the loving obedience of Jesus Christ and thus serve as a living sign of God's redemptive purposes for the world.

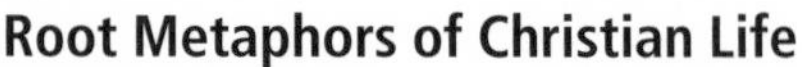

Root Metaphors of Christian Life

1. Community
. . . being an alternative model of life witness to the world.

2. Cross
. . . living the way of Jesus through the community's life.

3. New Creation
. . . exhibiting the firstfruits of the coming of God's future.

Richard B. Hays, *The Moral Vision of the New Testament*

How is the sign to be shown clearly? Richard Hays identifies three New Testament root metaphors that helpfully point the way.[44] First, believers should commit themselves to a community of faith. God is bringing into being a people, the church, that is called to embody an alternative order that stands as a sign of God's work in the world. God's will is not merely what I should do, but what we believers should be and do together as a corporate reflection of Christ. Second, this church reflection should be shaped by the cross since the death of Jesus is a New Testament paradigm of what it means to be faithful to God in this fallen world. We are to participate in Christ's sufferings (Phil. 3:10). The church is called to be a visible sign of self-giving love, taking up its cross, giving up itself so that Christ again becomes visible (2 Cor. 4:11), bearing the burdens of others and thus fulfilling the law of Christ (Gal. 6:2). Third, the community of the cross is to enjoy and embody the power of Christ's resurrection, thus showing in its life that, by the power and grace of God's Spirit, it is a forerunner of the new creation. The church that yields to the cross can anticipate the coming resurrection. While yet groaning for the full birth of God's tomorrow, it is privileged to receive and make visible the firstfruits of the Spirit (Rom. 8:22–23). The church is to be the cross-shaped community that knows new creation and dares to live the knowledge that the powers of this world are doomed and the age to come is already beginning to appear.

Right belief is essential for a distinctly Christian life. One must know the right story that narrates reality from God's perspective. But really knowing cannot be separated from truly living what one knows tentatively by faith. In addition, effective Christian witness happens best only when good fruit appears on the tree of right verbal confession. Announced Dietrich

Bonhoeffer, "If you would find *eternity*, give yourself to *time*. This seems a tremendous paradox: if you desire the eternal, give yourself to the temporal. If you desire God, hold fast to the world."[45] This does not mean being worldly in the sense of being defined by the world's fallenness; it does mean being Christlike in very present, practical, and relevant ways in the midst of the world's fallenness. That which lures the lost is the cosmetics of love, joy, and peace, in short, the lived evidence of life in God's Spirit.

Too many Christians are satisfied with simply experiencing the forgiveness of God's love. They need also to pursue holiness or Christlikeness by divine grace so that mission becomes possible. The issue is one of seeing and being seen. Robert Barron has written a whole book of theology around a single and significant thesis: Christianity is essentially a way of seeing. Holiness is seeing with the eyes of Jesus Christ. To truly be alive and then to truly live as a Christian, a person needs to come to vision through Christ. Jesus wants us "to open our eyes and see *him* . . . to see what God is doing in and through him. He himself *is* the Kingdom of God coming into the world with transformative power."[46] We are invited to participate in this transformation, to be changed by accepting this story as our own. We, then, adorn the Christian doctrine best by exhibiting its renewing life and so walking in God's ways that, when the world turns its attention to Christian believers, it is Christ who comes onto their screens.

What is the impact on your community of the presence and life of your congregation? What is the impact on your neighbors of the way your family lives its life? We Christians are to be the light of the world, sharers of the good news of Christ in word and deed. For some, you will be the only representative of Christ they will ever know. Is your witness attractive, respectable, believable, responsible? With what are you adorning the doctrine that you profess to believe? If the fruit of the Spirit is emerging within you, the beauty of Christ will shine in your life, and good news will go forth. This is truly living the Spirit's way.

Questions to Pursue

1. What is one particular example of living the Spirit's way in today's information age?
2. Give examples of what it might look like today for a Christian to be clothed with Christ.
3. What do hospitality and humor have to do with Christian spirituality?

4. Do you see similarities between the teaching of the famous fifteenth-century book *The Imitation of Christ* and the twentieth-century teaching of Georgia Harkness?
5. How does a sacrament (see the glossary) illustrate well the incarnational spiritual tradition?
6. Explain the contrast between the "worldly holiness" of biblical Christianity and the heretical teaching of Gnostics (see the glossary).
7. How do the three root metaphors of the intended Christian life help believers to be the right signs to the world?

7

Truly Abiding: The Spirit's Assurance

> God is Prologue, Plot, and Epilogue to the whole biblical story of creation's origin and redemption. . . . The continuing thrust of the story reveals the Spirit of God carrying forward that which God planned from eternity and provides in Christ. The dramatic birth of the church shifts the scene back and forth from the inner life of personal renewal of individual believers to the church's outer mission of peace, justice, and liberation. The new community of the Spirit, the church, is called to model for the world that which is yet to be.[1]

> The power of the age to come was being poured out upon the church for the accomplishment of a universal proclamation of the particular redemption in Jesus Christ, a proclamation in word and power and demonstration of the Spirit. . . . The vivid presence of the Spirit heightened expectation, propelled into mission, enlivened worship, and increased consecration in preparation for the appearance of the Lord of the harvest.[2]

Christians who are truly living (see chapter 6) gain an assurance from God's Spirit that allows them to abide, endure, and hope regardless of circumstances. One day faith will be sight, and all that is partial will be whole. One day all will be glory with nothing but rejoicing around the throne of God. But until then we anticipate by faith and at least taste the future glory by present life in the Spirit. And who is the Spirit? The Spirit is the presence of God who is providing a current pledge of what is yet to come (2 Cor.

5:1–5). There is urgent need to inform people that such a tasting is available now. Already a divine pledge can bring assurance about the future.

An old story comes to us from Greek mythology. Thetis, a sea nymph, was anxious that her infant son Achilles be invulnerable in battle when he grew to be an adult. She dipped him in the River Styx since its water was thought to confer invulnerability. There was only one problem, a big one as the story finally plays out. Thetis held the little boy by the heel as she dipped him, thoughtlessly keeping dry this small part of his body. Many years later, in the heat of battle, an arrow struck and killed this young man. Yes, it had struck him at his only vulnerable spot—his "Achilles heel." One such vulnerability that stalks many Christians is their inability to abide in the faith through the battles of life.

One of C. S. Lewis's famous presentations was made at Evensong at the Oxford University Church of Saint Mary. His subject was the joy a Christian should experience and the too-often sensed feeling of exile where there is a "desire for our own far-off country, which we find in ourselves even now." Lewis assured his audience that this longing will not go unsatisfied forever.

> At present we are on the outside of the world, the wrong side of the door. We discern the freshness and purity of morning, but they do not make us fresh and pure. We cannot mingle with the splendours we see. But all the leaves of the New Testament are rustling with the rumour that it will not always be so. Some day, God willing, we shall get in.[3]

The hopeful rumor may be whispering encouragingly in the Bible, but the glorious news does not reach most people convincingly, if at all.

The world (and even the church) is full of persons who can hardly make it, whose vulnerabilities are exposed, who long for a home they seem to have no way of reaching. They have few roots and little staying power in life. Hope is only a fleeting fancy. Their families often have come apart. They have trouble sustaining significant relationships. They have no place of importance to be nor anything of particular importance to do. They usually do not belong to a supportive community and cannot survive any more bad news. Having little hope for the future, they find it difficult to locate any meaning in or enthusiasm for life in the present. When one seems to be going nowhere, it is hard to put up with life. It is a struggle to go on at all. Being part of some destiny seems a mere delusion.

Many things are changing so fast that people are left reeling. What was impossible yesterday is ordinary today. What was sacred yesterday is widely discarded as no longer relevant. What we remember as simple is now complicated and fraught with new dilemmas and dangers. The rapid change brought on by technological advances is both exhilarating and disorienting, including such a change in the employment world that large numbers of dedicated and skilled workers have seen their long-term jobs disappear. The future seems unknown and ominous. Nuclear weapons are such a threat to the very existence of humanity that many young people despair of the future and do not prepare for much beyond living for the moment. Even so, Christians are to be instructed by their Hebrew roots. There is hope in all circumstances. There is life beyond exile. The future finally is the Lord's.

In the Meantime

The Spirit of God offers assurance so believers can abide whatever comes in the meantime. C. S. Lewis was right. The pages of the New Testament rustle with the rumor that exiles are coming to an end. A resurrection is on the way; eternal life is in the wind. There is hope in God! The Spirit comes to convict of sin and cleanse from all unrighteousness by revealing, forgiving, comforting, and sanctifying (2 Thess. 2:13). But the Spirit also awakens, inspires, and fills with "all joy and peace in believing," so that, by the power of the Spirit, believers might abound in hope (Rom. 15:13). The future is assured. Even so, the Christian hope is hardly restricted to an anticipated new world beyond time. Christian spirituality includes a call to social holiness in the present. Christian hope intends to motivate believers to spearhead the advance of God's reign in this present world through the transforming power of the Spirit. Two equally vital time references for Christians, then, are God's tomorrow and the church's responsibility in the meantime.

The Hebrew view of time and history is essentially linear and progressive. Whatever the present dangers and tragedies, history is going somewhere. In the final analysis, the big stream of human experience was initiated by God, is infused by God's redemptive working, and finally will be consummated by the God who transcends all time and has not lost control of the process. There is a goal, a glorious climax at the end of the age. There is hope. The faithful are to hold on and believe. We are never alone and the future is secure. However, God's time and our time often flow differently (Ps. 90:4). God's perceptions rarely match our own (Isa. 55:8). Even so, in faith believers can let go of everything because they are held tightly by God's enduring love. They can risk claiming nothing as their own because they know that they have been claimed as God's own and thus one day will have all things worth having. They can risk for Christ's sake because, as Jesus made plain, there is no real reason for a disciple to worry, and there is only one safe place to store up treasures. Seek first the reign of God, and all else that is good will come in due time (Matt. 6:33).

A key connection is between truly living the Christian life (chapter 6) and the concern for how best to truly abide in the difficult times prior to the ultimate victory of the reign of God. That which yet will be is to make a difference in the meantime.[4] At this very moment, the Spirit of Christ ministers to enable mission in this world—until the time of mission ends and a better world arrives. A proper looking forward toward God's *then* helps equip believers for serving faithfully in the *now* of God's world. There is a strong New Testament connection between the "last days" and the current ministry of the Holy Spirit. One can say that the Spirit is the initial presence of the future that God has promised. The present lives of Spirit-filled believers are themselves to be "a sign of the last days of the final fulfillment of the divine promises," a sign made possible because the Spirit is God's presence and power that functions "like a wind blowing from the future of God into our present."[5] And what comes from the future is deeply rooted in the church's past. Steven Land notes that "when the Pentecostals spoke of restoration, it was not primarily a restoration of this or that outward characteristic of the early church, but primarily the apostolic *power* and *expectancy*."[6] It is in the Spirit that believers find roots in yesterday, abilities for today, and enduring hope for tomorrow.

The Book of Revelation, full of references to the Hebrew Scriptures, is a continuing means of warning and assurance for Christians in the midst of threats to the church's very survival. There were significant problems both inside the early churches of Asia and outside from the threat of a dominant Roman rule and its perverted commitment to emperor worship. John is granted a divine vision that unfolds things that would come to pass. He knew that, because evil did not defeat Jesus on the cross, the church could successfully carry its cross in this world and would one day be granted a glorious resurrection. In this revelation one finds the ringing announcement that God is victorious, reigning both in and beyond human history. Believers threatened with persecution of whatever kind should be assured and live in hope. Rome may insist on the words "lord and god" being applied to its emperor, but believers in Christ know that kingdoms of this earth rise and fall. Finally, it will be God's Christ who overcomes. Only "you are worthy, our Lord and God, to receive glory and honor and power" (Rev. 4:11).

One of the great spiritual figures in all of church history is St. Augustine (354–430). He lived in a dramatic and frightening time. In the year 410, Rome was sacked, a signal that the mighty empire might be at the point of collapse. Like a latter-day Noah, Augustine constructed a theological ark in which the church could survive the terrible storm. While the world was reeling under crushing blows, Augustine

> turned to the deeper question of the relations between earthly cities, like Rome, which have their day, rising and falling like everything in time, and the Heavenly City or City of God, which is everlasting. This question occupied him for the next seventeen years, almost to the end of his life, and resulted in his great work of genius, *The City of God*, which directly or indirectly influenced the thought of Christians on what they owed to God and what to Caesar through the succeeding fifteen centuries.[7]

Another great spiritual leader, Dietrich Bonhoeffer, lived in a different time of world calamity. It was not just that in the 1930s and 1940s Germany was mildly deluded by some nationalistic rhetoric. It was, in fact, seeking to conquer the world with a morally sick man in charge of a seriously sick nation. In contrast to German churches that too easily accommodated themselves to the sad circumstance, Bonhoeffer instituted clandestine seminaries to educate pastors who would preach courageously the implications of the true gospel of Christ. He was martyred by the Nazis just as the monstrous war was drawing to a close. Hitler's Third Reich was to have lasted for a thousand years, but it was short-lived, while the gospel of Christ lives on. When the church realizes that this is the way of things, we can be strengthened to be faithful in the difficulties of the present. The last word is always the Lord's.

The Epistle to the Hebrews proclaims Jesus as the pioneer who already has arrived at the goal and now acts as the "perfecter of our faith" (Heb. 12:2), while his disciples journey on. Christians are pilgrims on an adventure of faith. It is a new exodus, a wilderness-toward-Canaan journey with God. Believers are on-the-way people, rescued by grace from all Egypts of oppression and sin, marching through the wilderness of this present world, always inspired and comforted by the promise of the coming Canaan of final rest in God's perfect and perpetual presence. This hope for and early foretaste of the coming Canaan of final consummation braces the resolve of the wilderness people to be faithful on the way. The future age already is invading the present evil age (Rom. 12:2; Gal. 1:4; 2 Tim. 1:9–10; Heb. 6:5). Christians do not wait until the second coming of Christ to experience the last things. Instead, they have been living in the last days since the inauguration of the reign of God now present through the Christ-Pentecost events recorded in Acts 2.

The Wonderful Bible Word

A wonderful biblical word about hope is sturdy enough to sustain believers for the roughest of roads and for all journeys of this life and beyond. The word is *hypomenō*. To the meaning of "dwelling" or "remaining" (*menō*) is added the prefix *hypo,* "under," resulting in the wonderful meaning of standing fast, being patient, sheltered safely, living within or under the sovereignty, protection, and control of another. The hope of abiding in and beyond this troubled world is an assurance that only the Spirit's presence and power can give. Here is one of the nobler and most reassuring of all New Testament words.

Usually translated "patience" or "endurance," in Jewish literature (e.g, Fourth Maccabees) *hypomenō* appears in settings of resistance to violent oppression. It means "spiritual staying power" that can nerve the faithful even to the death. The gospel of Christ, when lived faithfully in the Spirit, provides the ability to wait out a storm, to bear the load with hope, to walk in darkness with genuine anticipation of the dawn. Christians can be graced with a quality of faith that faces the harshest of winds without losing footing on solid ground. William Barclay recalls George Matheson who, having been stricken with blindness and disappointed in love, wrote a prayer pleading that he might accept his circumstances, "not with dumb resignation, but with holy joy; not only with the absence of murmur, but with a song of praise."[8] That is a request for Christ's kind of spiritual staying power.

Beginning as a despised, illicit religious sect, Christianity endured three hundred years of hostility and then emerged as the dominant force in the Roman Empire. Many of the earliest generations of Christians faced severe persecution and learned to trust in the truly sovereign God. Polycarp was born about A.D. 70 and knew eyewitnesses of Jesus, possibly including the apostle John. As an elderly bishop of the church about 156, he was arrested at the demand of an angry mob at a pagan festival and soon became the earliest Christian martyr we know of outside the New Testament.[9] Aggressive evil in God's world does bring suffering and raise questions that even sturdy faith finds hard to answer. But faith does have adequate answers.

The twentieth century witnessed a devastation of God's chosen people on a scale almost unimaginable. Elaine Emeth joined seminary classmates on a tour of infamous sites of the Holocaust where she witnessed "the horrifying testimony of Treblinka, prayed the Kaddish at a crematorium oven at Auschwitz, and wept at the grave of forty-five murdered Jewish orphans at Kieke, Poland."[10] Her conclusion was that the Holocaust forces Christians into new spiritual territory. Now any view of God that insists that God is in full control of all that happens is inadequate.[11] To be added to the usual images of God—Father, Good Shepherd, Savior, Advocate, etc.—is "truly vulnerable one and discomforter." Often there are no easy answers to the urgent "why" questions. Reports Emeth:

> The God I see after Auschwitz is not the comforting, rescuing God I wish for in my weakness. Instead, when my heart is broken open by suffering . . . I meet a more complex God: simultaneously truthful, powerful, vulnerable,

> suffering, and commanding—a God whom I can love and trust completely, but who also makes me quake. . . . An *un*comforting God does not provide easy, consoling answers to our pleading question, Why? A truly vulnerable God suffers with those who suffer, and risks everything for the ultimate victory of justice, wholeness, and peace. A *dis*comforting God demands our participation in the establishment of divine justice in our world.[12]

There may be no easy answers, but there is the promise of the abiding divine presence and the unshakable divine love. Mature Christian spirituality has learned to stay, to stay responsibly, and to never turn back.

Staying in God's Presence

Unfortunately, many of us Christians today have so absorbed the surrounding secular context that we function as aggressive capitalists, even in our spiritual lives. We strategize, count, plan, produce, consume, and think of time as money. If, however, we are to survive as God would have it, we would stop, focus, learn to live by grace and in hope, and practice the presence of God apart from any insistence on immediate utility.[13] Many of us routinely devote years to education and hardly invest minutes in serious spiritual formation; but it is only in spiritual growth that we have staying power in the faith. Surviving adversity demands spiritual maturity that comes only from intentional participation in the habits and graces divinely given for spiritual maturing.

Living increasingly within the purposes and promises of God is essential, although such a focus is seriously lacking among many Christians who live in wealthy secular environments. We are tempted to think constantly about strategy, program, efficiency, and market. We become more seeker-friendly than we are Christ-related. We want our pastors to be opportunistic chief executive officers of rapidly growing and complex organizations (local congregations). By contrast, above all we should be patiently practicing the presence of God if the church is really to be the church. We are warned that whoever runs ahead and does not continue in the teaching of Christ will not have the blessing of God (2 John 9). We also are promised that holding to Christ's teachings and living in his way is what yields true discipleship, sets free, and brings the deep knowledge of the truth of God (John 8:31). With such discipleship, freedom, and knowledge also comes joy. To abide in the love of Christ makes one's joy complete (John 15:9–11).

Practicing the presence of God requires sacred space that engages more than the human intellect. The private closet of prayer is one such space. It makes available the privacy needed to build a strong relationship with God. Another space consideration is the public space of the community of believers at worship. Today's inquirer after God may appreciate being made comfortable at church, but being a hospitable fellowship must include a plan for a conscious immersion of those at worship in a public space that inspires reverence for God. Without question, Christian spirituality is affected by the space in which spiritual reflection and nurture take place. In our visually oriented times, it is crucial that we recover the significance of the symbolic actions of worship, accompanied by the sounds of meaningful music and the sights of the arts.

Location, posture, and what fills eyes and ears have considerable spiritual significance. Worship leaders should seek "to feature the relational seating of God's people around the symbols of water, the pulpit, and the Table. These are the primary visual images of God's work in the history of salvation."[14] The "dwelling under" meaning of our biblical word calls for appropriate architecture in which to worship. Small group life can proceed almost anywhere. Public worship should occur, when possible, where the physical surroundings support theological assumptions. Great attention was given to the design of the ancient temple in Jerusalem because it was the special place of God's presence. Worship surroundings should enliven the senses and thus enable one to become aware of God's presence.

Surviving Responsibly

The biblical word *hypomenō* takes on much meaning as believers face difficulties in life. Required in such times is the ability to be patient, steadfast, waiting, and surviving because faith and hope outlast momentary trials. According to Paul, we can even rejoice in our present sufferings because we know that they produce a perseverance that enhances Christian character and enlivens Christian hope (Rom. 5:3–4). When faith is tested, the needed perseverance develops (James 1:2–4). The Hebrews were reminded:

> But recall those earlier days when, after you had been enlightened, you endured a hard struggle with sufferings, sometimes being publicly exposed to abuse and persecution, and sometimes being partners with those so treated. For you had compassion for those who were in prison, and you cheerfully accepted the plundering of your possessions, knowing that you yourselves possessed something better and more lasting. Do not, therefore, abandon that confidence of yours; it brings a great reward. For you need endurance, so that when you have done the will of God, you may receive what was promised. (Heb. 10:32–36)

Blessed is any believer who perseveres responsibly under trial, for when the test has been withstood and duty done, there will be a crown of life as promised by God for those who love and do the divine will (James 1:12).

Humans may have crucified Jesus, but God reversed the intended impact of that cruel action. In Jesus' resurrection, God defeated all evil forces and began a new creation. The sacrifice on the cross and the victory of the resurrection address human guilt as justification, provide the needed purity and power as sanctification, and assure the final consequences as eventual glorification. Jesus' resurrection made dramatically clear that the future belongs to God, that death does not have the last word, and that the power of God is greater than all the powers lurking in this evil world. We should ask, Are we as believers in Jesus Christ experiencing resurrection freedom and new Jesus-life in the Spirit? Where is the power of the Spirit that releases believers to risk-taking on behalf of Christ? To be in Christ is, by definition, to be responsible for participating in the mission of Christ. Is this now the case?

The life of the early Christians was essentially an eschatological existence. That is, they knew themselves to be living "between the times." Already, by God's grace, they had become people of God's future, privileged to be living the life of the future in the present age. The Gospel of John emphasizes that new existence in Christ, by the Spirit, is to be a present reality. Life under the reign of God is to be now, not merely a hope whose realization is reserved for the future. The believer already has made the transition out of death into life (John 5:24). Given this marvelous reality, are we now free enough of fears and ties to this world that we can be active representatives of the world to come? Maturing and enduring in Christian faith requires such freedom and responsibility. Henry Austin is credited with saying that "genius, that power which dazzles mortal eyes, is oft but perseverance in disguise." Who finally wins the prize when the race is the Christian spiritual life? The one who exercises self-control and is fixed on the wreath of victory which is imperishable (1 Cor. 9:24–27).

No Turning Back

Paradoxically, for Christians the spiritual quest is the pursuit of endurance while one remains open to the Spirit's gifting of that which makes endurance possible and worth all effort (1 Tim. 6:11). Paul showed the way with his endurance of many things (2 Tim. 3:10–11). Comfort and wisdom now can be found in realizing that we who pursue this Christian way are not alone. In fact, we are surrounded by a great cloud of witnesses who have walked this way before and now encourage us to "lay aside every weight and the sin that clings so closely, and let us run with perseverance the race that is set before us, looking to Jesus the pioneer and perfecter of our faith" (Heb. 12:1–2). The present worldly existence is not the Christian's real home, only the place of sojourning and serving. As an old song puts it, believers are "traveling through Emmanuel's ground to fairer worlds on high."

On this journey there is to be no turning back. We are called to fight the good fight of faith while wearing gentleness and exhibiting endurance (1 Tim. 6:11). Paul exhorts believers to "run in such a way that you may win [the heavenly prize]" (1 Cor. 9:24). Running properly ensures that "if we have died with him, we will also live with him; if we endure, we will also reign with him" (2 Tim. 2:11–12). Assurance comes from the Book of Revelation: "Because you have kept my word of patient endurance, I will keep you from the hour of trial that is coming on the whole world to test the inhabitants of the earth. I am coming soon; hold fast to what you have, so that no one may seize your crown" (3:10–11).

The phrase "eternal security" is often used in sermons and books to claim that ultimate and positive completing of the faith journey is assured once we start on the Christian way. But how do we actually gain a security that never ends? By never turning back. We are secure only in Christ; we remain in Christ only through abiding faith and faithfulness. Christians choose to live under the gracious reign of God. They dwell under God's sovereignty and reap the reward of endurance and fellowship with God both here and hereafter. The reward is for those who endure; divine resources make such endurance possible. Endurance is not inevitable, only wonderfully possible. Because Christ lives, so can we. One meaning of the word *hypomenō* is to "dwell under." How do believers survive satanic assaults? As the old song affirms:

Under His wings I am safely abiding;
Though the night deepens and tempests are wild,
Still I can trust Him; I know He will keep me;
He has redeemed me, and I am His child.[15]

The fact that Jesus told his disciples it was not for them to know the times and seasons (Acts 1:7) should be sufficient word to the wise not to make fools of themselves by constant speculation about the ways, places, and even dates of God's future actions. It is embarrassing to the Christian gospel when failed speculations are observed by the world and judged as failures of the faith itself. Biblically speaking, the primary purpose of a future faith vision is to provide believers with the wisdom and resolve needed for pursuing the life of discipleship in the present time.[16] The biblical prophet was divinely enabled to understand the then-current flow of historical events in terms of God's concerns, purposes, and involvements. The primary prophetic question should be: "What sort of persons ought you to be in leading lives of holiness and godliness?" (2 Pet. 3:11). The

God, the Final Victor

It matters not who we are or where we are, a holy God is a God in whom there is nothing to adulterate or diminish or alter the transcendent qualities which our weakness or our sinfulness need. *He is always God.* Nothing is ever missing from him if he is to be what all mankind must have to make and keep it truly human on the way to its fulfillment in him. Sometimes the best of us have days when our dearest friend must say, "you are not yourself today." That fact gives them a hard time and sends them away deprived of what they should have from us. BUT GOD IS ALWAYS GOD.

Albert Edward Day, *The Captivating Presence*

Did we in our own strength confide,
Our striving would be losing,
Were not the right Man on our side,
The Man of God's own choosing.
Dost ask who that may be?
Christ Jesus, it is He;
Lord Sabaoth His name,
From age to age the same,
And He must win the battle.

Martin Luther, "A Mighty Fortress Is Our God"

assurance that should bolster the courageous leading of such lives is this great affirmation of Jude 24:

> Now to him who is able to keep you from falling, and to make you stand without blemish in the presence of his glory with rejoicing, to the only God our Savior, through Jesus Christ our Lord, be glory, majesty, power, and authority, before all time and now and forever. Amen.

The Christian tradition is rooted deeply in its Hebrew heritage. This heritage is stamped with the seal of "not yet" and is inscribed with the preposition "until." Jewish believers were convinced that the sovereignty of God will become fully realized and visible. This makes possible the "until" of faith (Dan. 4:23–32; 7:1–22). The God of Israel is the coming God. The future, therefore, is the center of gravity of Israel's faith. Hope was the mainspring of her existence, the source of her vitality and optimism, pointing to the time of the resolution of all the ambiguities and inequities of the past and present (Isa. 40:9–10). In fact, the very structure of the Hebrew canon appears intended to keep hope alive. The last word always was "hold on, God is not done with us yet." Torah ends with Deuteronomy 34 where Moses dies and is buried in a location known only to God. He only saw the promised land from afar; nonetheless, the people would eventually enter in. The Prophets end with Malachi 4 and the promise of the return of Elijah who will turn the hearts of parents to their children and of the children to their parents. The Writings end with the story of King Jehoiachin. After the disaster of the exile, life for the people of God still remains possible. The future is open, and the life of Israel awaits what God still has in store.

In the annual cycle of the Christian year, the season of Advent is the recurring reminder of God's persistent and inevitable coming. It happened once and will happen again!

The Church Year: Advent—Again and Always

The Advent season begins the Christian year and then, a year later, begins it again. It is the season of joyful waiting for the coming of the Lord—first in the flesh of Jesus, then in the Word and Spirit of Jesus, and ultimately in the final coming of Jesus in full victory when every knee will bow. The season that anticipates God's fresh beginnings in the first-century coming of Jesus Christ also celebrates the promise that this same Jesus finally will return to consummate human history under his gracious rule. It prays for fulfillment: "Return to us, O God Almighty! Look down from heaven and see! Watch over this vine, the root your right hand has planted, the son you have raised up for yourself" (Ps. 80:14–15 NIV).

Repeating the cycle of the Christian year is necessary. Note the endless-circle graphic in chapter 1. How easily we forget, and how dependent the faith is on active and accurate remembering! After the long summer and fall, the many Sundays of ordinary time, the doubts, disappointments, and distractions of life in the world (and sometimes even in the church), a return to Advent allows a recapturing of the anticipation and vision. It is easy to become weary in well doing, discouraged by the darkness, worn out by the world. We can lose vital touch with faith in the Easter mystery. The world's evil fosters a numbness that tempts believers to live again as though the present is all there is, and things likely will have to stay the way they are. Returning to the biblical texts and worship themes of Advent encourages a new opening of oneself to God and a patient waiting in hope.

Throughout the Hebrew Scriptures, Israel is reminded of her identity by retelling her faith journey in light of God's gracious acts on her behalf. The Passover celebration, for instance, involves the recollection of Israel's mirac-

Holiness and Hope

In the early part of 1790 [John] Wesley wrote "The Wedding Garment." . . . In this sermon he pointed out once again that orthodoxy is a small part of religion and must not be mistaken for the very substance of the Christian faith, which is not a string of ideas or speculation of any sort, but holy love reigning in the heart. . . . Wesley's real comfort and his sure source of strength was not in anything he had done, no matter how noble or sacrificial. His comfort remained in what God had graciously done for him in Jesus Christ.

Kenneth J. Collins, *A Real Christian: The Life of John Wesley*

ulous exodus from Egypt. The Psalms often recall God's great acts of deliverance and providence that brought Israel into being and sustained her through all her hardships, suffering, and infidelities. The New Testament extends this process of memory by telling the stories of Jesus, the church's early expansion, the anticipation of ultimate deliverance and entrance into the new Jerusalem. The Bible affirms that believers are part of these wonderful stories and teaches that authentic Christian spirituality depends on recognizing and accepting one's personal place in the ongoing reality of this long trail of divine action.

Recalling the right story strengthens the believer's sense of identity and staying power. Memory bolsters the ability to survive, but only when remembering what God has done inspires actual willingness to participate in what God now is doing. Christianity is not simply a set of ideas and old memories—even though it has the best ideas and the most amazing memories available to humans. Christianity at its fullest and best is a way of life, a new relationship with God brought about in Christ through the Holy Spirit. To become a Christian necessarily includes both knowing the Christian story and entering into that story's ongoing impact as the definition of one's own existence. God came in Jesus Christ; God still comes in Jesus Christ; one day God in Christ will come to consummate all things. What a story! To become part of this story brings meaning, joy, and sustaining strength.

The Social Justice Tradition

The last of the six Christian spiritual traditions takes believers into the streets of life with the vision of a new world and the will to help bring it about. The Covenant Code (Exodus 21–23) features the whole of life being brought under the rule of God. Rich or poor, small or great, all Israelites were declared equal before God. The Hebrew tradition insists on compassion for the oppressed, disinherited, weak, poor, and afflicted. The reason was the Hebrew memory of God's goodness to them: "You shall not oppress a resident alien; . . . for you were aliens in the land of Egypt" (Exod. 23:9). To be spiritual in part is to be one with God's people as they join in God's mission to reveal the divine heart in holiness and righteousness.

Jesus was a committed Jew who took seriously the prophet's call to "let justice roll down like waters, and righteousness like an ever-flowing stream" (Amos 5:24). The will of God, and thus the assigned mission of God's people, is to work for shalom to prevail in all human relationships and social structures. Jesus put it clearly. On two great commandments hang all the law and prophets. Loving God with all of oneself and loving one's neighbor likewise are the two coordinate movements of the heart filled with God's love (Matt. 22:37–40). Leaving out the true loving of one's neighbor is to violate fundamentally the commandments in general.

We who believe in Jesus are not called to receive the Spirit of Jesus for ourselves alone. The Holy Spirit of God is the Spirit of mission. The will of God, as we know it from the life, death, and resurrection of Jesus, is the redemption of the world. A "spiritual retreat," then, is an oxymoron in the sense that truly being in God's Spirit is to be thrust into the world on mission as opposed to pulling away from the world in fear, cynicism, or disgust. In Acts 2, reception of the Spirit means proclaiming boldly the gospel of Jesus to all people, despite the differences of culture and language. When Paul speaks in 1 Corinthians of the gifts of the Spirit, he does so by relating these gifts to concrete service to neighbors. They are not the toys of self-service, but the tools that allow a faithful and fruitful presentation of the lordship of Jesus Christ.

E. Stanley Jones, beloved missionary to India, established the *ashram* (a Hindu word meaning "retreat") as a weeklong pattern of solitude and community building that was anything but an invitation to social irresponsibility or neglect of church mission. It reflected this attitude of Frank Laubach, found in his *Letters by a Modern Mystic:*

> I resolved that I would succeed better this year with my experiment of filling every minute full of the thought of God than I succeeded last year. And I added another resolve—to be as wide open toward people and their need as I am toward God. Windows open outward as well as upward. Windows open *especially* downward where people need the most![17]

To move inward in spiritual quest must not abandon but motivate and resource the outward thrust of love and justice. Parker Palmer is right:

> If we are to touch again the root reality of human unity, the inward quest is necessary, because the God who occupies the heart of our true self is the God at the heart of all other selves. And if our public action is not to lead to burn-out and despair, the inward quest is necessary once more, for it is inwardly that we renew the wellsprings of faith which sustain action. . . . We are not primarily responsible for shrewd analysis of problems, for strategic selection of means, for maximizing the chances of success. We are primarily responsible for turning to God, for attempting to know and do God's will. That will may lead us into actions which are not shrewd, strategic, or successful, as the life of Jesus suggests. But as Jesus' life demonstrates, human action which is faithful to God's will can have transforming effect.[18]

To really follow Jesus is to experience the inevitable tensions of being in a countercultural movement. The story of Jesus as told in the Gospel of Mark is a conflict-ridden tale. A key reason for the conflict is that Jesus and the good news about him were being made available to all people. He crossed normally fixed boundaries of geography and social, religious, and spiritual status. A wide range of people gathered and responded to his teaching (Mark 3:7). There were Galilean fishermen, tax collectors and sinners (2:13–17), a healed demoniac (5:1–20), a Gentile centurion (15:39), and many Galilean women (15:40–41). As the apostle Paul told the Galatians, the social results of faith in Jesus should be substantial, so much so that in the community of faith there no longer is to be any discriminatory distinction between men and women, Jew and non-Jew, slave and free. All have inherited the same promise, can participate in the same divine life, and thus are to be one in Christ Jesus (Gal. 3:28–29). On the campus of Asbury Theological Seminary in Wilmore, Kentucky, is a life-sized bronze statue of John Wesley. His hands are raised in the act of biblical proclamation. Part of the descriptive plaque reads, "With an Oxford mind and an Aldersgate heart, Wesley engaged sophisticated scholars and marginalized masses with equal ease." That is the Social Justice tradition of Christian spirituality.

The Hebrew tradition of Jesus and of all who are his is rich in this regard. A trilogy of its great words is *mishpat, hesed,* and *shalom*. Taught as God's will for the human community are a just and equitable distribution of the means of life (*mishpat*)[19] and doing the distribution with kindness and compassion (*hesed*), realizing that what the Lord requires is "to do justice, and to love kindness, and to walk humbly with your God" (Mic. 6:8). Doing the right thing in the right spirit is to be in the service of the grand vision of restoring God's intended wholeness, peace, unity, and balance to things in general (*shalom*). Faithfulness to this spiritual trilogy of divine mission began in the earliest Christian church with a significant council in Jerusalem that decided in favor of multiculturalism within a unified faith (Acts 15).

An internal difficulty of social justice soon arose and was solved quickly by naming and assigning deacons who were "full of the Spirit and of wisdom" (Acts 6:3).

There is always need for models of Christian persons who have lived a holistic gospel in the midst of competing cultures. There is one insightful record of eight such persons, ranging from William Goodell (1792–1878) and Julia A. J. Foote (1823–1900) to Clarence Jordan (1912–1969) and Orlando E. Costas (1942–1987).[20] All these truly spiritual Christians had experienced regeneration in Christ, maintained an intimate relationship with God,[21] were shaken out of an ethnocentric parochialism, lived out of a vision of human interrelatedness, developed a healthy criticism of the prevailing culture,[22] and challenged the adequacy of the religious institutions they knew. The nineteenth-century holiness revival fostered grateful people such as these who had renewed relationships with God that spilled over into renewed relationships among people. Reports church historian Douglas Strong:

> The inclusive fellowship of the nineteenth-century Holiness folk was evident, for instance, in the ecstasy of the campmeeting, where, at least initially, gender, racial, and class barriers were dismantled at the altar. Such overturning of traditional distinctions offered participants a glimpse of God's new creation—a model of personal and social transformation. Many have interpreted the campmeeting experience as highly individualistic when, in fact, it was a thoroughly social—and often multicultural—occasion. The religion of nineteenth-century revivalism was intensely personal, but never private.[23]

The social setting of church life is to be ordered rightly for the good of all. Richard Foster concludes:

> Social justice gives relevance and bite to the language of Christian love. Too often our talk about love is sentimental and soft. It needs to be toughened by the hard realities of absentee landlords and prostitute rings and drug smugglers and industrial spies and political pettifoggers. We cannot speak with integrity of loving our neighbor until we are prepared to face the structural violence that is built into many of our policies and institutions.[24]

The picture is not pretty, but it is where Jesus went and served.

In today's world, Christian evangelism must both announce and inaugurate the coming reign of God in all human affairs. Christian believers are called to witness with their mouths and model the witness with their lives. The challenge is great. Thanks to modern communications technology, popular culture has become intrusive and pervasive. Hardly any room of any home is without direct impact. This culture has become shockingly coarse and violent. There is real danger in constant consumption of junk food and junk culture. The environment shapes the way people think and act. For good reason, Charles Colson is troubled about the negative impact of culture on Christian spiritual lives today: "Pop culture (even Christian versions of it) may erode the skills and disciplines needed for a robust spiritual life."[25]

Followers of Jesus must not deny in word or deed the divine incarnation in Christ. Rather, we who would be disciples of the master, we who would move beyond mere religion, must be new creations in Christ and do all things under the reign of Christ. We must worship and work, be loved by God, and show God's compassion to the world, always enabled by the grace and gifts of God's Spirit now at work in us. As Brennan Manning puts it, "To write a letter of our lives over the signature of Jesus is to recognize his dying and rising as they are traced in *our* actions and carved in *our* hearts. In such a context, death will not be a new experience for us, *nor will resurrection!*"[26]

The Apostles' Creed

When it comes to the future, of what are Christians assured? The Apostles' Creed is modest in the information it affirms about the future. Many currently controversial subjects are left wholly unaddressed. There never has been any consensus in the church catholic about matters such as tribulation or millennium. What has gained wide Christian consensus and is central to the faith itself is the simple statement that Jesus will "come again to judge the living and the dead." The creed then adds two final phrases that fortify the believer's abiding in this life by the presence and power of the Spirit. There is the life yet to come! Still ahead is the "resurrection of the dead" and the "life everlasting." What is coming will be the completion of what already is. The hope of a coming resurrection is grounded in the accomplished resurrection of Jesus. To be with God forever will be an extension of the eternal life to be experienced now. In the corporate judgment of the church across the centuries, these straightforward affirmations and these alone are the Christian's hope and certainty. All else is mere speculation. Christ will return. We all will be raised and judged. There is life everlasting.

Christ's resurrection in the past and ours yet to come join to constitute a hope by which believers can live and a light by which they can see adequately for the discipleship demands of the present. The phrase "resurrection of the body" in the ancient creeds (Apostles' and Nicene) expresses the central genius of Christian faith. It has to do with the mystery that, while yet unrealized, is nonetheless an "assurance of things hoped for" (Heb. 11:1) based on the Jesus-past already known. The apostolic witness points directly at Jesus. He arose again by the power of God, actually and fully, with a new and real, although different body. He is "the firstborn from the dead" (Col. 1:18). We who belong to Christ will be next (1 Cor. 15:23). "Thanks be to God, who gives us the victory through our Lord Jesus Christ" (1 Cor. 15:57). The good news is that this resurrection victory that lies ahead is already at work in those who are in Christ (Eph. 1:19–20). Looking forward in faith leads to living now by faith in the potential of resurrection existence.

Jesus Christ is the Alpha and Omega. He spoke the originating word of creation (John 1:3), and he will announce the final word of consummation. He is the heart of the faith of Christians and what the Apostles' Creed is primarily all about. Because of Jesus, we know about God the Father. Through the Spirit of Jesus, we receive God's precious gift of life both here and hereafter.

One word in the Apostles' Creed speaks boldly to the religious pluralism of our time. Jesus is God's *only* Son. The original focus of this singularity apparently was a refutation of the Gnostics, who assumed a great chasm between a good God, an evil creation, and a series of intermediary beings who filled in the gap. To the contrary, Christian faith affirms a good God and an essentially good creation (apart from its sin). Intermediaries were not and are not needed. Jesus is the direct and full reflection of the creator God. He is the one and only Son in whom "the whole fullness of deity dwells bodily" (Col. 2:9; 1 Tim. 2:5).

An emphasis on the uniqueness of Jesus Christ is as crucial as it is increasingly unpopular today. As H. Ray Dunning says well:

> But to add "additional" truth to that already revealed in Jesus Christ, or to claim other ways of salvation than that provided by His work, is to move oneself outside the boundary of essential Christian truth. . . . There can be no authentic Christian teaching that is not consistent with the revelation in Christ. He alone is the Touchstone for truth, life, and salvation.[27]

Clark Pinnock agrees, adding the caution that the work of God's Spirit should not be limited inappropriately:

> It is possible on the basis of the particularity of Christ to propose a global theology. God has not left himself without witness anywhere, though he has revealed himself definitively in one particular human life [Jesus]. Moral and spiritual worth can be found in other faiths, yet God's revelation in Christ is of surpassing value, normative in relation to general revelation and universal in significance. Jesus is the incarnation of God, but the Spirit also sustains human relationships with God broadly. On this basis, we expect the Spirit to be drawing humanity into the range of Christ's saving work everywhere.[28]

The creed's phrase "the communion of saints" suggests that true religion is found primarily but not exclusively in the church of God. Authentic faith exists wherever there is real commitment to the will of God and to a Christlike life of truth and love. The Spirit of Christ is the heart of the church, but never its prisoner. Paul clearly affirms that the faith of Abraham, for example, relied on the promises of God and is the proper pattern for Christian faith—even though it was not an explicit commitment to Jesus. The norm God uses to judge all persons is Jesus Christ (Rom. 2:13–16), but all people are not judged by whether or not they actually knew Jesus and had made an explicit commitment to him.

With the church being granted a privileged but not singular place in the plan of God's saving work, it is clear that the people of God are themselves on journey. Belief in "one holy catholic and apostolic church" does not imply current perfection of this especially graced community of faith. What then does the confession affirm? It claims confidence that whatever happens, we who believe and are obedient are Christ's church, and the gates of hell will not prevail. We are not abandoned amid earthly struggle, but enjoy the grace of perseverance through the Spirit.[29] Who will sustain the church through all of its present difficulties and also through all that may yet come beyond our own time? According to Martin Luther:

> It is not we who can sustain the church, nor was it those who came before us, nor will it be those who come after us. It was, and is, and will be the one who says, "I am with you always, even to the end of time." As it says in Hebrews 13: "Jesus Christ, the same *yesterday, today,* and *forever.*" And in Revelation 1: "Who *was,* and *is,* and *is to come.*" Truly, he is that one, and no one else is, or ever can be.[30]

Being spiritually mature brings wisdom, but not all information; it enables right perspective without all of the details. Maturity learns to focus on Jesus and trust the Spirit, resting in the relationship rather than being anxious over what is not yet unavailable.

What do Christians know by faith about the future? The great ecumenical creeds affirm the following and only the following—all else is speculation. Jesus will come again. There will be a resurrection of the dead and a final judgment. There will be everlasting life with God for those who chose to reflect the life of the Spirit. The reign of God will have no end. Period. The hymn writer Daniel W. Whittle, having composed four stanzas that begin with "I know not," comes to the chorus with a confession of the central wisdom that he does know. He knows Jesus Christ, the wisdom of God made manifest to us. So he concludes with hope and joy:

> *But "I know whom I have believed,*
> *And am persuaded that He is able*
> *To keep that which I've committed*
> *Unto Him against that day."*[31]

Walk with the Spirit

The image of "passing through the land" comes to us from the earliest episodes of Israel's history (Gen. 12:1–9). A call is received from God to leave the known and journey in faith for the sake of the future. True believers become "resident aliens,"[32] spiritual sojourners in this present world. The faithful find their freedom and destiny in their willingness to move on as God directs. There is a crucial relationship between mobility and formation, being willing to journey with the great Shepherd and becoming spiritually formed in the process. God has promised to hallow our comings and goings in the best way possible: by joining us on the road.[33] When traveling on the road of life with Jesus, we find ourselves profoundly identified with the one who has nowhere to rest his head except on the heart of God. Why could Jesus manage to survive even though he always was on the edge? Because

> He ascends the cross, the place where two edges stand harshly angled to each other—the hardened immensity of human brokenness and the even more immense mystery of God's love. Jesus can live on the edge because he lives from a center radiant with God's love for him and for all creation. There his treasure lies, there his heart abides, from there the boundaries of his heart expand to transform every edge into a potential center of God's untamed grace.[34]

There is great comfort in the Lord's promise to preserve the church through time and to give the church the Spirit of truth who will guide it in all its struggles. And who is this Spirit?

> I invite us to view Spirit as the bond of love in the triune relationality, as the ecstasy of sheer life overflowing into a significant creation, as the power of creation and new creation, as the power of incarnation and atonement, as the power of new community and union with God, and as the power drawing the whole world into the truth of Jesus.[35]

Here is the power of assurance for tomorrow! Walking humbly with the Spirit is to be ever restless to know better the living God and to be ever more sensitive hearers of the Word of God. It is to seek the image of Christ as the dominant reality of one's own life. Being shaped into this image is the key to the future.

A wonderful example is E. Stanley Jones (1884–1973), who titled his 1968 autobiography *A Song of Ascents*. Like the psalms of ascent sung by ancient Hebrew pilgrims as they journeyed upward toward Jerusalem (Psalms 120–34), Jones narrates his lifelong spiritual pilgrimage. Writing at age eighty-

Prayer for Life's Restoration

It is hard to trust when we have been hurt. It is hard to hope again when we have known tragedy. It is hard to stop flinching, to stop responding to past pains. It is hard to face the present with an open heart. Help me, God. Restore me. Revive in me all the optimism that I once had. Remind me of the person I used to be. Help me to return to life, to openness, and to You, my God. Amen.

Naomi Levy, *To Begin Again*

three, he still understood himself to be in the midst of a continual process of being formed more fully into the likeness of Jesus Christ. When asked on which side of the twentieth-century theological divide he belonged, he responded that he was "not a fundamentalist or a modernist, only a Christian-in-the-making."[36] As a world evangelist,[37] he actively promoted a "first-hand contagious experience of the living Christ" that carried him "away from a self-preoccupied to a Christ-preoccupied life."[38] Being spiritual in the Christian sense comes down to living by the proper preoccupation, enlarging the area of one's conversion, taking in fresh territory every day.

Claiming fresh territory by faith is often difficult. Naomi Levy tells the moving story of Louis, one of only nine people to survive Auschwitz out of four hundred and fifteen people who were forcibly sent there from his village. On the fiftieth anniversary of his liberation, he helped erect a monument commemorating the deliverance. At the dedication ceremony, he read these words from the Book of Psalms: "The cords of death encompassed me, the grave held me in its grip. . . . Be at ease once again, my soul, for the Lord has dealt kindly with you. . . . I shall walk before the Lord in the land of the living." Levy concludes this from the experience of Louis:

> He taught me what it means to choose life even though you are haunted by death, to choose joy even though life is full of pain, to choose the future even though you are pursued by the past. . . . Our hope that the future can and will be different from the past, our faith that we have the capacity to remake our very selves, will allow us to move forward without cynicism and without bitterness.[39]

Choose life! Even in death, believers in Jesus are assured of life. Resurrection power does not originate with us, but it is ready to work in us by God's grace.

The metaphor of earnest money suggests a precious truth about the importance of what little has been gained now (primarily as a gift of God) and what finally will be realized (wholly God's gift). Earnest money is a partial payment that binds an agreement and obliges both the buyer and seller to complete the transaction. The gift of the Holy Spirit to the Christian believer is the first installment, as it were, of the infinite treasure that God plans to bestow when Christ returns to complete our salvation. So long as we abide in God, and God abides in us, we have the guarantee as well as the foretaste of heaven. "And do not grieve the Holy Spirit of God," Paul admonishes, "with which you were marked with a seal for the day of redemption" (Eph. 4:30). By constantly abiding, we turn away from wickedness, the Spirit's seal is ours, and we have the assurance of the fullness still to come.

We who truly believe do not know many of the whats, whens, or hows related to the final resolution of questions and evils of this world, but by faith we do know the *who.* That which finally will be is shaped by and in the control of the one who already has come and is known. Verse 1 of the hymn "I Know" by Charles Naylor and Andrew Byers testifies (emphasis added):

I know on Whom *my faith is fixed,*
I know in Whom *I trust;*
I know that Christ abides in me,
And all His ways are just.

The best faith-abiding is the posture of Christ-celebrating. Be sure of who, and the whats, whens, and hows will take care of themselves.

Both the Apostles' and Nicene Creeds end with a simple "Amen." In gratitude and hope, the whole assembly of believers is to express a "Yes!" and a "So be it!" to the God revealed to us as Father, Son, and Holy Spirit. We who believe "have been changed by this God who is the source of loving grace, who in Jesus is the initiative of loving grace, and who in the Spirit is the presence of loving grace."[40] Thus, we sing this gentle prayer to the Spirit of Christ as we endure the rigors of the journey of faith in this yet-troubled but soon-ending world.

Abide with me: fast falls the eventide;
The darkness deepens; Lord, with me abide:
When other helpers fail, and comforts flee,
Help of the helpless, O abide with me![41]

The abiding of God's Spirit is the heart and hope of Christian spirituality. Committed believers gratefully sing (with the personal emphasis added):

> *Blessed* assurance, *Jesus is* mine!
> *Oh what a* foretaste *of glory divine!*
> *Heir of salvation, purchase of God,*
> *Born of His Spirit, washed in His blood.*
>
> *This is* my *story,*
> *this is* my *song,*
> *Praising* my *Savior*
> *all the day long.*[42]

Therefore, since "we know that in all things God works for the good of those who love him, who have been called according to his purpose" (Rom. 8:28 NIV), "let us draw near to God with a sincere heart in full assurance of faith" (Heb. 10:22 NIV). We always are to remember this: "Those who trust in the LORD are like Mount Zion, which cannot be shaken but endures forever. As the mountains surround Jerusalem, so the LORD surrounds his people both now and forevermore" (Ps. 125:1–2 NIV).

In 1946 Harry Emerson Fosdick retired from the active ministry of the Riverside Church in New York City to be a Christian ambassador at large. He reported in his 1956 autobiography, *The Living of These Days,* that "expectancy about tomorrow looms larger than nostalgia about yesterday." Although elderly, he closed his personal memoirs with this: "Though I am an old man, I share at least a little the hopeful spirit of the young, facing life, as Lowell sang, with 'the rays of morn on their white Shields of Expectation.'"[43]

David Elton Trueblood concluded his 1974 autobiography, *While It Is Day,* this way:

> The writing of my memoirs at this particular time does not mean that I think my work is completed. The present time is simply a good one in which to write about the journey up to this point, attempting to do so while it is day. Both the price and the glory of our finitude are indicated by the fact that we do not arrive; we are always on the way.[44]

The final verse of the Bible clarifies why full assurance is not mere illusion and can withstand all obstacles to the Christian spiritual journey: "The grace of the Lord Jesus be with God's people. Amen!" (Rev. 22:21 NIV). Praise the Lord! Take courage! Life's sorrows can be endured. The church's mission can be accomplished. There is hope—at least in God. Ultimate divine meaning one day will overcome temporary human madness. No sickness or sorrow need mar the happiness that lies ahead. Christian faith knows that some day, with time behind us, eternity before us, and the redeemed of all ages around us, there will be heaven, our eternal home. Therefore, believers are to stand firm, giving themselves fully to the current work of the Lord, always aware that their work is not in vain (1 Cor. 15:58). Since the church acts under the Lord's mandate (Matt 28:19–20), the gates of hell cannot prevail against it (Matt. 16:18). The Word of God was before all time and will be when time is no more. Those who are faithful in the meantime, those who now hope and serve the God of hope, one day will find themselves home with God forever. Hallelujah!

Questions to Pursue

1. Does the world today look to you as ominous as the unknown future? Do you find the rapid technological changes both exhilarating and frightening?
2. What is the New Testament view of the relation between what will be eventually and what we Christians should be doing in the meantime?
3. Think about the subject of *hypomenō* ("spiritual staying power"). How does one gain eternal security?
4. How many Christian "Advents" are there? What value is there in repeating the cycle of the Christian year in the pattern of Christian worship?
5. What is the relationship between an ashram and the Christian call to social justice initiatives in the violent streets of today's world? Can one be on spiritual retreat and still be involved in relevant Christian mission?
6. According to the Apostles' Creed, what do Christians believe about the future?

8

Truly Growing: Paths to Sanctification

> Now, discipline always seems painful rather than pleasant at the time, but later it yields the peaceful fruit of righteousness to those who have been trained by it.
>
> Hebrews 12:11

> The noblest work of Christ is shaping Christian character. It is his desire to confirm us in his pattern and spirit of life. . . . The disciplines that we assume can bless our will and give it moral constancy to remain habitually directed to what we see in Christ. This is as it must be, thus linking our *active* consent with his inviting call to become more than we are.[1]

Christian spirituality rests on these foundations: God is, comes, reaches, graces, adopts, illumines, gifts, guides, and assures. Such a constellation of divine realities constitutes the vital dimensions of the Spirit's ministry and the Christian's spiritual life. The goals are transformation and mission. One of the great challenges of Christian spirituality is finding ways to help people make vital connections between faith and everyday life. Christianity must be made relevant by believers in today's schools, workplaces, and recreational centers, or it will cease to have much meaning and become an esoteric activity limited to one hour per week of mere religion behind church walls. Disciples of Jesus must have a theology that redeems the routines in ways that integrate what is believed with what is thought, felt, and done all week long.

Proven Paths to Sanctification

Before impacting our surroundings on behalf of Christ, it is crucial that the renewing potential of God's grace impacts our own lives. Believers are to be growing up into Christ, maturing in faith, and being gifted for spiritual service. This process of being set apart for God's service is called "sanctification." Being sanctified is not a doctrine to be reduced to a denominational slogan or hardened into a spiritual formula, and it must not be ignored. Robert Barron is right in saying that Christianity is, above all, "a way of *seeing* . . . [and] holiness is seeing with the eyes of Christ."[2] Such Christ vision comes only by divine grace coupled with an intentional pattern of nurturing the capacity for spiritual vision. The apostle Paul speaks of the necessity of the believer's spiritual training and active pursuit of righteousness (1 Tim. 4:7–10; 6:11–16).

We must be properly "set apart" before we can properly "set out" on Christian mission. There are some proven paths to sanctification. All that has gone before in this book is preparation for finding and walking these holiness paths. If Christians can come to know what it means to "pray without ceasing" (1 Thess. 5:17), "persevere in prayer" (Rom. 12:12), "pray in the Spirit at all times in every prayer and supplication" (Eph. 6:18), "continue steadfastly in prayer" (Col. 4:2 RSV), and "always to pray, and not to faint" (Luke 18:1 KJV), then life really will be redeemed for believers, and the faith will be attractive to many others. Unceasing prayer will help to "maintain spiritual poise," but balanced spiritual maturity can come into being only by cultivating the disciplines and practices that lead to "spiritual composure."[3] Gaining spiritual maturity can be as difficult as it is essential.

The subtitle of this book, *Moving beyond Mere Religion*, calls for a conscious move from theory to practice, from theological foundations to the actual life changes for which they call, from the legality of being justified before God to the sanctification that sets apart for God and pursues altered habits, values, and whole-life orientations. The desired move is from the routinely institutional to the intensely spiritual. But first, a major caution is in order.

The chapters of this book have sought to make and illustrate one central point. Questing after the fullness of Christian spirituality is necessarily dependent on Christian theology and church tradition. Apart from its Hebrew heritage, biblical base, and the beliefs and lives of Christian spiritual leaders across the centuries (see the list of select spiritual leaders in the back of the book), Christian spirituality easily becomes shallow, sentimental, faddish, foundationless, often feeble, and even foolish. A constant danger is thinking of "being spiritual" as having special feelings and practicing certain techniques thought likely to generate these feelings. By sharp

Plan for Spiritual Growth

Plan for spiritual growth in Christ. That people "accept Christ as their personal Savior" is *not* a sufficient goal for church life. . . . The goal is that persons mature in Christ. . . . The pastoral question of early Methodist preachers—"How is it with your soul?"—is the most important question we as the church can learn to ask each other in the twenty-first century. . . . The way we go about being the church should be determined by our agenda for enhancing people's spiritual health.

Gilbert W. Stafford, *Church of God: At the Crossroads*

contrast, we have affirmed that the practice of the Christian faith, while critical indeed, should be an outgrowth of the substance of the faith—thus, for instance, the frequent reference to the Apostles' Creed in chapters 2 through 7. Once spirituality is rightly grounded, however, it will only mature when the believer is intentional about inward growth and outward involvement in the real-life implications of the faith.

The Book of Hebrews speaks of a discipline by which believers can be spiritually trained and that results in the "peaceful fruit of righteousness" (Heb. 12:11). As Gilbert W. Stafford affirms in the above quotation, Christ wishes to shape Christian character in all disciples—a going on to sanctification. This shaping requires the habit of the active consent of the believer along the journey to being confirmed in Christ's pattern and spirit of life.

Does this imply salvation by works? Paul asked the Galatians if they had received the Spirit by works (Gal. 3:2). The implied answer was an obvious no. God is the gracious initiator and will faithfully continue the work of grace now begun (Phil. 1:6). All is by grace. Even so, Paul told believers to "work out your own salvation with fear and trembling" (Phil. 2:12). Believers are to be active cooperators in the process of spiritual formation. Cooperation is not the Galatian error of beginning in the Spirit and ending up with mostly human effort (3:3). A cycle of divine grace and human responsiveness is the ideal rhythm of growing into Christ.

What is the goal of such "working out"? It is to move beyond mere religion to vital Christian spirituality. It is being conformed to the image of Jesus Christ (2 Cor. 3:17–18). Note the testimony of Dwight L. Grubbs, who was liberated from the religious pressure to achieve and became more aware of the reality of the journey and the freedom of God's grace:

Prayer from the Tower

Lord, let's watch things, you and I,
from the grandstand of this steeple,
among the bells and pigeons of this tower.
We can see it all from here: the people,
houses, traffic among the cluttered streets
and down the cool boulevards.
Notice how no one looks up? They surely must know
that we are here, watching, waiting for them to need us
and return to the altar that we have kept polished and
dressed for the season of repentance.
Shall we continue to wait at this distance?
I could call down to them and announce a time for prayers.
I might even scatter messages to the street for them to
gather up like new money to redeem these sordid days.
I really should go down among them and bear the cup of
cold water and perhaps the bread. But the streets are
battle lines and here I am armed only with the paper word of the Lord.
Yet, it's marvelous how this tower gives me a kind of courage.
Thank you, Lord.
Lord?
LORD?!
. . . Amen.

Warren Lane Molton, *Bruised Reeds*[4]

> For me, it was a delightful awakening when I slowly became aware that my walk with the Lord need not be an uptight, screwed down, perfectionistic, human effort to *do right*. Thankfully, I learned about grace! Really, I think I'm a better person now, a healthier, more effective minister, and I enjoy life more. I am learning to accept the process. I am learning to accept myself as human and fallible. I daily rely on grace, and I deeply believe God loves me, "just as I am." In fact, I may not be as "religious" as I once was, but I believe I'm more spiritual.[5]

By grace, believers can and must mature in Christlikeness. One characteristic of Jesus was his practical love for others. He spoke in common parables and was a man of the streets. The troubling prayer of Warren Lane Molton, "Prayer from the Tower," questions any tendency of Christians to hide in theoretical towers of ideals and abstractions, waiting for the lost people of the world to rise to the theological occasion.

What and how are closely related but quite different questions. It is one thing to ask what Christian spirituality is, has been, and should be; it is another thing to determine effective ways of achieving what should and can be in the spiritual life. The first disciples asked Jesus how they should pray. He gave them a model prayer, a proper pattern of spiritual questing and maturing (Matt. 6:9–13). Disciples are still asking a range of such questions. The practical need persists. E. Glenn Hinson writes extensively about the proven paths of spiritual preparation for Christian leadership.[6] John Westerhoff learned that "the greatest concern and interest of laity and clergy is spirituality" because "burnout," "drain out," and "rust out" are widely experienced by church teachers and preachers who have neglected their spiritual lives.[7] How does one reverse all this dying in the midst of living the faith? Returning to the biblical revelation itself is an excellent place to begin. There we find numerous models for pursuing intentional spiritual growth.

Biblical Models of Spiritual Growth

God knows how we fragile humans are made (Ps. 103:13–14). Humans are alike and yet different. We have a wide range of learning styles, preferences, personalities, and divine gifts (1 Cor. 12:4–11). As the Myers-Briggs Temperament Indicator suggests, people differ in how they focus, in how they gather and organize information, and in their attitudes toward life. So it is natural to assume that the means of grace and the disciplines designed to stimulate spiritual growth will vary and should be adapted to individuals. Means to spiritual growth should not be stereotyped. We face the challenge of knowing ourselves well enough to approach our relationships wisely with God, the church, the world, and our own distinctive growth needs.[8]

Look again at chapters 2 through 7 of this book. Highlighted in each is a great New Testament word that illumines a key dimension of the Christian life and a great spiritual tradition of Christian church history that corresponds to one of the key aspects of the life and teachings of Jesus. These are not mere records of ancient language and dusty traditions. They are essential elements of what is necessary for Christian faith to be authentic, alive, and relevant today. They are places to begin to become a Christian as Jesus intends. Reading the Bible is basic and is assisted greatly by following the biblical texts that have been organized around the Christian year and then illumined by careful commentary. Note especially the excellent series of commentaries based on the texts of the New Revised Standard Version of the Bible prepared by Walter Brueggemann and others.[9]

If you wish to pursue the potential riches of the five spiritual movements in the history of the church in ways designed to nurture personal growth in small-group settings, refer to James Bryan Smith's *Spiritual Formation Workbook.* He presents the movements under these titles: "Discovering a Life of Intimacy with God" (Contemplative tradition); "Discovering a Life of Purity and Virtue" (Holiness tradition); "Discovering a Life of Empowerment through the Spirit" (Charismatic tradition); "Discovering a Life of Justice and Compassion" (Social Justice tradition); and "Discovering a Life Founded upon the Word" (Evangelical tradition). Beyond these traditions and emphases, we find that the Bible is rich with additional possibilities for knowing and growing in the faith. There are many helpful ways to proceed. Five that are especially biblical are (1) going to the altar with Isaiah, (2) singing with the psalmist, (3) praying the way Jesus said to pray, (4) fasting for reasons Jesus makes clear, and (5) sitting at the table with Jesus and becoming Christlike in the process.

1. To the Altar with Isaiah

Regarding the first of these biblical models, Stephen Seamands focuses on the key passage of Isaiah 6:1–8 "as a window through which we can catch a vision of the biblical understanding of holiness."[10] His book *Holiness of Heart and Life* opens the dimensions of Isaiah's spiritual experience in the temple with the chapters: "If My People Will Humble Themselves," "A Vision of a Holy God," "Opening Ourselves to God's Presence," "A People of Power," "Called to Purity," "Abounding in Love," "Experiencing God's Gracious Touch," and "Here Am I—Send Me!" This sequence of biblical emphases traces a spiritual path full of potential for any believer seeking a fuller life in Jesus Christ. Study this passage, and then walk this high road yourself. Much insight and spiritual growth is available to the one humbly kneeling in amazement and repentance before a holy God.

2. Singing with the Psalmist

Second, a Christian is encouraged to develop the discipline of singing with the psalmist. The Book of Psalms is a great spiritual treasure waiting to be explored. Walter Brueggemann has shown how a believer's spiritual journey goes through three stages and how three clusters of the psalms reflect the feelings, perceptions, agonies, and joys in each of these stages.[11] Wherever one is and whatever one is facing on the spiritual journey, there are psalms that show the way, pray your deepest longing, vent your strongest feelings, and shout your highest praise. Here is an important place to dwell.

The body of Isaac Watts (1674–1748) lies in the old cemetery opposite John Wesley's City Road Chapel in London, England, along with the remains of Susanna Wesley, William Blake, and John Bunyan. In 1719 Watts published *Psalms of David Imitated in the Language of the New Testament* which included his hymn "From All That Dwells below the Skies" (a paraphrase of Psalm 117). He also adapted Psalm 98 to compose the beloved "Joy to the World!" Following this lead, most major hymnals today include two or three dozen hymns based on the psalms. This is a great spiritual resource not to be neglected in public worship or private prayer. One body of Christians, the Reformed Presbyterian Church of North America, sings only from a psalter in worship services. This guarantees worship that is spiritually rich and truly biblical. I recall with gratitude many formal occasions during my student years at Geneva College when we began with this from Psalm 100: "All people that on earth do dwell, Sing to the Lord with cheerful voice; Him serve with fear; His praise forth tell; Come ye before Him and rejoice."

3. Praying the Jesus Way

Third, Steve Harper addresses the issue of proper praying with his book *Praying through the Lord's Prayer*.[12] He says that the Lord's Prayer given by Jesus to his disciples is more than an ancient set of words to recite in worship services. It really is a plan for Christian praying, a means to gaining Christian perspective on the issues of life, a primary path to spiritual formation and maturity. Praying should move through the following eight stages:

1. *Our Father*. Acknowledge the reality and presence of God, the wonderfully available divine parent who loves, comes, hears, desires relationship, and brings warmth and healing. The sovereign God is somehow ours. Amazing! To begin true prayer is to be newly amazed at being able to do such a thing.
2. *Who art in heaven*. Recognize that God is in the right place doing the right things. God is consistent, dependable, indeed is in heaven, neither removed from your circumstances nor trapped in them as you may feel you are. The holy one remains on high, high enough to have all human needs in right perspective and under control.
3. *Hallowed be thy name*. Celebrate and praise the great Father who is in heaven. God is the "I AM" of all life! We humans are fallen, but God stands in hallowed holiness. This God is with you, hearing you, lov-

ing you, gracing you. Rejoice, give thanks and praise, and be truly grateful. Show reverence where reverence is due.

4. *Thy kingdom come and thy will be done.* Seek God's perspective on the things of great concern to you. Life is not random chaos. There is a plan, God's will, that calls for your awareness and grateful obedience. Listen for what God wants, not what you want. The reign of Jesus Christ is the road to spiritual health and hope. Walk the kingdom road. Do the will of God, and the reign of God will surely come.
5. *Give us our daily bread.* Offer to God all your pressing concerns, asking for adequate provision in accord with the divine will and because of the divine love. Life is a table, and we wait at its foot as dependent children. The "us" means that the body of believers is to be both a praying and a sharing community. The bread is for the family. God often gives bread through the grateful generosity of blessed believers. When you ask for things, think also about the urgent needs of others.
6. *Forgive us.* Be honest and repentant, recognizing that your personal forgiveness will be in proportion to your willingness to forgive and serve others. Forgiveness is completely free—and will cost you everything.
7. *Lead us not into temptation.* Know that God is willing to deliver you from all evil. God's grace is sufficient. You will not face any testing that is beyond your divinely assisted ability to bear.
8. *For thine is the kingdom.* This final section of the prayer probably was not part of the original, but was soon added to the text by the church as its testimony, its doxology of praise. The accent is on the word *is.* The early church knew that God's reign had come upon it. The cross had proven stronger than sin. The resurrection of Jesus had proven stronger than death. So, end your prayer on the solid rock of assurance. God's power and glory are adequate for every test and for all time. Whatever the present, the future is the Lord's—and yours as you are in Christ. Amen. So be it!

This is the Christian prayer pattern. Its heart lies in this prayer of Andrew Murray, found in his book *With Christ in the School of Prayer:*

> Lord Jesus! Reveal me to the Father. Let His name, His infinite Father-love, the love with which He loved Thee, according to Your prayer, be in me. Then shall I say aright, "My Father!" Then shall I apprehend Your teaching, and the first spontaneous breathing of my heart will be: "My Father, Your Name, Your Kingdom, Your Will." Amen.[13]

Now for the challenge that has deep roots in the Hebrew heritage of Christians. The church has no higher calling than to realize its commission to be a house of prayer (1 Kings 8:22–53; Isa. 56:7). Unfortunately, Jesus found it otherwise in his day (Matt. 21:13). Churches find it easy to focus on being places for wholesome fellowship and fun, religious performances and platitudes, altruistic fund-raising and good works. But prayer? Usually prayer is limited to a formalized and small part of worship services. Most listen while a leader prays. In his *Prayer in the Hebrew Bible,* Samuel Balentine highlights the critical dimensions of the intended prayer life of the people of God, including that the church is to be "shaping the future of God." He means that the work of intercessory prayer can and should alter what God will and will not do in the world. To be silent is to be tragically negligent.[14] May churches be more houses of prayer than hangouts for play.

4. *Fasting and Praying*

At least as much is said in the Bible about fasting as about giving. The missionary activity of the church began in Antioch when Barnabas and Saul were commissioned: "Then after fasting and praying they laid their hands on them and sent them off" (Acts 13:3). Praying as Jesus instructed is to include fasting. He assumed the discipline of fasting for his disciples, but was careful to alert them both to its potential and its pitfalls (Matt. 6:16–18). There will be a rich reward if fasting is done in secret and for the right reasons, not as a pathetic public display of shallow piety—the reward of which is only passing public notice.

The point is not to look dismal and feel deprived. To the contrary, fasting as a Christian spiritual discipline can be a means of gathering spiritual resources. In the midst of the abstaining, fasting is an act of affirmation: "It is a way of waiting on God; it is an act of surrender. Fasting tends to induce within us an awareness of the spiritual dimension of life. Fasting is not a renunciation of life; it is a means by which new life is released within us. . . . Fasting allows a kind of self-death and resurrection."[15] What matters is not so much what we give up as what we gain in proportion to the emptying of self that we allow. As the Spirit gains possession of our attention and hearts, testimony is given that we really are children of God (Rom. 8:16).

For our consumer-oriented society, might it be a greater sacrifice to fast than to give? Might fasting involve more than the elimination of food? How difficult would it be for you to not look at any television or computer screen for one week in favor of much more looking into the biblical text? To what are we addicted other than to the presence, voice, and will of God? Fast. It is a way of focusing on God. It is not manipulation of God, but an intentional opening to him. It allows an inner solitude that sets aside time and space for undivided attention to God's presence, purposes, and provisions.

5. *Sitting at the Lord's Table*

Jesus said that disciples are to participate in this meal that reflects the Jewish Passover and commemorates his own death and resurrection (Luke 22:7–21). Participation is one means to spiritual growth. For instance, consider Christian holiness through this lens. There are three spiritually profound dimensions of the Lord's Supper. These form a virtual definition of what it means to be holy or truly set apart and on the path of life God intends. The supper of the Lord is:

1. *A Sanctifying Meal.* Believers are to be set apart for God's purposes. To remember in the biblical sense is to become vitally involved in the reality of what is remembered, so much so that Christ's death/resurrection story becomes the shaping power of present life. To be holy is to benefit from Christ's sacrificial life by becoming like Christ in his servant life. To sit at the table with Christ is to be set apart from preoccupation with self and shaped by a preoccupation with the cross, empty grave, and present reign of Christ (Gal. 2:20). We become our preoccupations. Believers are to live this story and thus become different from the world.
2. *A Social Meal.* There is to be no more Jew/Greek, slave/free, or male/female. To be holy in a Christian sense necessarily involves the social implications of Christlikeness. We are to "discern the body" when we eat and drink at the Lord's Table. Salvation involves more than forgiveness of past sins. It includes the righting of relationships and the forming of a new community—the body of Christ on earth. To sit at the table with Christ is to be one with all who sit at the table. The church's witness to the world should be "Behold how they love!" rather than "There are divisions" (1 Cor. 11).
3. *A Seditious Meal.* Let thy kingdom come, on earth as it is in heaven. To be in Christ and part of the Christ community is to participate in a new creation that is the radical antithesis of the values, structures, and dynamics of the world. Taking the meal of the Lord is subversive since it is joining a spiritual force working within the fallen world to undermine and renew it. To eat and drink with the Lord is to celebrate a foretaste of the reign of God still to come in its fullness. To sit at the table with Christ is to declare one's ultimate allegiance. Sir Thomas More's final words on the English scaffold were: "I die the

> king's good servant, but God's first!" First Peter 2:11 reports that Christians are "aliens and strangers in the world" (NIV).

In summary, to properly celebrate the meal of the Lord is to become: (1) committed to being a new creation in an unholy world; (2) consecrated to a life together in Christ that moves against the destructive, manipulative, dehumanizing values and structures of the world; and (3) determined by the grace of God to live out the victory of Christ's death until he comes, "seeking first the kingdom of God." Holy Christians are not self-centered, solitary, or safe; they are God-centered, community-minded, and confident of the final outcome.

Having gone to the altar with Isaiah, sung from the heart with the psalmist, learned the wisdom and power of praying as Jesus directs, including the related disciplines of fasting and sitting at the table with Jesus, a believer has an excellent beginning on the spiritual journey. Here is what Paul said to the Ephesians:

> You were taught to put away your former way of life, your old self, corrupt and deluded by its lusts, and to be renewed in the spirit of your minds, and to clothe yourselves with the new self, created according to the likeness of God in true righteousness and holiness. (Eph. 4:22–24)

How does one proceed with this big spiritual agenda of being renewed, clothed with the likeness of God? There are designated means, the potential of being filled with the fruit of the Spirit, and the privilege of receiving special gifts from God that equip for service. Renewal resources are close at hand.

Exercises, Fruit, and Gifts

Spiritual growth is not automatic. Maxie Dunnam's widely used *Workbook of Living Prayer* begins with this: "You are asked to give twenty to thirty minutes each day to *work* at making prayer a living experience."[16] Here is the crucial paradox. For the Christian, all is by grace; but divine grace typically works with active human cooperation and through divinely appointed means.

Randy Maddox points out a relative neglect of the various means of grace essential for spiritual growth and achieving full holiness of heart and life.[17] There is urgent need for motivation in holiness or the forming of Christian character ("holy tempers") through the intentional and systematic use of the divinely provided means of grace.[18] Jesus made clear that a serious disciple is to "take my yoke upon you, and learn from me"

The Goal of Spiritual Formation

In its specifically Christian sense, the word "spirituality" focuses on the "spiritual person" (*pneumatikos anthrōpos*) (1 Corinthians 2:14–15)—that is, the person who has faith in the risen Christ and is in the process of being renewed through the work of the Holy Spirit. In its Christian sense, "spirituality" is about the process of renewal and rebirth that comes about through the action of the Holy Spirit, which makes us more like Christ. It is about spiritual growth and development, and includes the development of just about every aspect of our life of Christian faith. The term also refers to the development of ways of reading and engaging with Scripture that are intended to nourish and sustain the life of faith, and especially to enable it to grow, even in adverse conditions.

Alister McGrath, *Beyond the Quiet Time*

(Matt. 11:29). Learning requires focus and effort. Holiness is necessarily related to practices that engender it. The practices generally happen in a committed community of faith, the church. They may be of many kinds, but one thing should be common to them all. Really learning Christian spirituality involves being with Jesus. "Stay awake with me," said Jesus (Matt. 26:38). "Follow me," he said often. If disciples gather in the name of Jesus, he said he will be in their midst (Matt. 18:20) to enable real worship and transformation.

Four examples should be helpful. Although the settings are different, much is the same. First, Jesus gathered a "small group" (the disciples) and patiently taught them (see the early chapters of Matthew). He urged them to be aware of and respond appropriately to the reign of God arriving in their midst with his own person and ministry. Second, in 1521 Ignatius Loyola underwent a profound spiritual crisis that led to his founding one of the great missionary movements in Christian church history, the Jesuits. His best-known writing is the *Spiritual Exercises* (1548), a work growing out of his own conversion and intended to lead others to find God as Ignatius himself had done—in the school of experience with the Christ of God. The attention of young believers had to be directed and exercised for spiritual benefit.

Third, in the eighteenth century, in the midst of institutionalized Lutheran orthodoxy, Philipp Jakob Spener discerned the urgent need for small-group life in the church. He established *collegia pietatis* (pious societies) in which pastors and laypeople could meet, study the Bible, and share their faith.

Fourth, the dramatic success of the great Wesleyan revival in eighteenth-century England was due to educational methods and structures of spiritual accountability as much or more than it was to new and dramatic doctrinal formulations. John Wesley believed that spiritual progress occurs when people participate faithfully in the right means of grace. What carried this spiritual revolution was Wesley's development of the class meeting. The idea matured in 1739 when an old armory, where royal cannon had been cast before an explosion in 1716, was bought and rebuilt by Wesley. He used it for a "spiritual explosion," the home of the Foundery Society, sometimes called the mother-church of Methodism. A "society" for Wesley was

> no other than a company of men [and women] having the form and seeking the power of godliness, united in order to pray together, to receive the word of exhortation, and to watch over one another in love, that they may help each other to work out their own salvation.[19]

The class meeting was a subdivision of the society, an intimate group of ten or twelve people who met weekly for personal supervision of their spiritual growth.

There is potential power in the focused spiritual life of a small group of searching disciples who function together within and alongside the church's life and in light of the wisdom of the larger church across the centuries. The emergence of megachurches today highlights anew the need for human-scale and intimate spiritual accountability groups. Do not try growing as a Christian all by yourself. If a supportive small group is not available, find a friend in the faith, a spiritual guide. André Gozier offers us all such a friend with his book *15 Days of Prayer with Thomas Merton* (1999).

Most contemporary Protestants have been influenced deeply by the spirituality of the sixteenth-century Reformation. Leaders like John Calvin moved the center of Christian living from the monastery to the public marketplace. Even so, there is value in spiritual retreats, as the ministry of Jesus makes clear (Luke 5:16). In the early twentieth century, E. Stanley Jones founded Christian *ashrams* (retreat centers for study and meditation) as one way of sharing Christ with higher-caste Hindus. He also utilized round-table conferences, as illustrated in his *Christ at the Round Table* (1928). Soon ashrams were convening across North America. They are weeklong, structured Christian retreats focusing on solitude and community building.

Similarly, in 1930 the beloved spiritual leader Glenn Clark founded Camps Farthest Out. Gatherings in isolated places were dedicated to discovering through play, work, and worship the wholeness of the abundant life that Christ has promised. Prayer is the foundation of these experiences on the way to physical, mental, and spiritual balance. Participants are encouraged in these camps to be "athletes of the spirit" who increasingly live in the present the coming reign of God. Clark's 1953 book *The Soul's Sincere Desire* is an articulate expression of the central role that prayer should have in every believer's life. To realize this potential, sometimes there is necessity for intense focus with fellow believers far away from life's ordinary rush and clutter. Sometimes retreat is available right in the midst of many people not of like mind. It is possible to be more than bored and gorged with too much food on a long airline flight. A little planning and focusing can turn the lengthy isolation into spiritual refreshment.

Evangelical Christians of recent generations usually have steered away from complex liturgies and monastic-like spiritual practices, preferring the disciplines of early rising, private prayer, family worship, and regular Bible reading. Many congregations convene weekly prayer meetings, host Bible-study groups, and exhort members to pray alone and with families. Apart from weekly worship, this is essentially the pattern of spiritual formation. Sometimes special-focus meetings, called "revivals," are convened, and instruction is given on how best to be world-denying in the quest to be truly Christian. But for many contemporary believers, this pattern is not enough. Alister McGrath has written *Beyond the Quiet Time* (1995) to help shape a practical evangelical spirituality. There are real limits to relying only on hearing a weekly sermon or two and trying to read the Bible and pray on your own. Discipline is necessary, group study is helpful, and linkage to the real world is required. Especially since the 1970s, John Stott in England and Carl F. H. Henry in the United States have led conservative Christians to a more open attitude toward culture in general. This has allowed politics and social concern to be viewed as part of the Christian's spiritual responsibility.

Many experiments in means for Christian spiritual formation have evolved in recent years. Included are the annual Praise Gatherings of Bill and Gloria Gaither in Indianapolis, the Promise Keepers movement for Christian men, the Academy for Spiritual Formation sponsored by the Upper Room, and the Renovaré renewal programs and publications of Richard Foster and his colleagues. Excellent anthologies of Christian spiritual readings (see bibliography) and workbooks are now in wide use in church group life. They include R. Eugene Sterner's *Keys to Spiritual Freedom* (1999), Maxie Dunnam's *Workbook of Living Prayer* (1994), and James Bryan Smith's *Spiritual Formation Workbook* (1993). Another key resource that greatly enriches the shallowness of typical devotions based on random Bible sampling is Bob and Michael Benson's *Disciplines for the Inner Life* (1989), which guides readers in daily Bible reading, praying, and sampling the wisdom of the Christian saints. Also, at least three habits or spiritual exercises have stood the test of time as biblically authentic, consistent with the perennial experiences of the saints, and above the shifting of time and place. They are (1) practicing the presence of God, (2) conforming to the will of God, and (3) being faithful to available grace. The many published guides now available assist in doing all three.

Righteousness is certainly not gained merely because a person participates in church life, but it rarely matures apart from such life. Note this from John Wesley's sermon "The Means of Grace": "By 'means of grace' I understand outward signs, words, or actions, ordained of God, and appointed for this end, to be the ordinary channels whereby he might convey to men preventing, justifying or sanctifying grace."[20] Wesley had confidence in those activities of the church that were designed to promote personal spiritual growth: the Lord's Supper, baptism, Bible reading, prayer, preaching, fasting, and confession. To the list of instituted means of grace, those thought to be established by Jesus for the life of all believers, Wesley added a list of "prudential" means like the class meeting. These were viewed as wise ways for helping to put people in touch with the dynamic power of God's grace. The real agent of change is the grace of God, but the activities or means of devotion enable this grace to become effective in actual life.[21]

When we seriously pursue the available means for spiritual growth, the result is the receiving of fruit and gifts. It is crucial to clarify what Christians are to seek and how they are to use whatever is received from the hand of God. To be holy is to have received the greatest gift from God. This is the indwelling presence of the Holy Spirit, God actually with and within the believer. We are judged holy only because of God's presence and the privilege of belonging to God in Jesus Christ through the Spirit. Sin can be avoided only because believers are being sanctified by divine presence and help. The presence of the Spirit and our obedient life in the Spirit are crucial to the maturing of individual Christians and to the health of the church. A lack of the power of Pentecost explains much of the emptiness the current church renewal and charismatic movements are seeking to fill. The emergence of the fruit of the Spirit (Gal. 5:22–23) should be a goal and is the privilege of all Christian believers, precisely because the fruit includes the expected expressions or reflections of the presence of the Spirit. The fruit are characteristics of the Spirit and thus are to be inherent in every Christian life that has moved beyond mere religion.

The gifts of the Spirit, however, are given only as the Spirit chooses, not as any person desires or has a right to expect. These divine gifts are intended primarily for service so the church may be strengthened and made more effective in its mission. Self-gratification by use of a divine gift or public exhibition of such a gift are inappropriate in church life (1 Cor. 14). Seek, yes, but seek for the indwelling of the Spirit and the spiritual fruit that flows from life in the Spirit. Remain open to divine gifts since they are the wisdom or ability that God may choose to give for the sake of the church's well-being and the salvation of the world. Spiritual gifts are tools for the tasks of ministry, not ornaments to create public amazement or badges to be worn so that superspirituality will be recognized and applauded. Remain open, but do not try to seek particular gifts or force expectation of such gifts on other believers. God will provide all that is needed, to whom and when he judges necessary. Thomas Oden summarizes well: "If the Spirit freely and sovereignly bestows *charismata* [grace gifts] of the Spirit, then it is not fitting for recipients to set their hearts upon receiving particular special gifts. Rather, they do well to receive gratefully whatever the Spirit offers (1 Cor. 12:11). We are commanded to be filled with the Holy Spirit (Eph. 5:18), not to seek to acquire particular gifts."[22]

Waiting before Working

In the sixteenth century, "radical" Christians protested against ecclesiastical deadness and a replacing of the life of the Spirit with an excessive and intolerable burden of human traditions and controls on civic and church life. There was just too much mere religion. Martin Luther rebelled against anything that suggested a works righteousness instead of salvation by grace through faith. Even so, shortly after the Protestant movement had gotten under way, the liabilities of unstructured piety were widely recognized by those very leaders bolting from Roman Catholicism. Luther himself produced *Seven Penitential Psalms with a German Translation* (1517); a *Short Form of the Ten Commandments, the Creed, and the Lord's Prayer* (1520); and his *Personal Prayer Book* (1522). Spiritual growth is not a substitute for salvation, but it is crucial and does not happen on its own.

So far as the preparation of new ministers was concerned, unfortunately a Protestant brand of scholasticism emerged that tended to feature academic concerns at the expense of spiritual formation. Then, seeking to correct the apparent weakness of the Protestant critique of the older monastic model of spiritual nurture, there arose in the seventeenth century a revitalization of Lutheran churches by renewed dependence on Bible study and the cultivation of the inner lives of believers in small cell groups (*collegia pietatis*). Philipp Jakob Spener, the father of German Pietism, was determined to again rescue churches from the deadening grip of "pharisaic orthodoxy." Such a determination was a continuance of the instruction given to the first disciples. Jesus had ordered them not to leave Jerusalem on their Christ mission until they had waited patiently "for the promise of the Father" (Acts 1:4). For the sake of authentic Christian identity and effective Christian mission, there is the importance of believers first experiencing a baptism "with the Holy Spirit" (Acts 1:5).

Cycles of spiritual deadness and then fresh renewal continue over time. The nineteenth century witnessed a major holiness revival in North America and Great Britain. With the opening of the twentieth century, there came the beginnings of a pentecostal movement that now has greatly influenced world Christianity with a fresh Spirit orientation. In January 1959, Pope John XXIII, announcing plans for the Second Vatican Council of the Roman Catholic Church, prayed that the windows of that ancient church be newly opened to God's breath. His intent was that the divine would sweep away deadness and unleash refreshing renewal in the Christian community. God has been faithful to such openness. The Catholic-Protestant divide now has been breached at numerous points, especially with the common concern for serious spiritual formation among believers. There is no magic formula for gaining spiritual maturity. However, "rediscovery of the churches' ancient stores of wisdom in the 'New Pentecost' of Pope John XXIII offers hope that we can move into the future with some assurance about spiritual formation."[23] The common Christian prayer should be, "Welcome, Holy Spirit. Come anew and bring your own life that will set us free to be all that God intends."

Jesus was clear about his disciples waiting before they were to go out working for him in the world. The work to be done would put them on the world's margins; the only effective way to accomplish the task was to be instruments shaped and directed by the Spirit of the Christ. Life in the Spirit, then, is to precede ministry through the Spirit. Paul came to know that, although faithful followers of Jesus risk being viewed as the rubbish of the world (1 Cor. 4:13), they can do all things that God intends when they are divinely strengthened (Phil. 4:11–13). The required strengthening, inspiring, and gifting is the work of the Spirit, the work for which we are to wait. To be spiritual Christians is to be doing Christ's work in the world after having waited for the doing of the Spirit's work in our own hearts.

Unfortunately, Alister McGrath is right. There is real danger that "evangelicals will be so busy doing things for God that they will crowd him out of their very activities. Our desire to do things for God can easily get in the way of God's desire to do something for us."[24] Those Protestant believers most opposed to salvation by works are as tempted in that direction as anyone else. The most orthodox believers can easily participate in mere religion. We are to be still if we are to know that God is God (Ps. 46:10). We are to wait on the Spirit before we can become agents of the Spirit.

To be Pentecost people in the world requires first having been in an upper room where the fire fell and hearts were set ablaze. In the fire of the Spirit, mere religion dissolves, authentic spirituality emerges, and the true life of God shines forth. The good news is that Jesus Christ, having died on the cross and risen from the dead, dies no more. He now sits at the right hand of the Father and has become for us the life-giving Spirit (1 Cor. 15:45). Away with mere religion. Bring on the new life available in the Spirit of Jesus!

Questions to Pursue

1. If spiritual growth is God's intention and can occur only by his grace, why and how should believers plan for it?
2. Does your own personality, dominant learning style, and particular gifting by God mean that spiritual growth for you may profit from some means and in some settings more than others?
3. Which of the biblical models of spiritual growth previewed in this chapter seems to have the most immediate potential for you personally? Will you discipline yourself to follow this path in the days ahead?
4. Are you sure you understand the crucial difference between the fruit and gifts of the Spirit? If not, look into this chapter again.
5. Have you participated in any of the spiritual growth settings mentioned in this chapter (Praise Gatherings, Promise Keepers, Camps Farthest Out, etc.)? If not, get involved with something that structures and stimulates your spiritual growth.
6. Many believers are very active. For what should one wait before it is time to work for Christ?

Glossary

Asceticism

Derived from the Greek term *askēsis* ("discipline"), asceticism refers to a wide variety of forms of self-discipline used by Christians to deepen their knowledge of themselves and their commitment to God. Jesus' teaching in the Sermon on the Mount stresses the need for self-effacement in order to acquire the things of the Spirit. He said, "If any want to become my followers, let them deny themselves and take up their cross daily and follow me. For those who want to save their life will lose it, and those who lose their life for my sake will save it" (Luke 9:23–24).

Some Christians have sought to increase their spirituality by living lives of celibacy and severe self-discipline, sometimes in remote places. Withdrawal to the wilderness has biblical precedent in Elijah, John the Baptist, and the time of testing and temptations of Jesus. Often the desert was seen as a place for the renewal and purification of the covenant community, a refuge from the state and the formalized trappings of religion. Origen interpreted the desert wanderings of Israel as a type of Christian spiritual life, characterized by separation from sin, withdrawal from the world, and growth through wrestling with temptation. In the 280s, Anthony of Egypt withdrew and became a spiritual model for many. By the fourth century, the Egyptian desert was heavily populated with Christian ascetics seeking authentic spiritual experiences. Later, monastic reform movements looked to the desert fathers as models and established spiritual communities in isolated locations. The *Sayings of the Fathers* (dating from the fifth century) records many of the teachings of these early spiritual pilgrims of the desert. A key resource is *The Life of Anthony*, a famous biography by Saint Athanasius written in 357.

Usually involved in this desert asceticism was a dualism of body and spirit. By disciplining the body, presumably one could enhance the life of the spirit. Christian ascetics of many cultures and centuries have withdrawn in one form or another to "subdue the flesh," imitate Christ, and protest the arid institutionalization and accommodation of the church to the surrounding society.

Awakenings

Often significant spiritual revivals have been referred to as "awakenings" (believers and others had "fallen asleep" spiritually and now were being renewed in large numbers). In recent centuries, given their Christian founding and tendency to move excessively toward the rational, most major awakenings have been associated with prominent college and university campuses located in France, England, and the United States. Early examples occurred at the University of Paris in seventeenth-century France and the Holy Club at Oxford, England, in the eighteenth century. In 1877 the Cambridge Inter-Collegiate Christian Union was founded and became the forerunner of the InterVarsity Christian Fellowship (D. L. Moody visited Cambridge in 1882 and fanned this revival).

In North America, the First Great Awakening was a series of revivals in the American colonies between 1725 and 1760. An especially significant evangelist was George Whitefield who came from England to travel throughout the colonies calling people to repentance and faith in Christ. He helped plant evangelical Christianity on American shores and prepare the colonies religiously for the trials of the coming revolutionary age. Princeton University, the University of Pennsylvania, Rutgers, Brown, and Dartmouth were some of the significant schools created as a result of this awakening. This awakening cut across denominational lines, and some have argued that it created a mood of tolerance that made possible the first amendment to the Constitution of the United States.

The Second Great Awakening came nearly a half-century later in another series of dramatic revivals in which preachers adopted emotional appeals for conversion to Christ and pressed for immediate decisions. Rather than the Calvinistic emphasis and the Eastern seaboard location of most of the First Awakening, this second one involved Congregationalists in New England, Presbyterians in the Old Northwest, and Methodists and Baptists on the Southwestern frontier. The dramatic Cane Ridge Revival (1801) in frontier Kentucky helped launch the Stone/Campbell (Disciples) movement, and the "Haystack Prayer Meeting" (1806) helped birth the American foreign missionary movement. This awakening touched Yale (1802), Princeton, and other great campuses. Later in the nineteenth century, the Holiness movement featured revival activity in many places, including scores of rural campgrounds, New York City with Phoebe Palmer, and Oberlin College in Ohio where revivalist Charles G. Finney was president. This Holiness movement soon spread to England and helped initiate the Keswick movement.

One prominent revival event of the twentieth century that gained national media attention began at Asbury College in 1970 and spread quickly to Anderson College (University) and elsewhere.

Charismatic Movement

Charisma and *charismatic* are terms associated with the gifting of the Holy Spirit in the lives of Christian believers. A particular precedent is the Pentecost events recorded in Acts 2. Many Christians over the centuries have assumed that gifts like healing and tongues ended after the apostolic age. However, since the early twentieth century, such gifting has become a central teaching of large numbers of Christians and has greatly influenced their theological emphases and worship patterns. These patterns often feature immediate divine presence and an experiencing of the Holy Spirit's power, including being "baptized" in the Spirit and sometimes being enabled to speak in "tongues."

Beginning in 1901 with the Bible school of Charles Parham in Topeka, Kansas, and then in 1906–9 at the Azusa Street Mission in Los Angeles, emerging from the ministry of African-American minister William J. Seymour, large "pentecostal" denominations (Assemblies of God, Church of God [Cleveland, Tenn.], etc.) emerged. Pentecostal or charismatic emphases found their way into most mainline Protestant and Roman Catholic bodies worldwide. This major development was helped by the founding in 1952 of the Full Gospel Businessmen's Fellowship International and the media in the U.S. (e.g., Pat Robertson's *700 Club* and the Christian Broadcasting Network).

Often it is thought that the charismatic movement is mostly about speaking in unknown tongues. This is hardly accurate or fair. The essence of "pentecostalism" is an emphasis on the direct and personal awareness of the indwelling presence and power of the Spirit of God. The "charismatic" believer seeks to be inspired and empowered for witness by the abundance of spiritual life as described in the Book of Acts and certain of the Epistles of the New Testament. Experiences of personal transformation and special gifting by the Spirit of God are understood to be divine doorways into the intended fullness of life that is available to the believer. This fullness often involves various "manifestations" of the Spirit, although these should always be characterized by a prevailing love of the Word of God and a concern to live by the power of the Spirit for the sake of the church's ministry.

Steven J. Land has written helpfully about pentecostal spirituality in terms of its apocalyptic vision, missionary fellowship, and trinitarian transformation. He concludes with this:

> Because the Holy Spirit brings the life of the kingdom of God into the present, passivity and cultural pessimism are minimized as people are empowered for ministry. . . . Indeed, the expectancy of the coming fullness of righteousness, peace, and joy feeds the activism. . . . Pentecostalism holds much promise for the future, if it remains open to the Spirit who indwells the people of God and moves all things toward their consummation in Jesus Christ.[1]

For Paul and his New Testament writings, the charismata are grace-gifts from God given to individual believers for the well-being and ministry effectiveness of the whole church (1 Cor. 12:7). When great emphasis is placed on these gifts, issues often arise about the proper role of experience in Christian faith, the intended nature of authority in the church, and the proper means for believers to come to know spiritual truth. Pentecostalism has brought both fresh life and considerable controversy and divisiveness to contemporary church.

Christian Calendar

There is a "theology of the calendar."[2] Christians live between time and eternity, celebrating in time the initial presence of eternity. Christians have found it helpful, even necessary, to keep track of time by routinely remembering God's work among us (see the calendar graphic in chapter 1). Spiritual timekeeping is crucial to Christian identity and living. As Stookey says, "The great festivals of the church celebrate in our present experience what has occurred or what we resolutely believe will happen. . . . We keep these occasions in order that God may work in us through them and in our world through us" (33).[3] For Christians, the new creation accomplished in Jesus Christ has produced a new organizing principle for the calendar (before Christ and after Christ). Worship is on the first day of the week and is to establish the meaning for the rest of the week.

Early in Christian church history, the believing community began to follow the pattern of its Hebrew heritage by establishing an annual cycle of remembrance celebrations that highlight the key elements of the Christian faith (a context for meaningful worship and a tool for constant instruction concerning the foundations of the faith). Easter is primary since the resurrection of Jesus was the dramatic event that interprets all else. It is followed by Pentecost, Advent, Christmas, Epiphany, Lent, Holy Week, and back to Easter. The church has devised systematic plans of Bible reading across a year that are sensitive to the Christian calendar and thus guide the reader in the whole message of Scripture in relation to the whole of time (God's past actions, present actions, and soon-coming actions). These plans are called "lectionaries."

Christian spirituality is to be nurtured by regular participation in such worship of God. Literally meaning "the people's work," *liturgy* usually refers to the written text and set forms of Christian worship services, particularly the Eucharist (Lord's Supper). Through use of such texts and worship patterns, the people of God "work" at glorifying God and being transformed by God through worship and learning. Liturgical patterns vary widely. The very formal ones are "high church." The relatively informal ones are "low church." There are, however, no nonliturgical churches. All groups of believers somehow pattern their approaches to and growth in God. Liturgy, then, is the frame within which attention to the risen Lord, now present in our midst, recasts our perspective on ourselves and others. It is the context for spiritual formation. Often including Scripture and prayer, sermon and sacraments, music and silence, its many facets function like windows through which we are better able to glimpse the profile of Jesus Christ and to become clothed ourselves with Christ.

Deism

The term *deism* is used to refer to the beliefs of a group of English writers, especially those of the seventeenth century, whose rationalism perceived God as the divine creator who no longer maintains immediate involvement with the life of creation. This is the watchmaker theory—God made the watch, and now it runs on its own according to certain laws of nature that God built into the universe. Traditional theism as biblically defined counters deism, picturing God as actively involved with the world process. Various schools of contemporary Christian theism (freewill and process, as examples) actively refute the tendency of deism to distance God from the current life of the fallen creation. Some of the founding fathers of the United States (George Washington, Benjamin Franklin, and Thomas Jefferson) were influenced by deistic thinking. Spiritual life usually affirms the nearness and involvement of God.

Gnosticism

The word *gnosticism* comes from the Greek word *gnōsis,* meaning "knowledge." Adherents to diverse gnostic movements, particularly influential in the second-century Christian church, believed that devotees had gained a special kind of spiritual enlightenment, a higher level of knowledge not accessible to the uninitiated. Gnostics tended to emphasize the spiritual realm over the material, often claiming that the material is inherently evil and hence to be escaped. This spiritual-material dualism usually regarded the creator of the cosmos as an ignorant or malevolent lesser deity who is mistakenly regarded as God by the Judeo-Christian tradition. Since the Hebrew tradition allowed no such dualism, the gnostic attempt was to separate Christians from their Jewish roots. Some interpreters see the Book of 1 John as an effort to refute gnostic teaching. The early church father Irenaeus wrote vigorously against the Gnostic movement, seeing it as a significant threat to the infant church. About 140–150, for example, Marcion attempted to encourage a total discontinuity between the Old and New Testaments, claiming that the God of the Old Testament was not the same as the Father of Jesus. Marcion was excommunicated c. 144.

Modern/Postmodern

The spiritual life of Christians necessarily interacts with and often is significantly shaped by the prevailing culture that forms the immediate context of a believing community. Enlightenment or modern culture, so influential on the general public during recent generations in the West, has assumed that what is reasonable and scientifically measurable becomes the standard of truth and reality. The truth is seen as a harmonious unity that can be penetrated by reason since the structures of reality and of the human mind correspond. The goal is to bring human life into conformity with the laws of nature that can be identified by human research and reason. Once identified and followed, continuous improvement in personal and social life is possible, even likely. Rational objectivity is possible and sets one free of church authority and on the path of probing and controlling the world for good.

Functioning in a Christian setting, this modernist philosophy was used by John Locke (1632–1704) to argue that Christianity, once freed of unnecessary dogmatic baggage, is the most reasonable form of religion (*The Reasonableness of Christianity*, 1695). Christian theology thus became a discovery and cataloging of facts of divine revelation found in the Bible. The faith itself came to function much like a science, with religious knowledge turned into rational propositions that have logical coherence. The Bible, in effect, was modernized. It became more mechanical, precise, impersonal, and subject to human mastery—something in substantial contrast with the Hebrew roots of Christian faith.

In the early years of the twenty-first century, it is increasingly clear that this modern worldview has weakened significantly. Reality appears to be more complex than the rigid categories of human rationality. Intellectual knowledge has not delivered the good life. Progress and peace obviously are not the natural followers of rational thinking and living. Neutral truth observers appear more shaped by their contexts than they have realized. What is emerging from the disintegration of the modern is a postmodernism. Theologian Millard Erickson (*Postmodernizing the Faith*, 1998) offers seven motifs of this emerging postmodernism. These motifs have obvious implications for Christian spirituality.

1. The objectivity of knowledge is denied. Knowledge is not a neutral means of discovery. The knower is conditioned by the particularities of his or her situation.
2. Knowledge is uncertain. The idea that knowledge can be erected on some bedrock of indubitable first principles ("Foundationalism") must be abandoned.
3. All-inclusive systems of knowledge are impossible. Systems that seek to interpret reality for all people for all times are impossible and should be abandoned.
4. The inherent goodness of knowledge is not a given. Modern people have not saved the world with the immensity of contemporary knowledge, but often have turned it to destructive ends.
5. Progress is not inevitable. Increased knowledge and cultural change can lead backwards. Newer is different, but not necessarily better.
6. Truth is a community reality. We must abandon the model of the isolated knower as the ideal and move to community-based knowledge. All truth is defined by and for some community.
7. Truth is to be known through multiple means (not simply or even primarily through reason and the scientific method). Intuition, for instance, is a legitimate means of knowing.

While such perspectives disturb various aspects of the status quo in some Christian circles, they open fresh doors for renewed biblical understanding. The central role of spiritual life in the midst of church life is growing clearer. A new relationalism is encouraging stimulating thinking about God and the world (see the work of Gregory Boyd, Clark Pinnock, and John Sanders, for instance).

Monasticism

Given the Latin root *mono,* meaning "one" or "alone," monasticism in large part means a Christian spirituality practiced in isolation, alone, or at least in a restricted community apart from the world and usually separate from the opposite sex. It is a specialized way of life, frequently a part of the Roman Catholic and Eastern Orthodox traditions, usually emphasizing life-in-community, poverty, celibacy, silence, contemplation, and structured common worship. Renunciation is seen as key to spirituality. Featured is the quest for a loss of self for the sake of increasing one's spiritual awareness and the implications of the love of Christ. Residents of these cloistered communities (monasteries) are monks or nuns, Christians especially committed to internalizing Scripture and engaging in prayer through faithfulness to the "offices" or set times of daily worship. The whole of life is oriented towards the reign of God and the life of Christ in the soul. Accompanying such asceticism is the desire for service of others, whether through the ministry of prayer, study, teaching, or active love in care for brother monks, sister nuns, visitors, or the needy.

Rise of structured settings for the monastic life came in part from the secularization of the church after Emperor Constantine (c. 275–337). Anthony of Egypt (c. 251–356) is called the "father of monks." He responded to this statement of Jesus: "If you wish to be perfect, go, sell your possessions, and give the money to the poor, and you will have treasure in heaven; then come, follow me" (Matt. 19:21). He gave away the land inherited from his father and lived on the desert margin of his village. His amazing story is told in the *Life of St. Anthony* by Athanasius (357). In the sixth century, St. Benedict of Nursia (c. 480–547), the father of Western monasticism, compiled for his monks at Italy's Monte Cassino the *Rule of St. Benedict.* This provided a practical and spiritually uncompromising guide that eventually was employed in the lives of monks of the West generally. It highlights the attitudes of humility and unreserved obedience to God and calls for regular prayer, silence, and habitual attention to the Word of God. Monks are to love each other and bear with the diversity and weakness of the brothers as together they engage in the rhythm of prayer, work, and study of God's Word. The oldest Trappist monastery in the United States, Gethsemani in rural Kentucky (founded 1849), still follows the Benedictine tradition and was the home of the most famous of its monks, Thomas Merton (1915–1968).

Mysticism

The Greek word *mystikos* refers to the "mystery" of God's love now made accessible to us in Jesus Christ. People are called to belong to the "fellowship of the mystery" (Eph. 3:9 KJV). Concerned for immediate, direct, and unmediated access to a loving relationship with God, mysticism seeks a personal, experiential, and contemplative knowledge of the divine. The search usually is characterized by the language of union with God in ways not heavily reliant on the use of human reason or the support of church institutions and traditions. At its core is the human individual who seeks and finds relationship with the absolute. John of the Cross (1542–1591) is well known for his tripartite division of the mystic way. It is the triple way of purgation, illumination, and union.

Much in the recent Western world has suggested the more scientific approach to truth that argues that if it cannot be seen, heard, or measured, likely it does not exist. Mystics remind us that there is far more reality beyond the physical senses than can be experienced by them. In the "dark night of the soul," by God's grace one can experience the ecstasy of love. The mystical focus is on the inward and experiential. Christian mystics often are emphatic about progress in love and about perfect love in union with God being the goal of all true religion.

Pantheism/Panentheism

Here are two words that are similar in sound and yet significantly different in meaning. *Pantheism* (Greek for "everything is God") is the belief that God and the universe are essentially identical. Many religions, including Hinduism, view divine reality and the world as closely connected. Sometimes it is said that God is the soul of the universe, and the universe is the body of God. Pantheistic views have often challenged classic Christian thought. One kind of pantheism tends to absorb creation and time into God (as in Hegel). Others tend to absorb God into creation and time (as in Wieman). All tend to erase the crucial difference between God and all that is temporal.

More compatible with orthodox Christianity is *panentheism* which, while also viewing God as close to and even permeating the entire universe, declares that God's being is greater than and not exhausted by the universe. God is *in* but not *of* (or the same as) the world, close to but not identical with the world. Process theology emphasizes the closeness and sometimes tends toward pantheism. For a careful analysis of the positives and negatives of process theology, see Barry L. Callen, *Clark H. Pinnock: Journey toward Renewal* (2000), chapter 5. Jürgen Moltmann's thought may be characterized as panentheism (God is *in* all) as opposed to pantheism (God *is* all) and atheism (God is *dissolved* in the all).

At issue is the proper balance between the sovereignty and independent existence of God (God existed prior to the creation) and the divinely chosen interaction of God with the creation. For a good study of models viewed from the perspective of classic Christianity, see Terrance Tiessen, *Providence and Prayer* (2000).

Pietism

Especially associated with certain German writers in the seventeenth century, Pietism is an approach to Christianity that emphasizes the personal appropriation of faith and the need for holiness in Christian living. Believing that the sixteenth-century Protestant Reformation had bogged down in dogmatics, polemics, and institutional rigidity, the Pietists offered concrete proposals for Bible study and increased lay participation. The fresh focus was on the practical and mystical appropriation of the grace of God. The German word *Pietismus* was an uncomplimentary nickname bequeathed to posterity by Pietism's detractors. The idea for the name might have come from Philipp Jakob Spener's *Pia Desideria*, the preface to an important 1675 book by Johann Arndt. This writing and its passionate call for church reformation is regarded as the precipitating event in the birth of German Pietism. Often viewed negatively as subjectivism, individualism, and otherworldliness, the core concerns of Pietism have often functioned as well-springs of new life in the church. See Dale Brown, *Understanding Pietism* (1996).

Sacrament

A *sacrament* is often thought of as a church practice or rite that is believed to have been instituted by Jesus himself and is intended to be part of Christian life in all times. Protestants generally identify two (baptism and the Lord's Supper), while Roman Catholicism recognizes seven (baptism, confirmation, Eucharist, marriage, ordination, penance, and unction). Some Christians, including Quakers, argue against any mandatory church rites, focus on their own spiritual essence, and speak of the whole universe as "sacramental" (permeated by and a conveyor of spiritual perception, life, and divine grace). When particular practices are identified and made central in Christian worship, they are thought to demonstrate God's use of material things to make present and visible the invisible realm of the Spirit. A sacrament often is defined as "an outward and visible sign of an inward and spiritual grace." But a sign in this case is believed by many Christians to do more than only recall and represent a pivotal past; it also effects what it signifies. In the Lord's Supper, for instance, participants clearly do remember the great sacrifice of God in Jesus Christ. But they also are privileged to participate with the really present Jesus, the perfect sacrament of God. The result of such grace-filled participation is that the humbled believer is also to become a sign of divine grace in the present world.

Notes

Introduction

1. Donald Bloesch, *The Holy Spirit: Works and Gifts* (Downers Grove, Ill.: InterVarsity, 2000), 21–22. Bloesch insists there are two serious threats to authentic Christian faith in the twenty-first century. One is a cold formalism that quenches the Spirit and the other an excessive pentecostalism that easily becomes a new formalism that also can be bereft of the sanctifying presence of the Spirit of God. He tries to build bridges between Word and Spirit that, in their union, ensure authenticity in Christian spiritual life.

2. Wesley D. Tracy et al., *The Upward Call: Spiritual Formation and the Holy Life* (Kansas City: Beacon Hill, 1994), 9–10.

3. See the excellent interpretation of the work of Thomas Aquinas by Robert Barron, *Thomas Aquinas: Spiritual Master* (New York: Crossroad, 1996).

4. Karl Rahner, "The Spirituality of the Future," in *The Practice of the Faith*, ed. K. Lehmann and A. Raffelt (New York: Crossroad, 1986), 22.

5. I use the six spiritual streams identified by Richard Foster in his *Streams of Living Water: Celebrating the Great Traditions of Christian Faith* (San Francisco: HarperSanFrancisco, 1998). They are the evangelical, charismatic, contemplative, holiness, incarnational, and social justice traditions.

6. Geoffrey Wainwright, *Doxology: The Praise of God in Worship, Doctrine, and Life* (London: Epworth, 1980), preface.

7. This is a central thesis of Bloesch, *Holy Spirit*. He sees today's Christian challenge as the rediscovery of the complementarity of logos and Spirit, while maintaining the subordination of Spirit to logos (which he judges to be the clear biblical pattern).

8. In the 1880s, a similar call to radical Christian reformation was ignited in large part by the ministry of Daniel S. Warner (1842–1895). The result became known as the Church of God (Anderson) movement.

9. A. W. Tozer, *The Pursuit of God* (1948; reprint, Camp Hill, Pa.: Christian Publications, 1982). Born in the hills of western Pennsylvania, longtime pastor of the Southside Alliance Church in Chicago (beginning in 1928), and editor of *The Alliance Witness* (beginning in 1950), Tozer was a twentieth-century prophet calling the church to simplicity and godliness.

10. Robert Bellah et al., *Habits of the Heart: Individualism and Commitment in American Life* (Berkeley: University of California Press, 1985), 221.

11. See John Howard Yoder, *The Politics of Jesus*, 2d ed. (Grand Rapids: Eerdmans, 1994).

12. Martin E. Marty, *The Irony of It All, 1893–1919*, vol. 1 of *Modern American Religion* (Chicago: University of Chicago Press, 1986), 2.

13. See Barry L. Callen, *Seeking the Light: America's Modern Quest for Peace, Justice, Prosperity, and Faith* (Nappanee, Ind.: Evangel, 1998).

14. See especially Stanley Grenz, *A Primer on Postmodernism* (Grand Rapids: Eerdmans, 1996); Henry Knight, *The Future for Truth: Evangelical Theology in a Postmodern World* (Nashville: Abingdon, 1997); and Robert Webber, *Ancient-Future Faith: Rethinking Evangelicalism for a Postmodern World* (Grand Rapids: Baker, 1999).

15. Editorial, quoting Nancy Joseph, *The Herald/Bulletin* (Anderson, Ind.), 30 July 2000, E1.

16. Kenneth J. Collins, ed., *Exploring Christian Spirituality: An Ecumenical Reader* (Grand Rapids: Baker, 2000).

17. Sandra Schneiders, "Theology and Spirituality: Strangers, Rivals, or Partners?" *Horizons* 13 (1986): 266.

18. Lawrence S. Cunningham and Keith J. Egan, *Christian Spirituality: Themes from the Tradition* (New York: Paulist, 1996), 7. They add, "Christian spirituality is concerned not so much with the doctrines of Christianity as with the ways those teachings shape us as individuals who are part of the Christian community who live in the larger world" (7).

19. John Wesley, "The Way to the Kingdom," in *Works of John Wesley*, vol. 1, ed. Albert Outler, Bicentennial Edition (Nashville: Abingdon, 1984), 220–21.

20. Note Kenneth J. Collins's recent biography of John Wesley titled *A Real Christian: The Life of John Wesley* (Nashville: Abingdon, 1999).

21. Clark H. Pinnock, *Flame of Love: A Theology of the Holy Spirit* (Downers Grove, Ill.: InterVarsity, 1996), 47, 83.

22. Justo L. Gonzalez, *Out of Every Tribe and Nation* (Nashville: Abingdon, 1992), 115.

23. See William M. Greathouse, *Wholeness in Christ: Toward a Biblical Theology of Holiness* (Kansas City: Beacon Hill, 1998).

24. Stanley Hauerwas and William Willimon, *Resident Aliens: Life in the Christian Colony* (Nashville: Abingdon, 1989), 48–49, 171.

25. Bill Gaither, as quoted in *The Herald Bulletin* (Anderson, Ind.), 6 May 2000.

26. Kenneth Leech, *True Prayer: An Invitation to Christian Spirituality* (New York: Harper and Row, 1980; Harrisburg, Pa.: Morehouse, 1995), 11.

Chapter 1: *Truly Open: The Spirit's Reaching*

1. John Sanders, *The God Who Risks: A Theology of Providence* (Downers Grove, Ill.: InterVarsity, 1998), 282.

2. Donald G. Bloesch, *The Crisis of Piety: Essays toward a Theology of the Christian Life*, 2d ed. (Colorado Springs: Helmers and Howard, 1988), xii, emphasis added.

3. For instance, see the helpful but controversial book by Clark Pinnock et al., *The Openness of God: A Biblical Challenge to the Traditional Understanding of God* (Downers Grove, Ill.: InterVarsity, 1994).

4. Hans Küng, *Credo: The Apostles' Creed Explained for Today*, trans. John Bowden (New York: Doubleday, 1993), 11.

5. For the dramatic story of one man's journey through established theological systems to a more biblical vision of God, see Barry L. Callen, *Clark H. Pinnock: Journey toward Renewal* (Nappanee, Ind.: Evangel, 2000).

6. This insight and many others are included by J. B. Phillips in his *Ring of Truth: A Translator's Testimony* (Wheaton: Harold Shaw, 1977).

7. Elton Trueblood explains that a person is a center of consciousness who has awareness, purposes, knowledge, and caring. He says, "God may be *more* than a Person and probably is, though we do not really know what that means, but unless He is at least as personal as we

are, He is not One to whom we can pray" (*A Place to Stand* [New York: Harper and Row, 1969], 72).

8. Kenneth Leech, *Experiencing God: Theology as Spirituality* (San Francisco: Harper and Row, 1985).

9. John Sanders, *The God Who Risks: A Theology of Providence* (Downers Grove, Ill.: Inter-Varsity, 1998). Clark Pinnock comments as follows in his endorsement of Sanders's book: "Some people have gotten the impression that God is an unblinking cosmic stare or a solitary metaphysical iceberg, and they naturally have difficulty relating to God as a loving, interacting Person. This book will help them overcome such misconceptions and greatly advances the case for the openness model of God."

10. Simon Chan, *Spiritual Theology: A Systematic Study of the Christian Life* (Downers Grove, Ill.: InterVarsity, 1998), 49.

11. Pinnock, *Openness of God,* 105.

12. Jody Veenker, "Spirituality without Religion," *Christianity Today,* 6 December 1999, 34–35. The occasion of this judgment was a widely publicized U.S. tour by the Dalai Lama and his urging of a Buddhist-like tolerant spirituality without any necessary God assumption. The article criticizes this popular preoccupation of so many today as "pop Buddhism's buffet of low-commitment, high-touch beliefs" (34).

13. For an extended historical and social exploration of these decades (and the 1940s and 1950s that preceded them), see Barry Callen, *Seeking the Light: America's Modern Quest for Peace, Justice, Prosperity, and Faith* (Nappanee, Ind.: Evangel, 1998).

14. Wade Clark Roof, *A Generation of Seekers: The Spiritual Journeys of the Baby Boom Generation* (San Francisco: HarperSanFrancisco, 1993), 4–5.

15. D. A. Carson, *The Gagging of God: Christianity Confronts Pluralism* (Grand Rapids: Zondervan, 1996), 567. While Carson writes extensively about what he considers core biblical theology, this present work relies in part on the Apostles' Creed as representative of what the Christian community across the centuries has identified as basic Christian beliefs.

16. Lawrence S. Cunningham and Keith J. Egan, *Christian Spirituality: Themes from the Tradition* (New York: Paulist, 1996), 2.

17. Chan, *Spiritual Theology,* 78.

18. Stanley Grenz, *Revisioning Evangelical Theology: A Fresh Agenda for the Twenty-First Century* (Downers Grove, Ill.: InterVarsity, 1993), 42.

19. Dale W. Brown, *Understanding Pietism,* rev. ed. (Nappanee, Ind.: Evangel, 1996), 22.

20. Donald Bloesch, *Wellsprings of Renewal: Promise in Christian Communal Life* (Grand Rapids: Eerdmans, 1974), 12–13.

21. For instance, note the excellent book *Spirituality in an Age of Change: Rediscovering the Spirit of the Reformers* by Alister McGrath (Grand Rapids: Zondervan, 1994). His "age of change" reference is to the sixteenth century, and his thesis is that Christians facing the unknowns of the twenty-first century "need to return to our evangelical roots in the Reformation and be refreshed, challenged, and nourished by our past" (14). Says McGrath, "With the Reformation, the formative centers of spirituality gradually shifted from the monasteries to the marketplace" (26).

22. Clark H. Pinnock, "Evangelical Theology in Progress," in *Introduction to Christian Theology,* ed. Roger Badham (Louisville: Westminster John Knox, 1998), 77, 82. The full story of Pinnock's own journey is found in Callen, *Clark H. Pinnock.*

23. Thomas C. Oden, *The Word of Life: Systematic Theology,* vol. 2 (San Francisco: HarperSanFrancisco, 1989), preface.

24. Bloesch, *Crisis of Piety,* 6.

25. Richard Foster, *Streams of Living Water: Celebrating the Great Traditions of Christian Faith* (San Francisco: HarperSanFrancisco, 1998), xv.

26. D. Elton Trueblood, *The Essence of Spiritual Religion* (1936; reprint, New York: Harper, 1975), x.

27. James S. Stewart, *A Man in Christ: The Vital Elements of St. Paul's Religion* (New York: Harper and Row, n.d.), 21.

28. For an extensive overview of the history, beliefs, and practices of the Believers Church tradition, see Barry L. Callen, *Radical Christianity: The Believers Church Tradition in Christianity's History and Future* (Nappanee, Ind.: Evangel, 1999).

29. McGrath, *Spirituality*, 31–32.

30. Marvin Wilson, *Our Father Abraham: Jewish Roots of the Christian Faith* (Grand Rapids: Eerdmans; Dayton, Ohio: Center for Judaic-Christian Studies, 1989), 159.

31. Helmut Thielicke, *A Little Exercise for Young Theologians* (Grand Rapids: Eerdmans, 1962), 37.

32. Dwight L. Grubbs, *Beginnings: Spiritual Formation for Leaders* (Lima, Ohio: Fairway, 1994), 12–15.

33. McGrath, *Spirituality*, 9. He went on to say (12), "It is all very well to stress the total sufficiency of the gospel and to focus on God as he has made himself known and available in Jesus Christ. But that gospel is addressed to sinful human beings who need all the help they can get to live by its precepts and harness its power in their lives."

34. As quoted by Kenneth Collins, *A Real Christian: The Life of John Wesley* (Nashville: Abingdon, 1999), 152.

35. Joseph D. Driskill, *Protestant Spiritual Exercises: Theology, History, and Practice* (Harrisburg, Pa.: Morehouse, 1999), xii, 30, 6.

36. Thomas Merton, *New Seeds of Contemplation* (Norfolk, Conn.: New Directions, 1972), 197–98.

37. J. I. Packer, "An Introduction to Systematic Spirituality," *Crux* 26, no. 1 (March 1990): 6.

38. Bloesch, *Crisis of Piety*, xii.

39. Evelyn Underhill, *The School of Charity: Meditations on the Christian Creed* (New York: Longmans, Green, 1954), 4.

40. Hans Urs von Balthasar, "The Gospel as Norm and Test of All Spirituality in the Church," *Concilium* (1969): 16.

41. Wilson, *Our Father Abraham*, 8.

42. Excerpt from the hymn "All Creatures of Our God and King" by Francis of Assisi.

43. Excerpt from the hymn "Lead On, O King Eternal" by Ernest Shurtleff.

44. Stephen Barton, *The Spirituality of the Gospels* (Peabody, Mass.: Hendrickson, 1992), 28–29.

45. See the chapter "On the Margin with the Master" in Callen, *Radical Christianity*.

46. Howard A. Snyder, *The Radical Wesley and Patterns of Church Renewal* (Downers Grove, Ill.: InterVarsity, 1980), preface.

47. John Wesley, "Of Former Times," in *The Works of John Wesley*, ed. Thomas Jackson (London: John Mason, 1829–31), VII: 165.

48. David McKenna, *A Great Time to Be a Wesleyan!* (Kansas City: Beacon Hill, 1999), 13.

49. Stephen A. Seamands, *Holiness of Heart and Life* (Nashville: Abingdon, 1990), 71, 73.

50. Clark Pinnock, *Flame of Love: A Theology of the Holy Spirit* (Downers Grove, Ill.: InterVarsity, 1996), 9–10.

51. See Callen, "Starting with the Spirit," chapter in his *Radical Christianity*.

52. Seamands, *Holiness of Heart and Life*, 14.

53. See Kallistos Ware, *The Orthodox Way*, rev. ed. (Crestwood, N.Y.: St. Vladimir's Seminary Press, 1995), 21–23.

54. See H. Richard Niebuhr, *Christ and Culture* (New York: Harper and Row, 1951) and Geoffrey Wainwright, "Types of Spirituality," in *The Study of Spirituality*, ed. Cheslyn Jones,

Geoffrey Wainwright, and Edward Yarnold (New York: Oxford University Press, 1986), 592–605.

55. A paraphrased version of this creed is arranged in four verses and set to the tune of the Austrian Hymn. It thus becomes a singable affirmation of Christian faith. See Janet Lindeblad Janzen, *Songs for Renewal* (San Francisco: HarperSanFrancisco, 1995), 6.

56. William Barclay refers to the Apostles' Creed as an expansion of Matthew 28:19 where Jesus directs believers to make disciples of all nations, baptizing in the name of the Father, Son, and Holy Spirit. This creed is "constructed to state the Church's belief on the great basic matters of the faith, which were the foundations of all missionary preaching" (*The Apostles' Creed for Everyman* [New York: Harper and Row, 1967], 11).

57. Jacob Neusner, *The Way of Torah,* 5th ed. (Belmont, Calif.: Wadsworth, 1993), 111.

58. Merrill Abbey, *The Shape of the Gospel: Interpreting the Bible through the Christian Year* (Nashville: Abingdon, 1970), 7.

59. See, e.g., John H. Westerhoff III, *A Pilgrim People: Learning through the Church Year* (Minneapolis: Seabury, 1984). In response to the question of why a Christian community of faith should use a lectionary to guide in the Bible's use in worship over time, Marion Soards et al. answer, "Simply put, the use of a lectionary provides a more diverse scriptural diet for God's people, and it can help protect the congregation from the whims and prejudices of the pastor or other worship planners" (*Preaching the Revised Common Lectionary: Year A, Lent/Easter* [Nashville: Abingdon, 1992], 9).

60. For a serious exploration of the themes of purity and power in the Wesleyan and Pentecostal traditions, see the *Wesleyan Theological Journal* 34, no. 1 (spring 1999).

61. See, e.g., Alan Kreider, *Journey towards Holiness: A Way of Living for God's Nation* (Scottdale, Pa.: Herald, 1987).

62. McKenna, *A Great Time.*

Chapter 2: *Truly Summoned: The Spirit's Presence*

1. Jürgen Moltmann, *The Spirit of Life: A Universal Affirmation* (Minneapolis: Fortress, 1992), x–xi.

2. As quoted by Malcolm Muggeridge, *A Third Testament* (Boston: Little, Brown, 1976), 136–37.

3. See Robert Barron, *Thomas Aquinas: Spiritual Master* (New York: Crossroad, 1996), especially chapter 2, "The Strangeness of God."

4. Howard Thurman, *Deep Is the Hunger* (Richmond, Ind.: Friends United, 1951), 147.

5. Anthony Bloom, *Beginning to Pray* (New York: Paulist, 1970), 25.

6. Harry Emerson Fosdick, *What Is Vital in Religion* (New York: Harper, 1955), 1.

7. Ibid., 8. Fosdick had a nervous breakdown when young and found God in his personal wilderness. Without this breakdown, he reports (9) that he would never have written his classic 1949 book *The Meaning of Prayer.*

8. Warren Lane Molton, *Bruised Reeds* (Valley Forge, Pa.: Judson, 1970), 27.

9. John S. Mogabgab, editor's introduction, *Weavings* 13, no. 2 (March/April 1998): 2.

10. Steven J. Land, *Pentecostal Spirituality: A Passion for the Kingdom* (Sheffield, England: Sheffield Academic Press, 1993), 222–23.

11. Frank Laubach, *Letters by a Modern Mystic* (1937; reprint, Syracuse, N.Y.: New Readers, 1979), 23.

12. Howard Thurman in *Disciplines for the Inner Life,* by Bob Benson and Michael W. Benson, rev. ed. (Waco: Word, 1985; Nashville: Generoux/Nelson, 1989), 7.

13. Barry L. Callen, ed., *Sharing Heaven's Music: The Heart of Christian Preaching* (Nashville: Abingdon, 1995). These essays on homiletics are in honor of the Rev. James Earl Massey, sometimes called the "prince" of contemporary Christian preachers.

14. John Wesley, *The Principles of a Methodist Farther Examined* (1746). A recent biography of John Wesley by Kenneth J. Collins is titled *A Real Christian: The Life of John Wesley* (Nashville: Abingdon, 1999).

15. Thomas Oden, *The Living God*, Systematic Theology, vol. 1 (San Francisco: Harper and Row, 1987; Prince Press edition, 1998), 67–68.

16. John Calvin, *Institutes of the Christian Religion*, 3.1.1.

17. See Barry L. Callen, *God as Loving Grace* (Nappanee, Ind.: Evangel, 1996), 137–44. See also Walter Brueggemann, *Genesis*, Interpretation commentary series (Atlanta: John Knox, 1982).

18. Note the familiar American folk hymn that asks, "Were you there when they crucified my Lord? . . . O! Sometimes it causes me to tremble, tremble, tremble."

19. Moltmann, *Spirit of Life*, 17.

20. Robert Webber, *Ancient-Future Faith: Rethinking Evangelicalism for a Postmodern World* (Grand Rapids: Baker, 1999), 27.

21. Richard Foster, *Streams of Living Water: Celebrating the Great Traditions of Christian Faith* (San Francisco: HarperSanFrancisco, 1998). The streams are the evangelical, charismatic, contemplative, holiness, incarnational, and social justice traditions.

22. Laurence Stookey, *Calendar: Christ's Time for the Church* (Nashville: Abingdon, 1996), 122.

23. Excerpt from the hymn "Come, Thou Long-Expected Jesus" by Charles Wesley. To this might well be added the cry of the Lord's Prayer: "Thy kingdom come, thy will be done on earth."

24. While this is a reasonable assumption, the facts are not completely clear or undisputed. Some early traditions in Asia Minor speak of the Lord's death, resurrection, and conception as all being in the Passover season, with the passing of nine months suggesting a late December birth of Jesus.

25. See Walter Brueggemann, *Hope within History* (Atlanta: John Knox, 1987).

26. Cunningham and Egan, *Christian Spirituality*, 148.

27. Undoubtedly the twentieth century's most prominent prophet of solitude as preparation for prophetic ministry is Thomas Merton (1915–1968). See R. A. Cashen, *Solitude in the Thought of Thomas Merton* (Kalamazoo, Mich.: Cistercian, 1981).

28. The Gnostics taught that Jesus only seemed to be an actual human being. For them, God's holiness meant that the divine would not directly touch the bodily life of this fallen creation.

29. Timothy George, "If I'm an Evangelical, What Am I?" *Christianity Today*, 9 August 1999, 62.

30. Foster, *Streams of Living Water*, 192, 206.

31. An understandable Roman Catholic critique of the faith-alone focus is that too often it leads Christians to a life of relative disinterest in serious spiritual growth, what Dietrich Bonhoeffer called "cheap grace" that avoids the critical issue of sanctification. To address this concern, Puritanism soon sought to graft aspects of patristic and medieval spirituality onto the Reformation base of justification by faith.

32. In their book *Who Needs Theology? An Invitation to the Study of God*, Roger Olson and Stanley Grenz helpfully address differences between the primary and secondary in Christian believing (Downers Grove, Ill.: InterVarsity, 1996), especially in chapter 2, "Not All Theologies Are Equal."

33. Billy Graham, *Just As I Am: The Autobiography of Billy Graham* (San Francisco: HarperSanFrancisco; Grand Rapids: Zondervan, 1997), 729.

34. Theodore Jennings Jr., *Loyalty to God: The Apostles' Creed in Life and Liturgy* (Nashville: Abingdon, 1992), 12.

35. Note that the systematic theology written by Barry L. Callen (*God as Loving Grace*) is structured around the trinitarian view of God. The three parts of this work are (1) Sovereign: The God who stands and creates, the source of loving grace; (2) Savior: The God who stoops and saves, the Christ initiative of loving grace; and (3) Spirit: The God who stays and sustains, the presence of loving grace.

36. Stuart Briscoe, *The Apostles' Creed: Beliefs That Matter* (Wheaton: Harold Shaw, 1994), 79–80.

37. Clark H. Pinnock, *Flame of Love: A Theology of the Holy Spirit* (Downers Grove, Ill.: InterVarsity, 1996), 113–14.

38. A recent example of this criticism is Mark Noll's *The Scandal of the Evangelical Mind* (Grand Rapids: Eerdmans, 1994). For strong critiques of aspects of Noll's perspective, see the *Wesleyan Theological Journal* 32, no. 1 (spring 1997): 157–92.

39. Douglas Strong, "Sanctified Eccentricity: Continuing Relevance of the Nineteenth-Century Holiness Paradigm," *Wesleyan Theological Journal* 35, no. 1 (spring 2000): 18.

40. One body emerging from this Holiness movement was the Church of God (Anderson). It particularly stresses the church unity that should be the result of holiness renewal. See John W. V. Smith, *The Quest for Holiness and Unity: The History of the Church of God* (Anderson, Ind.: Warner, 1980); and Barry L. Callen, *Following the Light* (Anderson, Ind.: Warner, 2000).

Chapter 3: *Truly Amazed: The Spirit's Extravagance*

1. Rufus M. Jones, *Studies in Mystical Religion* (London: Macmillan, 1909), xv.

2. Vladimir Lossky, *The Mystical Theology of the Eastern Church* (Crestwood, N.Y.: St. Vladimir's Seminary Press, 1976), 42.

3. C. S. Lewis, *Surprised by Joy* (San Diego: Harcourt Brace Jovanovich, 1955), 220ff.

4. Barbara Brown Taylor, "A Great Cloud of Witnesses," *Weavings* 3, no. 5 (September/October 1988): 34.

5. These comments of Douglas Steere are summarized by E. Glenn Hinson in *Spiritual Preparation for Christian Leadership* (Nashville: Upper Room, 1999), 183–86. Also see Hinson's biography of Steere titled *Love at the Heart of Things* (Nashville: Upper Room, 1998).

6. John Sanders, *The God Who Risks: A Theology of Providence* (Downers Grove, Ill.: InterVarsity, 1998), 251.

7. Gregory A. Boyd, *God of the Possible: A Biblical Introduction to the Open View of God* (Grand Rapids: Baker, 2000), 96.

8. Excerpt from the hymn "Love Divine, All Loves Excelling" by Charles Wesley.

9. Excerpt from the hymn "Wonderful Grace of Jesus" by Haldor Lillenas.

10. Excerpt from the hymn "Grace Greater than Our Sin" by Julia Johnston.

11. Thomas Oden, *The Transforming Power of Grace* (Nashville: Abingdon, 1993), 15, 17, 19.

12. Gabriel Fackre, *Ecumenical Faith in Evangelical Perspective* (Grand Rapids: Eerdmans, 1993), 121.

13. Annie Johnson Flint, "He Giveth More Grace" (Kansas City, Mo.: Lillenas, 1941, 1969).

14. See Walter Brueggemann, *The Message of the Psalms: A Theological Commentary* (Minneapolis: Augsburg, 1984).

15. John H. Westerhoff III, *A Pilgrim People: Learning through the Church Year* (Minneapolis: Seabury, 1984), 71–83.

16. Robert Webber, ed., *The Complete Library of Christian Worship*, vol. 5, *The Services of the Christian Year* (Nashville: Star Song, 1994), 80.

17. Laurence Hull Stookey, *Calendar: Christ's Time for the Church* (Nashville: Abingdon, 1996), 80.

18. Westerhoff, *Pilgrim People*, 11.

19. M. Basil Pennington Jr., "The Call to Contemplation," *Weavings* 11, no. 3 (May/June 1996): 33. Also see Rodney Clapp, "Remonking the Church," *Christianity Today,* 12 August 1988, 20–21; and Robert Barron, *Heaven in Stone and Glass: Experiencing the Spirituality of the Great Cathedrals* (New York: Crossroad, 2000).

20. Dom Helder Camara in *Disciplines for the Inner Life,* by Bob Benson and Michael W. Benson, rev. ed. (Waco: Word, 1985; Nashville: Generoux/Nelson, 1989), 74.

21. Stephen C. Barton, *The Spirituality of the Gospels* (Peabody, Mass.: Hendrickson, 1992), 1.

22. Jürgen Moltmann, *The Spirit of Life: A Universal Affirmation* (Minneapolis: Fortress, 1992), 42–43.

23. See Winfried Corduan, *Mysticism: An Evangelical Option?* (Grand Rapids: Zondervan, 1991), where such a definition is offered in the context of the caution that no experience should supersede biblical revelation as authoritative for the Christian (32).

24. See Robert G. Tuttle Jr., *Mysticism in the Wesleyan Tradition* (Grand Rapids: Zondervan, Francis Asbury, 1989).

25. This pilgrimage of John Wesley is well recounted by Tuttle, *Mysticism in the Wesleyan Tradition.*

26. The idea of union with God requires careful clarification. For a biblical call to it, note 2 Peter 1:4 and John 10:34–35 (reflecting Psalm 82:6). Eastern Christianity, consistently emphasizing such union or *theosis,* repudiates any hint of pantheism—a real equating of God, humans, and creation. Believers in Jesus Christ do not come to participate in the very essence or nature of God nor do they lose their humanity in the process of being united with God. The emphasis is on sanctification or being transformed so that believers reflect the likeness of God in their lives (because it is the Spirit of God who now lives in them). Here is the key Christian confession as reported in Galatians 2:19–20: "I have been crucified with Christ; and it is no longer I who live, but it is Christ who lives in me. And the life I now live in the flesh I live by faith in the Son of God, who loved me and gave himself for me."

27. This phrase or the similar "in the Lord" occurs in Paul's writings 164 times. James Stewart says, "The heart of Paul's religion is union with Christ" (*A Man in Christ: The Vital Elements of St. Paul's Religion* [New York: Harper and Row, n.d.], 147). He adds, "Only when union with Christ is kept central is sanctification seen in its true nature, as the unfolding of Christ's own character within the believer's life; and only then can the essential relationship between religion and ethics be understood" (152–53).

28. Donald Bloesch, *The Struggle of Prayer* (Colorado Springs: Helmers and Howard, 1988), 155.

29. Henri Nouwen, *In the Name of Jesus: Reflections on Christian Leadership* (New York: Crossroad, 1989), 28–30.

30. See the classic study by Stewart, *A Man in Christ.*

31. See James Earl Massey, *Spiritual Disciplines: Growth through the Practice of Prayer, Fasting, Dialogue, and Worship* (Grand Rapids: Zondervan, Francis Asbury, 1985).

32. Daniel B. Clendenin, *Eastern Orthodox Christianity: A Western Perspective* (Grand Rapids: Baker, 1994), 151.

33. E. Stanley Jones, *The Christ of the Indian Road* (New York: Grosset and Dunlap, 1925), 179.

34. Excerpt from the hymn "Moment by Moment" by Daniel W. Whittle.

35. Frank C. Laubach, *Letters by a Modern Mystic* (1937; reprint, Syracuse, N.Y.: New Readers, 1979), 11.

36. Thomas Merton, *The Seven Storey Mountain* (Garden City, N.Y.: Garden City Books, 1948; New York: Harcourt Brace, 1998).

37. Thomas Merton, *New Seeds of Contemplation* (Norfolk, Conn.: New Directions, 1972), 1.

38. Henri Nouwen, *Making All Things New: An Invitation to the Spiritual Life* (San Francisco: Harper and Row, 1981), 54.

39. Georgia Harkness, *Mysticism: Its Meaning and Message* (Nashville: Abingdon, 1973), 54.

40. Georgia Harkness, *Foundations of Christian Knowledge* (Nashville: Abingdon, 1955), 153.

41. Richard J. Foster, *Streams of Living Water: Celebrating the Great Traditions of Christian Faith* (San Francisco: HarperSanFrancisco, 1998), 51. Foster suggests some "venues for solitude," like taking predawn walks, trying a month of commuting with the car radio left off, and sitting in silence "doing nothing, having nothing, needing nothing" (56–57).

42. Alister E. McGrath, *I Believe: Exploring the Apostles' Creed* (Downers Grove, Ill.: InterVarsity, 1998), 37.

43. C. S. Lewis, as quoted by Stuart Briscoe, *The Apostles' Creed: Beliefs That Matter* (Wheaton, Ill.: Harold Shaw, 1994), 63.

44. Richard J. Foster, *Prayer: Finding the Heart's True Home* (San Francisco: HarperSanFrancisco, 1992), 81, 89.

Chapter 4: *Truly Belonging: The Spirit's Act*

1. R. Eugene Sterner, *Keys to Spiritual Freedom* (Anderson, Ind.: Warner, 1999), 5, 16.

2. For an exposition of Christian theology from the perspective of God's intended community, see Stanley Grenz, *Theology for the Community of God* (Nashville: Broadman and Holman, 1994).

3. See Gregory A. Boyd, *God of the Possible: A Biblical Introduction to the Open View of God* (Grand Rapids: Baker, 2000).

4. See Barry L. Callen, *Clark H. Pinnock: Journey toward Renewal* (Nappanee, Ind.: Evangel, 2000), 100–106, 127–73.

5. George A. Buttrick, *Prayer* (Nashville: Abingdon, 1942), 15, 22–23.

6. John Killinger, *You Are What You Believe* (Nashville: Abingdon, 1990), 86.

7. John S. Mogabgab, Introduction to *Weavings* 4, no. 1 (January/February 1989): 2.

8. Marvin R. Wilson, *Our Father Abraham: Jewish Roots of the Christian Faith* (Grand Rapids: Eerdmans; Dayton, Ohio: Center for Judaic-Christian Studies, 1989), 9.

9. James Muilenburg, *The Way of Israel: Biblical Faith and Ethics* (New York: Harper, 1961; New York: Harper Torchbook edition, 1965), 57.

10. Note, for instance, that the journey metaphor is central for a classic Christian work like John Bunyan's *The Pilgrim's Progress* (published in two parts, 1678 and 1684).

11. Stephen Barton, *The Spirituality of the Gospels* (Peabody, Mass.: Hendrickson, 1992), 100.

12. Clark H. Pinnock, *Flame of Love: A Theology of the Holy Spirit* (Downers Grove, Ill.: InterVarsity, 1996), 47.

13. Thomas Jackson, ed., *The Works of the Rev. John Wesley, A.M.* (London: Wesleyan Conference Office, 1872), 5:12; 6:5f.; 5:252.

14. Richard Foster, *Streams of Living Water: Celebrating the Great Traditions of Christian Faith* (San Francisco: HarperSanFrancisco, 1998), 84.

15. For a good presentation of the challenges facing serious Christians today, see Stanley Hauerwas and William Willimon, *Resident Aliens: Life in the Christian Colony* (Nashville: Abingdon, 1989).

16. Henri Nouwen, *Reaching Out: The Three Movements of the Spiritual Life* (Garden City, N.Y.: Doubleday, 1975), 112.

17. This writer graduated from Geneva College, where the lyrics judged acceptable for Christian worship are restricted to those of the Hebrew psalms. See *The Book of Psalms for Singing* (Pittsburgh: Reformed Presbyterian Church of North America, 1973). For instance, Psalm 100 is structured into four stanzas, with the first reading:

All people that on earth do dwell,
Sing to the Lord with cheerful voice;
Him serve with fear, His praise forth tell;
Come ye before Him and rejoice.

18. See Wilson, *Our Father Abraham*, 185–90.

19. Stanley Hauerwas, *Sanctify Them in the Truth: Holiness Exemplified* (Nashville: Abingdon, 1998), 77–78, 89.

20. A classic presentation of the early Methodist model of church discipline is found in D. Michael Henderson, *John Wesley's Class Meeting: A Model for Making Disciples* (Nappanee, Ind.: Evangel, 1997). There is still widespread attraction to classic communities of serious Christian discipline. See, e.g., Dianne Aprile, *The Abbey of Gethsemani: Place of Peace and Paradox* (Trout Lily, 1998). This volume chronicles 150 years in the life of America's oldest Trappist monastery, a lovely setting in rural Kentucky that was home to Thomas Merton and to which thousands go on spiritual retreat each year.

21. Pinnock, *Flame of Love*, 229.

22. These crucial meanings are explained well in Howard A. Snyder, "The Church as Holy and Charismatic," *Wesleyan Theological Journal* 15, no. 2 (fall 1980): 7–32.

23. See James D. G. Dunn, *Jesus and the Spirit* (London: SCM, 1975), 341.

24. The May/June 2000 issue of *Weavings* is devoted to an exploration of Christian humility.

25. Jürgen Moltmann, *The Spirit of Life: A Universal Affirmation* (Minneapolis: Fortress, 1992), 81.

26. Laurence Stookey, *Calendar: Christ's Time for the Church* (Nashville: Abingdon, 1996), 74.

27. Pinnock, *Flame of Love*, 9.

28. Foster, *Streams of Living Water*, 70–71.

29. Ibid., 83–84.

30. The available literature is rich in both autobiographies and biographies. Note, e.g., the fine biographies of John Wesley (Kenneth Collins, *A Real Christian: The Life of John Wesley* [Abingdon, 1999]) and Charles Wesley (T. Crichton Mitchell, *Charles Wesley: Man with the Dancing Heart* [Kansas City: Beacon Hill, 1994]). A wonderful source of biographical sketches and holiness testimonies is found in Melvin Dieter, ed., *The Nineteenth-Century Holiness Movement* (Kansas City: Beacon Hill, 1998). More contemporary works include *Corrie Ten Boom: Her Story* (New York: Inspirational, 1995) and the autobiographies of Howard Thurman (*With Head and Heart*, Harcourt Brace Jovanovich, 1979) and Elton Trueblood (*While It Is Day*, Harper and Row, 1974). These are but a few biographies available detailing the lives of the saints.

31. Excerpt from the hymn "The Bond of Perfectness" by Daniel S. Warner.

32. A. W. Tozer, *The Pursuit of God* (1948; reprint, Camp Hill, Pa.: Christian Publications, 1982), 96.

33. Charles E. Brown, *A New Approach to Christian Unity* (Anderson, Ind.: Warner, 1931), 170.

34. Stookey, *Calendar*, 150.

35. Foster, *Streams of Living Water*, 106.

36. See Barry L. Callen, *Radical Christianity: The Believers Church Tradition in Christianity's History and Future* (Nappanee, Ind.: Evangel, 1999).

37. See Donald Dayton, *Theological Roots of Pentecostalism* (Lanham, Md.: Scarecrow, 1987; Peabody, Mass.: Hendrickson, 1991). Dayton sees Pentecostalism as part of "an ongoing struggle to understand and make vital for our own time the meaning of the New Testament" (35). He sees as inadequate the interpreting of Pentecostalism "primarily in terms of its most characteristic feature, glossolalia, or 'speaking in tongues'" (15). Rather, it should be seen as an

outgrowth of Methodist emphases and nineteenth-century holiness revivals. Also see Steven J. Land, *Pentecostal Spirituality: A Passion for the Kingdom* (Sheffield, England: Sheffield Academic Press, 1993).

38. J. I. Packer, *Keep in Step with the Spirit* (Grand Rapids: Revell, 1984), 185–97.

39. See Snyder, "The Church as Holy," 7–32.

40. The articles were "A Truce Proposal for the Tongues Controversy" (8 October 1971); "The New Pentecostalism: Reflections by a Well-Wisher" (14 September 1973); and "Opening the Church to the Charismatic Dimension" (12 June 1981). For the full story of Clark Pinnock's theological and spiritual journey, see Callen, *Clark H. Pinnock.*

41. Samuel Powell and Michael Lodahl, eds., *Embodied Holiness: Toward a Corporate Theology of Spiritual Growth* (Downers Grove, Ill.: InterVarsity, 1999).

42. As quoted by Mary Bosanquet, *The Life and Death of Dietrich Bonhoeffer* (New York: Harper and Row, 1968), 80. See Bonhoeffer's *Life Together* (New York: Harper and Row, 1954) where he says, "Let him who cannot be alone beware of community. . . . Let him who is not in community beware of being alone. . . . One who wants fellowship without solitude plunges into the void of words and feelings, and one who seeks solitude without fellowship perishes in the abyss of vanity, self-infatuation, and despair" (77–78).

43. If the intended holiness of the church is an ongoing reflection of the activity of God in Jesus Christ, Theodore Jennings Jr. helpfully notes that the resulting social reality is expressed in "(a) the inclusion and reconciliation of the diverse peoples and cultures of the earth, (b) the empowerment and incorporation of diverse gifts and ministries in the Body of Christ, and (c) the corresponding abandonment of the ways of division and enmity within the community and the demonstration of those spiritual fruits which produce love within the community" (*Loyalty to God* [Nashville: Abingdon, 1992], 187–88).

44. The entire July/August 1988 issue of *Weavings,* titled "Life Together," seeks to explore the role of community in faith development.

45. Simon Chan, *Spiritual Theology: A Systematic Study of the Christian Life* (Downers Grove, Ill.: InterVarsity, 1998), 102–3.

46. At the heart of John Wesley's paradigm of Christian spiritual formation was the class meeting. See Henderson, *John Wesley's Class Meeting.*

Chapter 5: *Truly Knowing: The Spirit's Eyes*

1. Donald Bloesch, *The Holy Spirit: Works and Gifts* (Downers Grove, Ill.: InterVarsity, 2000), 24.

2. See Robert D. Ballard, *The Eternal Darkness* (Princeton, N.J.: Princeton University Press, 2000).

3. D. Elton Trueblood, *The Knowledge of God* (New York: Harper, 1939), 1.

4. Kallistos Ware, *The Orthodox Way* (1979; rev. ed. Crestwood, N.Y.: St. Vladimir's Seminary Press, 1995), 8.

5. Ansel Adams, *Yosemite and the Range of Light* (Boston: Little, Brown, 1979).

6. Anselm of Canterbury in William Barclay, *William Barclay: A Spiritual Autobiography* (Grand Rapids: Eerdmans, 1975), 37.

7. Howard Thurman, *With Head and Heart: The Autobiography of Howard Thurman* (San Diego: Harcourt Brace Jovanovich, 1979), 226.

8. David Wells, *No Place for Truth, or, Whatever Happened to Evangelical Theology?* (Grand Rapids: Eerdmans, 1993).

9. For two excellent sources for exploring a more spirituality-based identity, see Stanley Grenz, *Revisioning Evangelical Theology: A Fresh Agenda for the Twenty-First Century* (Downers Grove, Ill.: InterVarsity, 1993) and Henry Knight III, *A Future for Truth: Evangelical Theology in a Postmodern World* (Nashville: Abingdon, 1997).

10. Marvin R. Wilson, *Our Father Abraham: Jewish Roots of the Christian Faith* (Grand Rapids: Eerdmans; Dayton, Ohio: Center for Judaic-Christian Studies, 1989), 136.

11. Abraham Joshua Heschel, *Man Is Not Alone: A Philosophy of Religion* (New York: Farrar, Straus and Young, 1951), 74, 91.

12. Wilson, *Our Father Abraham,* 153.

13. William J. Abraham, *Canon and Criterion in Christian Theology* (Oxford: Clarendon, 1998).

14. Brennan Manning, *The Signature of Jesus,* rev. ed. (Sisters, Ore.: Multnomah, 1996), 26, 28.

15. Clark Pinnock, "Biblical Texts, Past and Future Meanings," *Wesleyan Theological Journal* 34, no. 2 (fall 1999): 143. Pinnock adds, "Revelation is neither contentless experience (liberalism) nor timeless propositions (conservatism). It is the dynamic self-disclosure of God, who makes his goodness known in the history of salvation, in a process of disclosure culminating in Jesus Christ. Revelation is not primarily existential impact or infallible truths but divine self-revelation that both impacts and instructs. . . . It is our introduction to a Person. Jesus said, 'Whoever has seen me has seen the Father' (John 14:9). Revelation is addressed not only to the intellect but to the whole person" (*Flame of Love: A Theology of the Holy Spirit* [Downers Grove, Ill.: InterVarsity, 1996], 226).

16. M. Robert Mulholland Jr., *Shaped by the Word: The Power of Scripture in Spiritual Formation* (Nashville: Upper Room, 1985).

17. Dwight L. Grubbs, *Beginnings: Spiritual Formation for Leaders* (Lima, Ohio: Fairway, 1994), 31–32.

18. For detail on how this approach to knowing is related to the current postmodern mindset and contrasts with the modern approach, see "Modern/Postmodern" in the glossary of this volume.

19. Abraham, *Canon and Criterion,* 23.

20. Ibid., 27.

21. Ibid., 466–67.

22. Pentecostal scholar Cheryl Bridges Johns contends that in the present environment of our postmodern world, "the scandal of letting go and letting God is the most intellectually respectable position available" ("Partners in Scandal: Wesleyan and Pentecostal Scholarship," *Wesleyan Theological Journal* 34, no. 1 [spring 1999]: 16).

23. Blaise Pascal (1623–1662) took on the task of defending Christian faith against the rationalistic arrogance of those who believed that they could live without God or could mold the divine purposes to their own ends. Pascal denounced the pretentions of many early scientists. He insisted in his *Pensées* that humans are great only as they realize that they are wretched.

24. Trueblood, *The Knowledge of God,* 144–54.

25. Ware, *Orthodox Way,* 8.

26. D. Elton Trueblood, *Robert Barclay* (New York: Harper and Row, 1968), 1–2. While George Fox was the founding genius of the Quakers, Trueblood attributes Robert Barclay with this movement's long survival because Barclay gave credible intellectual structure to what at first was mainly grassroots spiritual enthusiasm.

27. Gregory of Nyssa (c. 330–395) is one of the most important writers of the Christian East. His spiritual writings stress the inability of the human mind to fully comprehend the mystery of God.

28. The movement in question is the Church of God (Anderson), and the dynamic that allows the special "seeing" is experienced holiness. As the primary pioneer of this movement said in lyrics that form beloved songs of this movement, "Fill me with Thy Spirit, Lord, Fully save my longing soul; Through the precious cleansing blood, Purify and make me whole." Given such experienced holiness or perfect love, there should then come the following which connects love to seeing the church: "How sweet this bond of perfectness, The wondrous love

of Jesus! A pure foretaste of heaven's bliss, O fellowship so precious!" (Daniel S. Warner, "The Bond of Perfectness," in *Worship the Lord: Hymnal of the Church of God* [Anderson, Ind.: Warner, 1989], 330).

29. A whole issue of *Weavings* (July/August 1996) is dedicated to the theme of "Praying the Bible."

30. Lawrence LaPierre, "A Model for Describing Spirituality," in *Exploring Christian Spirituality*, ed. Kenneth Collins (Grand Rapids: Baker, 2000), 74.

31. Helmut Thielicke, *A Little Exercise for Young Theologians* (Grand Rapids: Eerdmans, 1962), 1, 8.

32. As quoted by Daniel Clendenin, *Eastern Orthodox Christianity: A Western Perspective* (Grand Rapids: Baker, 1994), 139.

33. Excerpt from the hymn "Open My Eyes, That I May See" by Clara H. Scott.

34. Albert Schweitzer, *The Quest of the Historical Jesus* (New York: Macmillan, 1950), 403.

35. Harry Emerson Fosdick, *What Is Vital in Religion* (New York: Harper, 1955), 96.

36. Alister McGrath, *Spirituality in an Age of Change: Rediscovering the Spirit of the Reformers* (Grand Rapids: Zondervan, 1994), 104.

37. Excerpt from the hymn "I Know Whom I Have Believed" by Daniel W. Whittle.

38. Jürgen Moltmann, *The Spirit of Life: A Universal Affirmation* (Minneapolis: Fortress, 1992), 47.

39. Ibid., 61.

40. McGrath, *Spirituality in an Age of Change*, 163–65.

41. Some interpreters argue that, despite Luther's obvious emphasis, he did hold together the *Christ-for-us* of Lutheran orthodoxy and the *Christ-in-us* of later Lutheran pietism.

42. The major themes of the Eastern church tradition are union with God, silent prayer, emphasis on the Holy Trinity in devotion and life, and synergy (divine-human cooperation in redemption). The union emphasis is not pantheism, but a sharing in the divine life as enabled by grace.

43. Nehemiah Curnock, ed., *The Journal of the Rev. John Wesley, A.M.*, 8 vols. (London: Robert Culley, 1909), 1:83.

44. John Wesley, *A Plain Account of Christian Perfection*, vol. 11 of *The Works of John Wesley*, 14 vols. (Grand Rapids: Baker, 1979), 366.

45. Wesley D. Tracy et al., *The Upward Call: Spiritual Formation and the Holy Life* (Kansas City: Beacon Hill, 1994), 12.

46. John Bunyan, *Pilgrim's Progress* (1678–1684). Teresa of Ávila (1515–1582), a Spanish Carmelite nun, wrote a famous book on prayer titled *Interior Castle*. In the spirit of Bunyan's *Pilgrim's Progress*, she uses allegory to describe the obstacles and joys of the Christian spiritual journey.

47. See, for instance, Daniel S. Warner, *Bible Proofs of the Second Work of Grace* (1880; reprint, Prestonsburg, Ky.: Reformation, 2002).

48. Donald W. Dayton, *Theological Roots of Pentecostalism* (Lanham, Md.: Scarecrow, 1987; Peabody, Mass.: Hendrickson, 1992).

49. See Melvin Dieter, ed., *The Nineteenth-Century Holiness Movement* (Kansas City: Beacon Hill, 1998).

50. Ibid., 303–6.

51. Hannah Whitall Smith, *The Christian's Secret of a Happy Life* (Grand Rapids: Revell, Spire, 1952), 46.

52. Alan Richardson, *Creeds in the Making: A Short Introduction to the History of Christian Doctrine* (Philadelphia: Fortress, 1981), 8.

53. From John Wesley's *Journal* for May 24, 1738.

54. A. W. Tozer, *The Pursuit of God* (1948; reprint, Camp Hill, Pa.: Christian Publications, 1982), 20.

Chapter 6: *Truly Living: The Spirit's Way*

1. J. Horace Germany, *At Any Cost: The Story of a Life in Pursuit of Brotherhood* (Anderson, Ind.: Warner, 2000).

2. Stanley Hauerwas, *Sanctify Them in the Truth: Holiness Exemplified* (Nashville: Abingdon, 1998), 187.

3. The famous book by Thomas à Kempis (c. 1380–1471) on Christian spirituality is titled *The Imitation of Christ.*

4. See the whole January/February 1996 issue of *Weavings,* which is on the theme "Clothed with Christ."

5. William J. Seymour, "Marks of Fanaticism," *The Apostolic Faith* 1, no. 2 (October 1906): 2.

6. Henri Nouwen, *Reaching Out: The Three Movements of the Spiritual Life* (Garden City, N.Y.: Doubleday, 1975), 46.

7. Christine D. Pohl, *Making Room: Recovering Hospitality as a Christian Tradition* (Grand Rapids: Eerdmans, 1999), 8.

8. Stephen Barton, *The Spirituality of the Gospels* (Peabody, Mass.: Hendrickson, 1992), 102. See J. Koenig, *New Testament Hospitality: Partnership with Strangers as Promise and Mission* (Philadelphia: Fortress, 1985), 85–123.

9. Merle Strege, *Tell Me the Tale: Historical Reflections on the Church of God* (Anderson, Ind.: Warner, 1991), 6.

10. John Mogabgab, editor's introduction, *Weavings* 9, no. 1 (January/February 1994): 3.

11. See Esther de Waal, *Seeking God: The Way of St. Benedict* (Collegeville, Minn.: Liturgical, 1984). Note also that the Abbey of Gethsemani in Kentucky is a monastery with a ministry of hospitality. For many years I have been welcomed there for retreats with graciousness and without charge.

12. Frederick Buechner, *Peculiar Treasures: A Biblical Who's Who* (San Francisco: Harper-SanFrancisco, 1979), 172–73.

13. Barry L. Callen, ed., *Sharing Heaven's Music: The Heart of Christian Preaching* (Nashville: Abingdon, 1995), 125.

14. Ibid., 133.

15. Dimensions of this hilarious Christian life are explored in the November/December 1994 issue of *Weavings,* titled "Hilarity."

16. For an extended discussion of Jesus and humor, see David Elton Trueblood, *The Humor of Christ* (New York: Harper and Row, 1964).

17. Excerpt from the song "I Then Shall Live" by Gloria Gaither.

18. Jürgen Moltmann, *The Spirit of Life: A Universal Affirmation* (Minneapolis: Fortress, 1992), 40.

19. John H. Westerhoff III, *A Pilgrim People: Learning through the Church Year* (Minneapolis: Seabury, 1984), 34, 41.

20. Richard Foster, *Celebration of Discipline: The Path to Spiritual Growth* (San Francisco: Harper and Row, 1978).

21. Evelyn Underhill, *The School of Charity: Meditations on the Christian Creed* (New York: Longmans, Green, 1954), 15–16.

22. Georgia Harkness, *The Church and the Immigrant* (New York: George Doran, 1921), 100–101. An excellent biography of Harkness is Rosemary Skinner Keller, *Georgia Harkness: For Such a Time as This* (Nashville: Abingdon, 1992).

23. Barry L. Callen, *God as Loving Grace* (Nappanee, Ind.: Evangel, 1996), 193.

24. Brennan Manning, *The Signature of Jesus,* rev. ed. (Sisters, Ore.: Multnomah, 1996), 8.

25. Vatican Council II of the Roman Catholic Church now has also sought to reclaim the concept of the laity as the people of God.

26. Martin Luther, *Appeal to the German Nobility* (1520).

27. Martin Luther, *The Freedom of a Christian* (1520).

28. Dietrich Bonhoeffer, *Letters and Papers from Prison*, ed. Eberhard Bethge, enl. ed. (New York: Macmillan, 1971), 380–83.

29. For a full introduction to the radical reformation, see Barry L. Callen, *Radical Christianity: The Believers Church Tradition in Christianity's History and Future* (Nappanee, Ind.: Evangel, 1999). John Wesley showed a close affinity with this tradition (see Howard Snyder, *The Radical Wesley and Patterns of Church Renewal* [Downers Grove, Ill.: InterVarsity, 1980]).

30. Alan Kreider, *Journey towards Holiness: A Way of Living for God's Nation* (Scottdale, Pa.: Herald, 1987), 15.

31. Ibid., 242.

32. Philip Yancey, "The Holy Inefficiency of Henri Nouwen," *Christianity Today*, 9 December 1996, 80.

33. Henri Nouwen, *In the Name of Jesus: Reflections on Christian Leadership* (New York: Crossroad, 1989), 17, 22.

34. Donald Kline, *Susanna Wesley* (Lima, Ohio: C.S.S. Publishing, 1980), 42. Reflecting in his later years, John Wesley recalled with such appreciation his mother's educational practices with the children that he asked her to collect for him the principal rules she had practiced.

35. Richard Foster, *Streams of Living Water: Celebrating the Great Traditions of Christian Faith* (San Francisco: HarperSanFrancisco, 1998), 262–63.

36. Laurence Stookey, *Eucharist: Christ's Feast with the Church* (Nashville: Abingdon, 1993), 95–96.

37. In 1963, Martin Luther King Jr. published a series of his sermons under the title *Strength to Love* (New York: Harper and Row).

38. Martin Luther King Jr., as quoted by Wayne Phillips, "Negroes Pledge to Keep Boycott," *New York Times*, 24 February 1956, 8.

39. See Dorothy Day, *The Long Loneliness: The Autobiography of Dorothy Day* (New York: Harper, 1952).

40. H. Ray Dunning, *A Layman's Guide to the Apostles' Creed* (Kansas City: Beacon Hill, 1995), 19.

41. This is the classic phrase of the German theologian Dietrich Bonhoeffer. Similarly, William Temple of England once said, "Christianity is the most materialistic of all religions" (taking seriously the creating and re-creating God).

42. Theodore Jennings Jr., *Loyalty to God: The Apostles' Creed in Life and Liturgy* (Nashville: Abingdon, 1992), 226.

43. Excerpt from the hymn "Are You Adorning the Doctrine?" by Charles W. Naylor.

44. Richard B. Hays, *The Moral Vision of the New Testament* (San Francisco: HarperSanFrancisco, 1996), 193–205.

45. Mary Bosanquet, *The Life and Death of Dietrich Bonhoeffer* (New York: Harper and Row, 1968), 70. Emphasis added.

46. Robert Barron, *And Now I See . . .* (New York: Crossroad, 1998), 3.

Chapter 7: *Truly Abiding: The Spirit's Assurance*

1. Barry L. Callen, *Faithful in the Meantime: A Biblical View of Final Things and Present Responsibilities* (Nappanee, Ind.: Evangel, 1997), 264.

2. Steven J. Land, *Pentecostal Spirituality: A Passion for the Kingdom* (Sheffield, England: Sheffield Academic Press, 1993), 72–73.

3. C. S. Lewis, *The Weight of Glory and Other Addresses* (New York: Macmillan, 1980), 16–17.

4. See Callen, *Faithful in the Meantime.*

5. Theodore Jennings Jr., *Loyalty to God: The Apostles' Creed in Life and Liturgy* (Nashville: Abingdon, 1992), 172.

6. Land, *Pentecostal Spirituality,* 53–54. Emphasis added.

7. Malcolm Muggeridge, *A Third Testament* (Boston: Little, Brown, 1976), 49.

8. William Barclay, *A New Testament Wordbook* (New York: Harper, n.d.), 61.

9. *The Martyrdom of Polycarp* is the earliest extant record of a martyrdom beyond the biblical record. It was a letter intended to circulate among early churches, along with other materials compiled by Marcion. It is presumed to be based on eyewitness accounts.

10. Elaine V. Emeth, "Lessons from the Holocaust: Living Faithfully in the Midst of Chaos," *Weavings* 13, no. 2 (March/April 1998): 17.

11. In the ultimate sense, God is of course in control of all things, or he would not be God. However, in granting relative freedom to humans, God has chosen not to determine and manipulate all things—at least not for now. See Barry L. Callen, *Clark H. Pinnock: Journey toward Renewal* (Nappanee, Ind.: Evangel, 2000), chapter 5.

12. Emeth, "Lessons from the Holocaust," 17. Also see the extensive study of Christian theism by John Sanders, *The God Who Risks: A Theology of Providence* (Downers Grove, Ill.: InterVarsity, 1998); Callen, *Clark H. Pinnock,* chapter 5.

13. Note the famous Christian spiritual classic titled *The Practice of the Presence of God* by Brother Lawrence (1692). Beginning in 1666, this resident of a Carmelite order in Paris, France, worked in the kitchen, blending work and prayer and calling himself "a servant of the servants of God."

14. Robert E. Webber, *Ancient-Future Faith: Rethinking Evangelicalism for a Postmodern World* (Grand Rapids: Baker, 1999), 108.

15. Excerpt from the hymn "Under His Wings" by William O. Cushing.

16. See Callen, *Faithful in the Meantime.*

17. Frank C. Laubach, *Letters by a Modern Mystic* (1937; reprint, Syracuse, N.Y.: New Readers, 1979), 9.

18. Parker J. Palmer, *The Company of Strangers: Christians and the Renewal of America's Public Life* (New York: Crossroad, 1992), 155.

19. A vigorous contemporary call for such equitable distribution is Ronald J. Sider, *Rich Christians in an Age of Hunger* (Downers Grove, Ill.: InterVarsity, 1977).

20. See Douglas M. Strong, *They Walked in the Spirit: Personal Faith and Social Action in America* (Louisville: Westminster John Knox, 1997), 120–23.

21. It is common today to deride otherworldly piety in favor of identifying with the oppressed of the world in their struggle for liberation. But, as Donald Bloesch rightly says, "It is possible to go so far in this direction that we lose sight of the fact that meaningful identification with the oppressed rests upon a prior identification with the Savior of the oppressed" (*The Struggle of Prayer* [Colorado Springs: Helmers and Howard, 1988], 166).

22. Humility in the early desert tradition of Christianity was in part a witness against the power and splendor of what had quickly become an imperial Christianity in league with the secular Roman Empire.

23. Douglas Strong, "Sanctified Eccentricity: The Continuing Relevance of the Nineteenth Century Holiness Paradigm," *Wesleyan Theological Journal* 35, no. 1 (spring 2000): 18.

24. Richard Foster, *Streams of Living Water: Celebrating the Great Traditions of Christian Faith* (San Francisco: HarperSanFrancisco, 1998), 178.

25. Charles Colson and Nancy Pearcey, *How Now Shall We Live?* (Wheaton: Tyndale, 1999), 467.

26. Brennan Manning, *The Signature of Jesus,* rev. ed. (Sisters, Ore.: Multnomah, 1996), 107, emphasis added.

27. H. Ray Dunning, *A Layman's Guide to the Apostles' Creed* (Kansas City: Beacon Hill, 1995), 31.

28. Clark H. Pinnock, *Flame of Love: A Theology of the Holy Spirit* (Downers Grove, Ill.: InterVarsity, 1996), 207.

29. Ibid., 222.

30. Martin Luther, as quoted by Alister McGrath, *Spirituality in an Age of Change: Rediscovering the Spirit of the Reformers* (Grand Rapids: Zondervan, 1994), 196.

31. Excerpt from the hymn "I Know Whom I Have Believed" by Daniel W. Whittle.

32. See Stanley Hauerwas and William Willimon, *Resident Aliens: Life in the Christian Colony* (Nashville: Abingdon, 1991).

33. See the November/December 1991 issue of *Weavings,* which develops the theme, "Passing through the Land."

34. Editor's introduction, *Weavings* (July/August 1998): 2.

35. Pinnock, *Flame of Love,* 247.

36. E. Stanley Jones, *A Song of Ascents: A Spiritual Autobiography* (Nashville: Abingdon, 1968), 17, 44.

37. See David Bundy, "The Theology of the Kingdom of God in E. Stanley Jones," *Wesleyan Theological Journal* 23, nos. 1–2 (spring–fall 1988): 58–80.

38. Jones, *A Song of Ascents,* 110, 80–82. Jones authored many other books full of wisdom and resources for spiritual insight and growth. Among them are *Conversion, Growing Spiritually, Christian Maturity,* and *Abundant Living.*

39. Naomi Levy, *To Begin Again* (New York: Ballantine, 1998), 156–57.

40. Barry L. Callen, *God as Loving Grace* (Nappanee, Ind.: Evangel, 1996), 340.

41. Excerpt from the hymn "Abide with Me" by Henry F. Lyte.

42. Excerpt from the hymn "Blessed Assurance" by Fanny Crosby.

43. Harry Emerson Fosdick, *The Living of These Days* (New York: Harper and Row, 1956), 312–13, 319.

44. David Elton Trueblood, *While It Is Day* (New York: Harper and Row, 1974), 161–62.

Chapter 8: *Truly Growing: Paths to Sanctification*

1. James Earl Massey, *Spiritual Disciplines: Growth through the Practice of Prayer, Fasting, Dialogue, and Worship* (Grand Rapids: Zondervan, Francis Asbury, 1985), 116.

2. Robert Barron, *And Now I See: A Theology of Transformation* (New York: Crossroad, 1998), 1.

3. Simon Chan, *Spiritual Theology: A Systematic Study of the Christian Life* (Downers Grove, Ill.: InterVarsity, 1998), 141.

4. Warren Lane Molton, *Bruised Reeds* (Valley Forge: Judson, 1970), 91. Warren was a student colleague of mine in Chicago during the troubled late 1960s.

5. Dwight L. Grubbs, *Beginnings: Spiritual Formation for Leaders* (Lima, Ohio: Fairway, 1994), 36–37.

6. E. Glenn Hinson, *Spiritual Preparation for Christian Leadership* (Nashville: Upper Room, 1999).

7. John H. Westerhoff, *Spiritual Life: The Foundation for Preaching and Teaching* (Louisville: Westminster/John Knox, 1994), x–xi.

8. Note, for instance, Reginald Johnson, *Your Personality and the Spiritual Life* (Wheaton: Victor, 1995).

9. Walter Brueggemann, Charles Cousar, et al., *Texts for Preaching: A Lectionary Commentary Based on the NRSV* (Louisville: Westminster John Knox, 1993—Year B; 1994—Year C; 1995—Year A).

10. Stephen A. Seamands, *Holiness of Heart and Life* (Nashville: Abingdon, 1990), 18.

11. See Walter Brueggemann, *The Message of the Psalms: A Theological Commentary* (Minneapolis: Augsburg, 1984); and Patrick Miller, ed., *The Psalms and the Life of Faith* (Minneapolis: Fortress, 1995).

12. Steve Harper, *Praying through the Lord's Prayer* (Nashville: Upper Room, 1992).

13. As quoted in Bob Benson and Michael W. Benson, *Disciplines for the Inner Life*, rev. ed. (Waco: Word, 1985; Nashville: Generoux/Nelson, 1989), 239.

14. Samuel E. Balentine, *Prayer in the Hebrew Bible: The Drama of Divine-Human Dialogue* (Minneapolis: Fortress, 1993), 284.

15. Massey, *Spiritual Disciplines*, 66–67.

16. Maxie Dunnam, *The Workbook of Living Prayer* (1964; Nashville: Upper Room, 1994), 11. Compare James Bryan Smith, *A Spiritual Formation Workbook* (San Francisco: HarperSanFrancisco, 1991, 1993).

17. Randy Maddox, "Reconnecting the Means to the End: A Wesleyan Prescription for the Holiness Movement," *Wesleyan Theological Journal* 33, no. 2 (fall 1998): 31.

18. A good overview of the means of grace as they traditionally have been understood in the Wesleyan tradition is found in Dean G. Blevins, "The Means of Grace: Toward a Wesleyan Praxis of Spiritual Formation," *Wesleyan Theological Journal* 32, no. 1 (spring 1997): 69–83. See also Kenneth Collins, *Soul Care: Deliverance and Renewal through the Christian Life* (Wheaton: Victor, 1995). Collins explores "Abiding in the Kingdom of God" by detailing in chapters 7 and 8 the personal and public "disciplines of the liberated life" that are necessary "to thrive, spiritually speaking, by receiving the ongoing grace of the One who is beyond us" (11).

19. As quoted by D. Michael Henderson, *John Wesley's Class Meeting: A Model for Making Disciples* (Nappanee, Ind.: Evangel, 1997), 84.

20. John Wesley, *The Works of John Wesley*, 3d ed. (Peabody, Mass.: Hendrickson, 1986), 5:187.

21. See Blevins, "The Means of Grace," 69–83.

22. Thomas C. Oden, *Life in the Spirit* (San Francisco: HarperSanFrancisco, 1992), 66.

23. Hinson, *Spiritual Preparation*, 35.

24. Alister McGrath, *Beyond the Quiet Time: Practical Evangelical Spirituality* (Grand Rapids: Baker, 1995), 11.

Glossary

1. Steven J. Land, *Pentecostal Spirituality: A Passion for the Kingdom* (Sheffield, England: Sheffield Academic Press, 1993), 222–23.

2. Laurence Stookey, *Calendar: Christ's Time for the Church* (Nashville: Abingdon, 1996), 11.

3. Ibid., 33.

Select Spiritual Leaders of the Christian Tradition

Years of Life	Name	Affiliation
c. 70–c. 160	Polycarp	Early bishop and martyr
120–202	Irenaeus	A father of the church
c. 155–220	Clement of Alexandria	A father of the church
185–254	Origen	A father of the church
c. 251–356	St. Anthony of Egypt	"Father of monks"
c. 331–396	Gregory of Nyssa	A father of the church
354–430	St. Augustine	A father of the church
1090–1153	Bernard of Clairvaux	Roman Catholic
1182–1226	Francis of Assisi	Roman Catholic
1225–1274	Thomas Aquinas	Roman Catholic
1380–1471	Thomas à Kempis	Roman Catholic
1483–1546	Martin Luther	Roman Catholic/Lutheran
1491–1556	Ignatius of Loyola	Roman Catholic
1496–1561	Menno Simons	Anabaptist/Mennonite
1509–1564	John Calvin	Reformed/Presbyterian
1515–1582	Teresa of Ávila	Roman Catholic
1611–1691	Brother Lawrence	Roman Catholic
1613–1667	Jeremy Taylor	Anglican
1623–1662	Blaise Pascal	Mathematician, mystic
1624–1691	George Fox	Quaker (Friends)
1628–1688	John Bunyan	Baptist
1635–1705	Philipp Jakob Spener	Lutheran
1679–1735	Alexander Mack	Brethren
1703–1791	John Wesley	Anglican/Methodist
1703–1758	Jonathan Edwards	Congregational
1707–1788	Charles Wesley	Anglican/Methodist
1714–1770	George Whitefield	Anglican
1720–1772	John Woolman	Quaker (Friends)

Years of Life	Name	Affiliation
1745–1816	Francis Asbury	Methodist
1807–1874	Phoebe Palmer	Methodist
1818–1855	Søren Kierkegaard	Danish philosopher
1820–1915	Fanny Crosby	American hymn writer
1824–1914	Daniel Steele	Methodist
1828–1905	J. A. Wood	Methodist
1829–1890	Catherine Booth	Salvation Army
1832–1911	Hannah Whitall Smith	Quaker/Presbyterian
1842–1895	Daniel S. Warner	Church of God (Anderson)
1863–1948	Rufus M. Jones	Quaker (Friends)
1870–1922	William J. Seymour	Pentecostal
1875–1941	Evelyn Underhill	Anglo-Catholic mystic
1881–1944	William Temple	Anglican
1884–1973	E. Stanley Jones	Methodist
1884–1970	Frank Laubach	Congregational
1886–1960	John Baillie	Church of Scotland
1891–1974	Georgia Harkness	Methodist
1892–1980	George A. Buttrick	Presbyterian
1893–1941	Thomas Kelly	Quaker (Friends)
1897–1980	Dorothy Day	Roman Catholic
1897–1963	A. W. Tozer	Christian and Missionary Alliance
1898–1963	C. S. Lewis	English professor, novelist
1900–1981	Howard Thurman	Baptist
1900–	D. Elton Trueblood	Quaker (Friends)
1901–1995	Douglas V. Steere	Quaker (Friends)
1906–1945	Dietrich Bonhoeffer	Lutheran
1906–1982	J. B. Phillips	Anglican
1910–1997	Mother Teresa	Roman Catholic
1912–	R. Eugene Sterner	Church of God (Anderson)
1915–1968	Thomas Merton	Roman Catholic
1926–	J. I. Packer	Anglican Evangelical
1928–	Donald G. Bloesch	United Church of Christ
1929–1968	Martin Luther King Jr.	Baptist
1930–	James Earl Massey	Church of God (Anderson)
1932–1996	Henri Nouwen	Roman Catholic
1933–	Dwight L. Grubbs	Church of God (Anderson)
1934–	Brennan Manning	Roman Catholic
1934–	Maxie Dunnam	United Methodist
1936–	M. Robert Mulholland Jr.	United Methodist
1936–	William J. Gaither	Church of God (Anderson)
1937–	Clark H. Pinnock	Baptist
1939–	Geoffrey Wainwright	United Methodist
1939–	Ronald J. Sider	Brethren in Christ
1942–	Gloria Gaither	Church of God (Anderson)
1942–	Richard Foster	Quaker (Friends)
1952–	Kenneth J. Collins	United Methodist
1953–	Alister McGrath	Anglican

Select Bibliography

Histories, Anthologies, Dictionaries, and Lectionary Commentaries

Bouyer, Louis. *A History of Christian Spirituality*. Vol. 1, *The Spirituality of the New Testament and the Fathers*. New York: Seabury, Crossroad, 1963.

———. *A History of Christian Spirituality*. Vol. 3, *Orthodox Spirituality and Protestant and Anglican Spirituality*. New York: Seabury, Crossroad, 1969.

Brueggemann, Walter, Charles Cousar, et al. *Texts for Preaching: A Lectionary Commentary Based on the NRSV*, Year A. Louisville: Westminster John Knox, 1995.

———. *Texts for Preaching: A Lectionary Commentary Based on the NRSV*, Year B. Louisville: Westminster John Knox, 1993.

———. *Texts for Preaching: A Lectionary Commentary Based on the NRSV*, Year C. Louisville: Westminster John Knox, 1994.

Castle, Tony. *The Perfection of Love: An Anthology from the Spiritual Writers*. London: Collins, 1986.

Christensen, Bernhard. *The Inward Pilgrimage: Spiritual Classics from Augustine to Bonhoeffer*. Minneapolis: Augsburg, 1976.

Collins, Kenneth J., ed. *Exploring Christian Spirituality: An Ecumenical Reader*. Grand Rapids: Baker, 2000.

Dunne, Sean. *Something Understood: A Spiritual Anthology*. Dublin: Marino, 1995.

Dupré, Louis, and Don E. Saliers, eds. *Christian Spirituality: Post-Reformation and Modern*. New York: Crossroad, 1989.

Foster, Richard, and Emilie Griffin, eds. *Spiritual Classics: Selected Readings*. San Francisco: HarperSanFrancisco, 2000.

Foster, Richard, and James Bryan Smith, eds. *Devotional Classics: Selected Readings*. San Francisco: HarperSanFrancisco, 1993.

Holmes, Urban T. *A History of Christian Spirituality*. New York: Seabury, 1980.

Holt, Bradley. *Thirsty for God: A Brief History of Christian Spirituality*. Minneapolis: Augsburg Fortress, 1993.

Jones, Cheslyn, Geoffrey Wainwright, and Edward Yarnold. *The Study of Spirituality*. New York: Oxford University Press, 1986.

Kepler, Thomas S., ed. *An Anthology of Devotional Literature*. Nappanee, Ind.: Evangel, 2000.

Leclercq, Jean, et al. *A History of Christian Spirituality*. Vol. 2, *The Spirituality of the Middle Ages*. 1968; reprint, Minneapolis: Seabury, 1982.

McGinn, Bernard, et al., eds. *Christian Spirituality: Origins to the Twelfth Century.* New York: Crossroad, 1985.

———, ed. The Classics of Western Spirituality: A Library of the Great Spiritual Masters. Numerous vols. New York: Paulist, 1978–.

Maas, Robin, and Gabriel O'Donnell. *Spiritual Traditions for the Contemporary Church.* Nashville: Abingdon, 1990.

Macquarrie, John. *Paths in Spirituality.* New York: Harper and Row, 1972; rev. ed., Harrisburg, Pa.: Morehouse, 1992.

Magill, Frank N., and Ian P. McGreal. *Christian Spirituality: The Essential Guide to the Most Influential Spiritual Writings of the Christian Tradition.* San Francisco: Harper and Row, 1988.

Mogabgab, John S., ed. *The Weavings Reader: Living with God in the World.* Nashville: Upper Room, 1993.

Raitt, Jill. *Christian Spirituality: High Middle Ages and Reformation.* New York: Crossroad, 1988.

Seen, Frank C., ed. *Protestant Spiritual Traditions.* New York: Paulist, 1986.

Tyson, John R. *Invitation to Christian Spirituality: An Ecumenical Anthology.* New York: Oxford University Press, 1999.

Van de Weyer, Robert. *Roots of Faith: An Anthology of Early Christian Spirituality to Contemplate and Treasure.* Grand Rapids: Eerdmans, 1997.

Wakefield, Gordon S., ed. *The Westminster Dictionary of Christian Spirituality.* Philadelphia: Westminster, 1983.

Journals Rich in Dimensions of Christian Spirituality

Journal of Pentecostal Studies

Pneuma

Spiritual Life (a Catholic quarterly)

Spiritus (journal of the Society for the Study of Christian Spirituality)

The Way: Review of Contemporary Christian Spirituality (published in England)

Weavings: A Journal of the Christian Spiritual Life

Wesleyan Theological Journal

Select Classics of Christian Spirituality Written before 1980

Athanasius, Saint. *The Life of Anthony.* 357.

Augustine, Saint. *The Confessions of St. Augustine.* c. 398.

———. *The City of God.* c. 413–426.

Baillie, John. *A Diary of Private Prayer.* 1936.

Barclay, William. *The Apostles' Creed for Everyman.* 1967.

Benedict, Saint Benedict of Nursia. *The Rule of St. Benedict.* c. 528.

Bloesch, Donald G. *Wellsprings of Renewal: Promise in Christian Communal Life.* 1974.

Bonhoeffer, Dietrich. *The Cost of Discipleship.* 1937; rev. ed., 1963.

———. *Life Together.* 1954.

Buechner, Frederick. *Peculiar Treasures: A Biblical Who's Who.* 1979.

Bunyan, John. *Pilgrim's Progress.* 1678, 1684.

Buttrick, George A. *Prayer*. 1942.

Chambers, Oswald. *My Utmost for His Highest*. 1935.

Clark, Glenn. *The Soul's Sincere Desire*. 1953.

Dunnam, Maxie. *The Workbook of Living Prayer*. Nashville: Upper Room, 1974.

Fosdick, Harry Emerson. *The Meaning of Prayer*. 1949.

———. *What Is Vital in Religion*. 1955.

Foster, Richard J. *Celebration of Discipline*. 1978.

Fox, George. *The Journal of George Fox*. 1694.

Harkness, Georgia. *Mysticism: Its Meaning and Message*. 1973.

Ignatius of Loyola. *Spiritual Exercises*. 1548.

Irenaeus. *Against Heresies*. c. 190.

Jones, E. Stanley. *A Song of Ascents: A Spiritual Autobiography*. 1968.

Jones, Rufus Matthew. *Practical Christianity*. 1899.

Kelly, Thomas R. *A Testament of Devotion*. 1941.

Kepler, Thomas S., compiler. *The Fellowship of the Saints*. 1948. Reprinted as *An Anthology of Devotional Literature*. 2001.

Kierkegaard, Søren. *For Self-Examination*. 1851.

King, Martin Luther, Jr. *Strength to Love*. 1963.

Laubach, Frank C. *Letters by a Modern Mystic*. 1937.

Law, William. *A Serious Call to a Devout and Holy Life*. 1728.

Lawrence, Brother. *The Practice of the Presence of God*. 1692.

Lewis, C. S. *Mere Christianity*. 1943.

Luther, Martin. *The Freedom of a Christian*. 1520.

Merton, Thomas. *The Seven Storey Mountain*. 1948.

———. *New Seeds of Contemplation*. 1962.

Muggeridge, Malcolm. *A Third Testament*. 1976.

Packer, J. I. *Knowing God*. 1973.

Palmer, Phoebe. *The Way of Holiness*. 1843.

Pascal, Blaise. *Pensées*. 1670.

Pinnock, Clark H. *Truth on Fire: The Message of Galatians*. 1972.

Sider, Ronald J. *Rich Christians in an Age of Hunger*. 1977.

Smith, Hannah Whitall. *The Christian's Secret of a Happy Life*. 1870.

Spener, Philipp Jakob. *Pia Desideria*. 1675.

Taylor, Jeremy. *The Rule and Exercise of Holy Living and Holy Dying*. 1650.

Thomas à Kempis. *The Imitation of Christ*. c. 1418.

Thurman, Howard. *Jesus and the Disinherited*. 1949.

Tozer, A. W. *The Pursuit of God*. 1948.

Trueblood, D. Elton. *The Essence of Spiritual Religion*. 1936.

———. *The Knowledge of God*. 1939.

———. *A Place to Stand*. 1969.

Underhill, Evelyn. *Mysticism*. 1911.

———. *The School of Charity: Meditations on the Christian Creed*. 1934.

Wesley, John. *The Journal of John Wesley*. 1735–90.

———. *A Plain Account of Christian Perfection.* 1766.

Woolman, John. *The Journal of John Woolman.* 1774.

Wynkoop, Mildred Bangs. *A Theology of Love: The Dynamic of Wesleyanism.* 1972.

Select Works on Christian Spirituality Written since 1980

Abraham, William J. *Canon and Criterion in Christian Theology.* Oxford: Clarendon, 1998.

Alexander, Donald L., ed. *Christian Spirituality: Five Views of Sanctification.* Downers Grove, Ill.: InterVarsity, 1988.

Balentine, Samuel. *Prayer in the Hebrew Bible: The Drama of Divine-Human Dialogue.* Minneapolis: Fortress, 1993.

Barron, Robert. *Thomas Aquinas: Spiritual Master.* New York: Crossroad, 1996.

Barton, Stephen C. *The Spirituality of the Gospels.* Peabody, Mass.: Hendrickson, 1992.

Benson, Bob, and Michael W. Benson. *Disciplines for the Inner Life.* Rev. ed. Waco: Word, 1985; Nashville: Generoux/Nelson, 1989.

Bloesch, Donald G. *The Crisis of Piety: Essays toward a Theology of the Christian Life.* 2d ed. Colorado Springs: Helmers and Howard, 1988.

———. *The Struggle of Prayer.* Colorado Springs: Helmers and Howard, 1988.

Bondi, Roberta C. *To Pray and to Love: Conversations on Prayer with the Early Church.* Minneapolis: Fortress, 1991.

Briscoe, Stuart. *The Apostles' Creed: Beliefs That Matter.* Wheaton: Harold Shaw, 1994.

Brown, Dale W. *Understanding Pietism.* Rev. ed. Nappanee, Ind.: Evangel, 1996.

Brown, Robert McAfee. *Spirituality and Liberation: Overcoming the Great Fallacy.* Louisville: Westminster, 1988.

Brueggemann, Walter. *The Psalms and the Life of Faith,* ed. Patrick Miller. Minneapolis: Fortress, 1995.

Callen, Barry L. *God as Loving Grace.* Nappanee, Ind.: Evangel, 1996.

———. *Radical Christianity: The Believers Church Tradition in Christianity's History and Future.* Nappanee, Ind.: Evangel, 1999.

———. *Authentic Spirituality: Moving beyond Mere Religion.* Grand Rapids: Baker, 2001.

Chan, Simon. *Spiritual Theology: A Systematic Study of the Christian Life.* Downers Grove, Ill.: InterVarsity, 1998.

Collins, Kenneth J. *Soul Care: Deliverance and Renewal through the Christian Life.* Wheaton: Victor, 1995.

———, ed. *Exploring Christian Spirituality: An Ecumenical Reader.* Grand Rapids: Baker, 2000.

Corduan, Winfried. *Mysticism: An Evangelical Option?* Grand Rapids: Zondervan, 1991.

Cunningham, Lawrence S., and Keith J. Egan. *Christian Spirituality: Themes from the Tradition.* New York: Paulist, 1996.

Dieter, Melvin, ed. *The Nineteenth-Century Holiness Movement.* Kansas City: Beacon Hill, 1998.

Driskill, Joseph. *Protestant Spiritual Exercises: Theology, History, and Practice.* Harrisburg, Pa.: Morehouse, 1999.

Dyck, Cornelius J. *Spiritual Life in Anabaptism.* Scottdale, Pa.: Herald, 1995.

Foster, Richard J. *Prayer: Finding the Heart's True Home.* San Francisco: HarperSanFrancisco, 1992.

———. *Streams of Living Water: Celebrating the Great Traditions of Christian Faith*. San Francisco: HarperSanFrancisco, 1998.

Graham, Billy. *Just As I Am: The Autobiography of Billy Graham*. San Francisco: HarperSanFrancisco; Grand Rapids: Zondervan, 1997.

Greathouse, William M. *Wholeness in Christ: Toward a Biblical Theology of Holiness*. Kansas City: Beacon Hill, 1998.

Grubbs, Dwight L. *Beginnings: Spiritual Formation for Leaders*. Lima, Ohio: Fairway, 1994.

Harper, Steve. *Praying through the Lord's Prayer*. Nashville: Upper Room, 1992.

Henderson, D. Michael. *John Wesley's Class Meeting: A Model for Making Disciples*. Nappanee, Ind.: Evangel, 1997.

Hinson, E. Glenn. *Spiritual Preparation for Christian Leadership*. Nashville: Upper Room, 1999.

Johnson, Reginald. *Your Personality and the Spiritual Life*. 1988; Wheaton: Victor, 1995.

Jones, Kenneth E. *Commitment to Holiness*. Anderson, Ind.: Warner, 1985.

Kreider, Alan. *Journey towards Holiness: A Way of Living for God's Nation*. Scottdale, Pa.: Herald, 1987.

Land, Steven J. *Pentecostal Spirituality: A Passion for the Kingdom*. Sheffield, England: Sheffield Academic Press, 1993.

Leech, Kenneth. *True Prayer: An Invitation to Christian Spirituality*. New York: Harper and Row, 1980; reprint, Harrisburg, Pa.: Morehouse, 1995.

———. *Experiencing God: Theology as Spirituality*. San Francisco: Harper and Row, 1985.

McGrath, Alister E. *Spirituality in an Age of Change: Rediscovering the Spirit of the Reformers*. Grand Rapids: Zondervan, 1994.

———. *Beyond the Quiet Time: Practical Evangelical Spirituality*. Grand Rapids: Baker, 1995.

———. *Christian Spirituality*. Malden, Mass.: Blackwell, 1999.

Macquarrie, John. *Paths in Spirituality*. 2d. ed. Harrisburg, Pa.: Morehouse, 1992.

Manning, Brennan. *The Signature of Jesus*. Rev. ed. Sisters, Ore.: Multnomah, 1996.

Massey, James Earl. *Spiritual Disciplines: Growth through the Practice of Prayer, Fasting, Dialogue, and Worship*. Grand Rapids: Zondervan, Francis Asbury, 1985.

Mitchell, T. Crichton. *Charles Wesley: Man with the Dancing Heart*. Kansas City: Beacon Hill, 1994.

Moltmann, Jürgen. *The Spirit of Life: A Universal Affirmation*. Minneapolis: Fortress, 1992.

Mulholland, M. Robert, Jr. *Shaped by the Word: The Power of Scripture in Spiritual Formation*. Nashville: Upper Room, 1985.

Nouwen, Henri. *Making All Things New: An Invitation to the Spiritual Life*. 1981.

Oden, Thomas C. *Life in the Spirit*. San Francisco: HarperSanFrancisco, 1992.

Packer, J. I. *Keep in Step with the Spirit*. Grand Rapids: Revell, 1984.

Palmer, Parker. *The Active Life: A Spirituality of Work, Creativity, and Caring*. San Francisco: Jossey-Bass, 1990.

———. *The Company of Strangers: Christians and the Renewal of America's Public Life*. New York: Crossroad, 1992.

Pannenberg, Wolfhart. *Christian Spirituality*. Philadelphia: Westminster, 1983.

Pennington, M. Basil. *Centering Prayer*. Garden City, N.Y.: Image Books, 1980, 1982.

Pinnock, Clark H. *Three Keys to Spiritual Renewal*. Minneapolis: Bethany, 1985. In Canada, *The Untapped Power of Sheer Christianity*. Burlington, Ont.: Welch.

———. *Flame of Love: A Theology of the Holy Spirit*. Downers Grove, Ill.: InterVarsity, 1996.

Powell, Samuel, and Michael Lodahl, eds. *Embodied Holiness: Toward a Corporate Theology of Spiritual Growth*. Downers Grove, Ill.: InterVarsity, 1999.

Smith, James Bryan. *A Spiritual Formation Workbook*. San Francisco: HarperSanFrancisco, 1993.

Sterner, R. Eugene. *Keys to Sp'ritual Freedom*. Anderson, Ind.: Warner, 1999.

Stookey, Laurence Hull. *Calendar: Christ's Time for the Church*. Nashville: Abingdon, 1996.

———. *Eucharist: Christ's Feast with the Church*. Nashville: Abingdon, 1993.

Strong, Douglas M. *They Walked in the Spirit: Personal Faith and Social Action in America*. Louisville: Westminster John Knox, 1997.

Tiessen, Terrance. *Providence and Prayer*. Downers Grove, Ill.: InterVarsity, 2000.

Tracy, Wesley D., et al. *The Upward Call: Spiritual Formation and the Holy Life*. Kansas City: Beacon Hill, 1994.

Tuttle, Robert G., Jr. *Mysticism in the Wesleyan Tradition*. Grand Rapids: Zondervan, Francis Asbury, 1989.

Wainwright, Geoffrey. *Doxology: The Praise of God in Worship, Doctrine, and Life*. London: Epworth, 1980.

Ware, Kallistos. *The Orthodox Way*. 1979; rev. ed., Crestwood, N.Y.: St. Vladimir's Seminary Press, 1995.

Westerhoff, John H. *Spiritual Life: The Foundation for Preaching and Teaching*. Louisville: Westminster/John Knox, 1994.

Willard, Dallas. *The Spirit of the Disciplines: Understanding How God Changes Lives*. San Francisco: Harper and Row, 1988.

Wilson, Marvin R. *Our Father Abraham: Jewish Roots of the Christian Faith*. Grand Rapids: Eerdmans; Dayton, Ohio: Center for Judaic-Christian Studies, 1989.

Index of Subjects and Persons

Abraham (OT patriarch), 38, 39, 62, 113, 166–67, 201
Abraham, William, 135, 137
adoption, 20, 107, 108, 109–17, 125, 129, 161, 179, 207
Advent, 48, 49, 66–67, 68, 71, 77, 90, 170, 194, 206, 228
Against Heresies, 262
All Saints Day, 121
Anabaptists, 31, 124, 174, 257
Anderson University, 21, 227
Anselm, Saint, 133
Anthony, Saint, 89, 222, 225, 232, 257, 261
Apostles' Creed, 13, 24, 33, 37, 47, 51, 66, 73–74, 77, 100, 101, 125, 126, 127, 129, 152, 178, 199, 200, 204, 206, 209
apostolic succession, 123
Asbury, college and seminary, 197, 227
asceticism, 89, 97, 136, 168, 225–26, 232
ashrams, 196, 206, 219
Ash Wednesday, 92
assurance, 20, 63, 64, 72, 93, 98, 100, 134, 139, 146, 148, 153, 183–206, 207, 214, 223
Athanasius, Saint, 89, 225, 232, 261
Augustine, Saint, 45, 71, 73, 145, 186–87, 257, 261

Barclay, William, 133, 188, 241 n. 56, 261
Belter Lectures, 21
Benedict, Saint, 166, 232, 257, 261
Bernard of Clairvaux, 31, 257
Bible (Scriptures), 20, 24, 31, 32, 38, 46, 55, 57–58, 60–61, 65, 83–84, 95, 96, 110, 117, 133, 136, 139, 141–42, 143, 164, 168, 169, 178, 195, 211–12, 215, 219, 220, 221, 228, 230
Blevins, Dean G., 254 n. 18
Bloesch, Donald, 22, 31, 37, 96, 143, 237 n. 7, 252 n. 21, 257, 261, 263
Bondi, Roberta, 263
Bonhoeffer, Dietrich, 14, 16, 22, 45, 126, 174, 180–81, 187, 242 n. 31, 247 n. 42, 251 n. 41, 258, 259, 261
Book of Common Prayer, 173
Booth, Catherine, 151, 258
Brethren of the Common Life, 171, 174, 176
Buechner, Frederick, 166, 261
Bunyan, John, 149, 213, 245 n. 10, 249 n. 46
Buttrick, David, 167, 258, 261
Buttrick, George, 35, 109, 258, 261

Callen, Barry L., 233, 238 n. 13, 238 n. 5, 239 n. 13, 239 n. 22, 240 n. 28, 240 n. 45, 240 n. 51, 241 n. 13, 242 n. 17, 243 n. 35, 243 n. 40, 245 n. 4, 247 n. 36, 247 n. 40, 250 n. 13, 251 n. 23, 251 n. 29, 252 n. 1, 252 n. 4, 252 n. 11, 252 n. 12, 252 n. 16, 253 n. 40, 263
Calvin, John, 45, 61, 72, 145, 163, 174, 219, 257

Camps Farthest Out, 219–20, 224
Cane Ridge Revival, 226
catholic, 32, 47, 49, 50, 65, 117, 125, 128, 199, 201
Catholic, Roman. *See* Roman Catholicism
Catholic Worker movement, 177
celibacy, 97, 225, 232
Chambers, Oswald, 80, 103, 261
Chan, Simon, 27, 128, 263
charismatic movement, 29, 50, 117–18, 122–24, 129, 147, 149, 212, 221, 227, 237 n. 5, 242 n. 21
Christian Broadcasting Network, 227
Christian Year, 13, 33, 48, 49, 51, 66, 90, 91, 122, 170, 194, 206, 211
Christmas, 48, 49, 66, 68, 71, 74, 90, 228
church, 9, 11, 12, 13, 14, 15, 16, 17, 18, 19, 20, 21, 22, 24, 28, 30, 31, 32, 33, 34, 37, 38, 41, 45, 47, 48, 49, 50, 52, 58, 60, 62, 64, 65, 66, 67, 72, 73, 74, 75, 76, 84, 85, 86, 87, 90, 91, 92, 95, 96, 97, 98, 102, 104, 107, 108, 109, 110, 112, 114, 120, 121, 122, 123, 124, 125, 126, 127, 128, 129, 132, 134, 136, 137, 139, 140, 141, 143, 144, 145, 146, 147, 149, 152, 153, 154, 157, 158, 160, 161, 162, 163. 166, 167, 170, 171, 173, 174, 175, 176, 177, 178, 179, 180, 183, 184, 185, 186, 187, 188, 189, 190, 194, 195, 196, 197, 198, 199, 200, 201, 202, 205, 206, 207, 208, 209, 211, 212, 213, 214, 215, 216, 218, 219, 220, 221, 222, 223, 226, 227, 228, 229, 230, 231, 232, 233, 234, 237, 241, 243, 246, 247, 249, 251, 252, 257, 258
church calendar, 49, 67
church polity, 129
Clark, Glenn, 26, 219–20, 261
Clement of Alexandria, 44, 257
Collins, Kenneth J., 17, 22, 195, 254 n. 18, 258
Colson, Charles, 198
community (church), 121, 143
Constantine, 44, 232
contemplation, 94–95, 99, 178, 232
Contemplative tradition, 21, 37, 93–94, 96, 97, 98, 99, 100, 122, 147, 212, 233, 237 n. 5, 242 n. 21
conversion, 30, 52, 71, 72, 73, 114, 135, 149, 203, 218, 226
Cooley, Evelyn, 9
Costas, Orlando, 198
Day, Dorothy, 177, 258
Dayton, Donald W., 247 n. 37
De Groote, Gerhard, 171
deification, 95, 96
deism, 229
desert fathers, 89, 225
De Waal, Esther, 166
Didache, 123, 127
discipleship, 12, 13, 18, 23, 30, 31, 32, 34, 40, 59, 82, 117, 129, 143, 148, 189, 192, 199
discipline, 17, 36, 68, 69, 89, 90, 91, 96, 99, 100, 117, 122, 129, 133, 142, 146, 148, 149, 157, 161, 171, 199, 207, 208, 209, 211, 212, 215, 217, 220, 224, 225, 246, 254
Dunnam, Maxie, 217, 220, 258
Dunning, H. Ray, 200

Easter, 48, 49, 67, 70, 76, 80, 89, 90–91, 92, 93, 101, 104, 118, 125, 129, 144, 146, 147, 169, 170, 194, 227
Eastern Orthodoxy, 20, 24, 94, 95, 96, 97, 99, 148, 176, 232
ecclesial canon, 137
Edwards, Jonathan, 72, 257
Elijah, 194, 225
enlightenment, 140, 142, 190, 230
Epiphany, 48, 49, 66, 69, 70, 71, 90, 228
Erickson, Millard, 231
eternal life, 26, 47, 66, 86, 131, 138, 185, 199
eternal security, 192, 206
Eucharist. *See* Lord's Supper
Evangelical tradition, 66, 71–73, 93, 122, 147, 212, 242 n. 21
experience, religious, 34, 97, 98, 115, 132, 140, 150, 155, 176, 212, 225
extravagance, 51, 79, 80, 81, 82, 83, 84, 85, 86, 100, 104

fasting, 69, 90, 91, 92, 97, 212, 215, 217, 221
Fiddler on the Roof, 169
Finney, Charles, 149, 227
First Great Awakening, 72, 226
Foote, Julia, 198
footwashing, 87, 176, 177
Fosdick, Harry Emerson, 55, 56, 81, 144, 205, 241 n. 7, 261

Foster, Richard, 33, 65, 103, 115, 123, 171, 176, 198, 220, 237 n. 5, 242 n. 21, 245 n. 41, 258, 259, 260, 261, 262
Fox, George, 14, 140, 248 n. 26, 257, 261
Francis of Assisi, 59, 257
Friends (Quakers), 14, 140, 163, 176, 234, 248 n. 26, 257, 258
fruit of the Spirit, 31, 45, 48, 65, 76, 92, 116, 122, 162, 180, 181, 217, 221, 224, 247 n. 43
Full Gospel Businessmen's Fellowship, 227

Gaither, Gloria, 20, 220, 258
Gaither, William (Bill), 20, 220, 258
Gandhi, Mahatma, 111, 177
Gardner College, 21
Germany, J. Horace, 160
Gethsemani, 232, 250 n. 11
gifts of the Spirit, 17, 31, 48, 71, 117, 118, 122, 123, 124, 125, 191, 196, 199, 204, 221, 222, 223, 224, 227
gnosticism, 70, 162, 168, 178, 182, 200, 229–30, 242 n. 28
Good Friday, 89, 93
Goodell, William, 198
grace, 7, 11, 12, 13, 14, 21, 24, 25, 27, 29, 44, 45, 53, 54, 60, 62, 63, 67, 71, 72, 74, 75, 76, 79, 80, 81, 82, 83, 84, 85–87, 88, 89, 90, 92, 93, 94, 95, 96, 100, 103, 107, 108, 110, 111, 112, 114, 115, 117, 118, 120, 122, 129, 132, 135, 136, 137, 138, 139, 141, 145, 148, 149, 150, 151, 154, 160, 164, 167, 171, 173, 176, 177, 180, 181, 187, 188, 189, 191, 199, 201, 202, 203, 204, 205, 207, 208, 209, 210, 211, 214, 217, 219, 221, 222, 224, 228, 233, 234, 235, 242 n. 31, 243 n. 45, 249 n. 42, 254 n. 18
Graham, Billy, 71, 73, 264
Great Commission, 74
Greathouse, William, 264
Gregory of Nyssa, 95, 249, 257
Grenz, Stanley, 30, 134
Grubbs, Dwight L., 22, 136, 209, 258, 264

Harkness, Georgia, 98, 99, 172–73, 182, 258, 261
Harper, Steve, 213, 264
Hauerwas, Stanley, 117, 125
Haystack Prayer Meeting, 226
Hebrew heritage, 228, 230, 231
Hebrew Scriptures, 38, 57, 144, 178, 186, 194
hedonism, 168
Henderson, D. Michael, 264
Henry, Carl F. H., 46, 220
Hindu, 16, 95, 98, 219, 233
Holiness movement, 14, 76, 149, 226, 227, 243
Holocaust, 188
Holy Club (Oxford), 226
holy places, 72
Holy Spirit, 24, 25, 27, 30–31, 32, 38, 42, 43, 46, 51–52, 59, 61, 63, 69, 74–76, 80, 99, 101, 117, 118, 123, 125, 140, 146, 147, 148, 150, 164, 176, 186, 196, 204, 218, 221–22, 227–28
holy week, 49, 90, 228
hospitality, 63, 163, 164–66, 177, 250 n. 11
humanism, 169
humor, 161, 166–68

icons, 176
Ignatius of Loyola, 218, 257, 262
illumination, 20, 22, 51, 66, 118, 131, 133, 136, 153, 233
image of God, 9, 11, 17, 18, 22, 30, 38, 83, 115, 147, 202, 209
Imitation of Christ, The, 171, 182, 262
incarnation, 18, 25, 42, 44, 45, 61, 62, 70, 90, 94, 102, 122, 199, 200, 202
Interior Castle, 249 n. 46
InterVarsity Christian Fellowship, 226
Irenaeus, 107, 230, 257, 262

Jesus, 16, 30, 40, 47, 54, 61–62, 64, 66–70, 74–75, 80, 82, 85–88, 90–93, 98, 100–103, 110, 111, 114–15, 118–19, 121–22, 125–27, 138, 140, 143, 146, 151, 152, 160, 164, 165, 168, 173, 178–79, 191, 194, 195, 196, 200, 201, 210–11, 213–14, 228
Jesus and the Disinherited, 165, 262
Job, 23, 55, 144, 167
John the Baptist, 69, 164, 225
Johns, Cheryl Bridges, 248 n. 22
Jones, E. Stanley, 98, 111, 196, 202, 219, 258, 262
Jones, Rufus, 262
Jordan, Clarence, 198

Kelly, Thomas, 57, 258, 262

Keswick movement, 151, 227
Kierkegaard, Søren, 54, 258, 262
King, Martin Luther, Jr., 163, 177, 258, 262
Kingdomtide, 170
knowing, 18, 33, 36, 37, 57, 131–55, 167, 173, 180, 212, 248 n. 18
knowledge, 13, 37, 85, 89, 113, 115, 132, 133–39, 142, 152, 154, 167, 180, 189, 225, 230–31, 233, 238 n. 7

laity, 174, 211, 251 n. 25
Land, Steven J., 186, 228, 264
Laubach, Frank, 59, 94, 98, 196, 258, 262
Lawrence, Brother, 53, 59, 77, 252 n. 13, 257, 262
lectionary, 49, 50, 170, 176, 241 n. 59
Leech, Kenneth, 27, 265
Lent, 48, 49, 90, 91–92, 228
Lewis, C. S., 81, 103, 184, 185, 258, 262
Life of Anthony, 89, 225, 261
liturgy, 15, 16, 175–76, 229
Locke, John, 230
Lord's Supper, 45, 102, 126, 127, 176, 177, 216, 221, 229, 234–35
love, 27, 33, 36, 28, 42, 45, 51, 54, 56, 60, 67, 71, 73, 75, 76, 81, 82–83, 84, 85–87, 88, 89, 96, 97, 99–100, 101, 108–10, 111, 112, 115, 122, 138, 141, 148–50, 159, 163, 165, 171, 177, 181, 189, 196, 210, 232, 233, 249 n. 28
Luther, Martin, 14, 45, 51, 55, 72, 77, 89, 145, 147, 163, 174, 177, 193, 201, 222, 249 n. 41, 257, 262

Mack, Alexander, 257
Maddox, Randy, 217
Mahan, Asa, 149
Manning, Brennan, 135, 158, 173, 199, 258, 265
Marcion, 178, 230, 252 n. 9
Massey, James Earl, 22, 241 n. 13, 258, 265
McGrath, Alister, 35, 36, 147, 218, 220, 223, 239 n. 21, 240 n. 33, 258, 265
McKenna, David, 41–42, 51
means of grace, 86, 137, 149, 211, 217, 219, 221
Menno Simons, 257
mere religion, 11, 13, 14, 15, 18, 19, 20, 22, 31, 35, 38, 43, 46, 47, 54, 58, 64, 65, 73, 74, 75, 76, 91, 98, 99, 115, 116, 128, 146, 154, 163, 170, 171, 173, 178, 179, 181, 183, 186, 191, 196, 197, 205, 206, 207, 208, 221, 222, 223
Merton, Thomas, 37, 94, 98, 99, 232, 242 n. 27, 246 n. 20, 258, 262
Methodism, 14, 42, 219
mission, 20, 25, 26, 32, 33, 34, 49, 52, 58, 64, 65, 73, 74, 75, 76, 91, 98, 99, 115, 116, 128, 146, 154, 163, 170, 171, 173, 178, 179, 181, 183, 186, 191, 196, 197, 205, 206, 207, 208, 221, 222, 223
Moltmann, Jürgen, 63, 146, 233, 265
monasticism, 128, 166, 232
Montanus, 123, 124
Moody, D. L., 226
Mulholland, Robert, 130, 258, 265
Murray, Andrew, 214
Muslim, 16
mysticism, 79, 95–96, 99–100, 136, 176, 232–33, 244 n. 23

Naylor, Charles, 139, 204
New Age, 16, 28, 95
Newton, John, 80
Niebuhr, H. Richard, 43–46, 52
Nouwen, Henri, 96, 98, 99, 116, 175, 258, 265

Oberlin College, 227
Ordinary Time, 48, 49, 170, 172, 194
Origen, 44, 225, 257

Packer, J. I., 37, 124, 258, 262, 265
Palmer, Parker, 196–97, 265
Palmer, Phoebe, 149, 150, 151, 227, 258, 262
panentheism, 95, 105, 233
Pannenberg, Wolfhart, 265
pantheism, 42, 95, 233, 244 n. 26, 249 n. 42
Parham, Charles, 227
Pascal, Blaise, 248 n. 23, 257, 262
Passover, 47, 91, 92, 119, 126, 194, 216, 242 n. 24
Pennington, M. Basil, 58, 94, 265
Pentecost, 19, 27, 47, 48, 49, 61, 71, 80, 92, 99, 118–19, 121, 125, 128, 129, 144, 145, 146–47, 150, 169, 170, 187, 221, 223, 227, 228, 247 n. 37
Pentecostalism, 12, 14, 20, 50, 124, 163, 186, 223, 227–28, 237 n. 1, 241 n. 60

persecution, 41, 44, 46, 84, 89, 131, 186, 188, 190
perseverance, 64, 190, 191, 201, 208
Peter, 71, 108, 115, 140, 141
Phillips, J. B., 24, 26, 88, 258
Pia Desideria, 31, 234, 262
Pietism, 13, 23, 31, 37, 72, 124, 149, 222, 234, 249 n. 41
pilgrimages, 36, 47, 72, 124, 149, 222, 234, 249 n. 41
Pilgrim's Progress, 249 n. 46, 261
Pinnock, Clark H., 18, 22, 42, 76, 109, 120, 124, 136, 200, 231, 239 n. 9, 248 n. 15, 258, 262, 265
Plato, 95, 113
Plotinus, 95
Polycarp, 188, 252 n. 9, 257
postmodernism, 12, 16, 29, 33, 34, 41, 58, 125, 230–31, 248 n. 22
poverty, 66, 70, 140, 173, 232
power, divine, 87
Praise Gatherings, 220, 224
prayer, 25, 26, 35, 36, 56, 59, 75, 83, 86, 95, 96, 100, 103, 109, 115–16, 138, 141–42, 143, 159, 166, 169, 171, 175, 189, 203, 208, 210–11, 213–14, 215, 217, 220, 223, 232
prayer meetings, 220, 226
prevenient grace, 74
process theology, 44, 233
Promise Keepers, 220, 224
Protestant Reformation, 13, 31, 72, 89, 123, 145, 147, 163, 174, 234
Psalms, 88–89, 93, 103, 116, 195, 202, 203, 212, 213, 246 n. 17
Puritanism, 13, 242 n. 31

Quakers. *See* Friends

Rahner, Karl, 12
religion, 14, 15, 16, 18, 28, 31, 34–35, 41, 54, 79, 80, 121, 135, 159, 165, 172, 175, 200, 225, 233, 244 n. 27
religious knowledge, 137, 230
Renovaré, 220
resurrection, 18, 19, 33, 47, 63, 65, 67, 75, 82, 87, 88, 90, 91, 92, 101, 104, 110, 118, 119, 122, 140, 147, 160, 170, 176, 177, 180, 185, 186, 191, 196, 199, 200, 201, 203, 214, 215, 216, 228, 242 n. 24
retreats, 196, 206, 219, 220, 246 n. 20, 250 n. 11
revelation, 15, 16, 18, 25, 30, 34, 38, 40, 46, 51, 59, 64, 65, 74, 108, 114, 115, 118, 126, 131, 134, 136, 138, 139, 140, 143, 175, 200, 211, 230, 244 n. 23, 248 n. 15
Robertson, Pat, 227
Roman Catholicism, 12, 20, 24, 31, 47, 120, 148, 222, 223, 234, 237, 242 n. 31, 251 n. 25
ruach, 69, 94, 169
Rule of Saint Benedict, 166

sacrament, 176, 182, 229, 234–35
saints, 9, 47, 56, 81, 94, 113–14, 120–22, 124, 125, 127, 128, 142, 146, 200, 220–21
Salvation Army, 151
sanctification, 13, 31, 45, 49, 72, 81, 91, 95–96, 148–49, 150, 151, 177, 191, 207–9, 242 n. 31, 244 n. 26, 244 n. 27
Sayings of the Fathers, 225
Scott, Orange, 149
Seamands, Stephen A., 42, 212
Second Great Awakening, 226
Sermon on the Mount, 89, 120, 225
Seymour, William J., 124, 227, 258
shalom, 60, 66, 93, 196, 197
Shively, Fredrick H., 22
Shoffner, Lena, 166
silence, 51, 55, 69, 94, 128, 176, 177, 229, 232, 245 n. 41
simplicity, 57, 171, 175, 237 n. 9
Smith, Hannah Whitall, 149, 151, 258, 262
Snyder, Howard A., 41
solitude, 69, 97, 99, 128, 171, 196, 216, 219, 242 n. 27, 245 n. 41, 247 n. 42
soul, 37, 38, 72, 89–90, 95, 120, 135, 147, 148, 151, 154, 169, 232, 233
Spener, Philipp Jakob, 31, 218, 222, 234, 257, 262
spiritual discernment, 139
spiritual estate, 173–74
spirituality, 11–22, 24–25, 27–38, 40–41, 43–47, 53, 58, 59, 65, 72, 76, 80, 84, 88, 94, 95, 98, 102, 110, 112, 114, 116, 117, 124, 128, 132, 142, 144, 145, 153, 157–58, 162, 163–64, 166, 169, 171, 172, 174, 185, 189, 190, 195, 205, 207,

208–9, 211, 218, 223, 225, 229, 231, 232, 239 n. 12
Steele, Daniel, 149–50, 155, 258
Steere, Douglas, 81, 258
Sterner, R. Eugene, 22, 108, 210, 258, 266
stewardship, 170
Stookey, Laurence, 119, 176, 228, 266
Stott, John, 220
Strong, Douglas M., 198, 266
submission, 117, 171
suffering, 24, 26, 27, 39, 45–46, 47, 54, 57, 70, 72, 86, 87, 88, 89, 125, 143, 144, 171, 174, 177, 178, 180, 188–89, 190
synagogue, 28, 116–17, 139
synergy, 249 n. 42

Taylor, Barbara Brown, 81
Taylor, Jeremy, 148, 257, 262
Temple, William, 25, 251 n. 41, 258
Teresa of Ávila, 249 n. 46, 257
theology, 11, 12, 19, 25, 28, 29
theosis, 95, 105, 244 n. 26
Thomas à Kempis, 171–72, 257, 262
Thoreau, Henry David, 133
Thurman, Howard, 55, 60, 133–34, 165, 258, 262
Tozer, A. W., 14, 60, 94, 121, 154, 237 n. 9, 258, 262
Tracy, Wesley D., 22, 266
Trinity, 18, 27, 32, 74, 102, 249 n. 42
Trueblood, D. Elton, 34, 138, 140, 205, 238 n. 7, 248 n. 26, 258, 262
truth, 13, 17, 19, 29, 33, 34, 36, 37, 51, 64, 65, 66, 71, 73, 84, 87, 88, 92, 99, 101, 125, 132, 133, 134–37, 139, 140, 141–43, 160, 189, 200, 201, 204, 228, 230–31, 233, 248 n. 15
Tuttle, Robert G., 266

Underhill, Evelyn, 37, 172, 258, 262

Wainwright, Geoffrey, 43, 258, 260, 266
Ware, Kallistos, 132, 139, 266
Warner, Daniel S., 121, 237 n. 8, 249 n. 28, 258
Watts, Isaac, 213
Weavings, 51, 261
Wells, David, 134
Wesley, Charles, 53, 80, 85, 88, 91, 104, 151, 159, 257
Wesley, John, 14, 18, 19, 21, 31, 36, 41–42, 45, 51, 60, 61, 95–96, 115, 117, 129, 148, 149, 151, 153, 160, 195, 197, 213, 219, 221, 247 n. 46, 251 n. 29, 251 n. 34, 257, 262
Wesley, Susanna, 175, 213
Wesleyan tradition, 13, 21, 41, 72, 124, 149, 219, 241 n. 60
Westerhoff, John, 90, 170, 211, 241 n. 59, 243 n. 15, 244 n. 18, 251 n. 19, 254 n. 7, 266
Whitefield, George, 226, 257
Wilkinson, Bruce, 56
Willard, Dallas, 266
Wilson, Marvin, 266
Wood, J. A., 149, 258
Woolman, John, 257, 262
worship, 13, 27, 35, 36, 48–49, 58, 67, 103, 113, 116, 138, 159, 162, 166, 175–76, 189–90, 199, 213, 218, 219, 220, 227, 228–29, 232, 234, 241 n. 59
Wynkoop, Mildred Bangs, 263

Yancey, Philip, 175
Yoder, John Howard, 237 n. 1

Index of Scripture

Genesis

1:1 74
2:7 58
3:19 92
4:1 139
11 119
12:1–4 62
12:1–9 202
17:17 167
28:16 54
37–50 62

Exodus

3:14 59
7:3 135
8:15 135
12–13 126
14 112
14:21 69
17:6 26
19:4 59
19:4–5 113
20:21 55
21–23 196
23:9 165, 196

Leviticus

11:44 81

Deuteronomy

6:4 57
7:7 116
10:19 63, 165
34 194

2 Samuel

7:24 60

1 Kings

3:9 58
8:22–53 215

1 Chronicles

4:10–11 56

Job

23:8–9 55
38:7 167

Psalms

1 88
1:1–2 99
9:1 103
13 88
27:4 59
30 88
30:12 103
34:8 135, 142
37 88
37:7 138
40 89
45:8 135
46:1 59, 61
46:4 21
46:7 59
46:10 59, 138, 223
47:1 159
63:5–7 154
71:21–22 63
74 88
80:14–15 194
82:6 99, 244 n. 26
90:4 185
95:6 97
98 213
100 213, 246 n. 17
103:13–14 211
106:1 103
114 39
120–134 202
125:1–2 205
126:1–2 167
139:23 146
145 88
149:3 159
150:3 159
150:4 159

Isaiah

1:11–17 35
6 104
6:1 82
6:1–8 42, 212
6:5 82
24–27 93
25:1 93
34:4 26
35:1–2 69
35:8 147
40:1–2 63
40:9 66
40:9–10 194
40:10 66
40:11 66
44:24 168
45:7 135
49:15 142
51:1 32
51:1–2 38, 113
55:8 185
55:8–9 62
56:7 215
60:1 70

Jeremiah

9:23–24 138
15:16 142
23:24 61
24:6–7 113
31:31–34 146
31:33 60, 146

Daniel

4:23–32 193
7:1–22 193

Hosea

6:6 138

Joel

2:1–2 92
2:13 92

Amos

5:21–24 35
5:24 196

Micah

6:8 35, 197

Habakkuk

3:2 135

Malachi

4 194
4:2 68

Matthew

1:18–25 26
2:16–18 70
4:1–11 69, 90
5:6 26
5:8 16, 135, 138
5:14–16 164
5:48 150
6:2 168
6:9 116
6:9–10 94
6:9–13 211
6:9–15 104
6:10 81
6:16–18 215
6:24 97

6:33 186
8:20 165
9:15 97
10:19–20 98
11:29 118, 218
12:34 16
16:18 206
18:19 61
18:20 218
19:21 232
20:33 54
21:13 215
22:15–22 163
22:37–40 196
23:5 168
23:24 168
23:37 25
24:28 168
25 161
25:31–46 177
25:34–40 165
26:26–29 126
26:29 97
26:38 218
27:46 57
28:19 74, 241 n. 56
28:19–20 128, 206
28:20 61, 98

Mark

1:11 70
1:24 144
2:13–17 197
3:7 197
5:1–20 197
8:34–35 171
8:35–36 158
9:24 144
9:33–37 171
10:35–45 171
10:45 171
14:36 101
15:34 144
15:39 197
15:40–41 197

Luke

1:4 139
1:14 164
1:46–55 70
1:47 164
2:10 164
3:22 70
4:14 69
5:16 219
6:41 168
7:33 69
7:36–50 165
9:23 89
9:23–24 225
9:28–36 115
9:60 168
10:21 164
12:6 101
14:16–24 63, 165
14:26 158
15:1–2 165
15:1–10 101
15:11–32 108, 110, 164
18:1 208
19:41–44 57
22:7–21 216
22:42 55
24:1–12 26
24:13–35 114
24:31 141
24:49 75
24:52–53 164
24:53 103

John

1:3 200
1:5 70
1:10–11 140
1:12–13 114
1:14 172
1:18 25
1:29 70
1:33–34 70
3:8 122
3:16 102
3:17 108
4 12
4:24 36
5:24 191
6:63 143
7:37–38 13
8:31 189
8:31–32 143
10:27 135
10:34–35 99, 244 n. 26
11:25–26 11
13:3–4 87
14:2–3 109
14:6–7 71
14:9 248 n. 15
14:16 61
14:18 108
14:26 61, 118
15:5 96
15:9–11 189
15:12 38
15:15 110
15:18–25 90
15:26 61
16:7 61
16:13 33
17:3 131, 138
17:21 42
19:28 26

Acts

1:4 222
1:4–5 146, 147
1:5 223
1:7 192
2 119, 187, 196
2:1–42 119
2:16–21 27
2:38 71
3:1–10 140
3:8–10 141
4:13 140
5:31 115
6:3 198
8:26–39 114
9 84
9:1–9 114
9:2 115
12:14 141
13:2 123
13:3 215
13:4 123
13:9–11 123
15 197
16:6–10 123
16:31 98
17:27 61
19:6 123
22:4 84

Romans

1:16 11, 62
1:32 140
2:13–16 201
4:16 38
5:1–5 27
5:3–4 190
5:20–21 56, 86
6:12–14 147
8:5 98
8:9 31
8:14 31
8:15 101
8:16 31, 215
8:22–23 180
8:23 45, 116
8:28 205
8:29 147
8:37 45
8:39 61
9:4 113
11:17–24 38
12:1 148
12:1–2 162
12:2 187
12:8 167
12:12 59, 208
15:7 165
15:13 185

1 Corinthians

1:18–31 45
1:25 87
1:27–30 167
2:13 136
2:14–15 218
3:6–7 76
3:21 168
4:10 45
4:13 223
4:20 123
5:7 90
5:7–8 91
9:24 192
9:24–27 191
10:17 126
10:31 169
11 216
12:3 118, 153
12:4–11 211
12:4–31 119

12:7 228
12:11 222
13 84, 88
13:3 159
13:12 96, 143
14 221
15:23 200
15:45 224
15:57 200
15:58 206

2 Corinthians

3:5–6 146
3:14–16 139
3:17–18 209
3:18 97, 119
4:11 180
4:17 88
5:1–5 183–84
5:17–18 71
6:6 51
12:9 86

Galatians

1:4 187
1:13 84
2:8–23 167
2:19–20 244 n. 26
2:20 157, 158, 216
3:1–5 167
3:2 209
3:3 209
3:7 38
3:8 113
3:27 163
3:28 126
3:28–29 197
4:5 114
4:6 101
4:7 114
4:8–10 167
4:19 11, 148, 171
5:5–6 119
5:6 38
5:13–25 119
5:22 122
5:22–23 221
6:2 180

Ephesians

1:3–5 107, 112
1:7–10 86
1:15–23 84
1:19–20 200
1:19–22 87
2:1–5 56
2:4 26
2:7 86
2:14 166
2:20 38
3:6 113
3:9 233
3:16 56
3:17–20 140
3:19 56, 85, 115
4:22–24 217
4:30 204
5:18 122, 222
6:10 63
6:12 90
6:13–17 163
6:17–18 59
6:18 208

Philippians

1:6 209
2:1–2 9
2:1–11 148
2:2 85
2:9–11 102
2:12 209
2:12–13 87
2:16 71
3:10 180
3:14 45
4:6 59
4:11–13 223

Colossians

1:6 141
1:15 172
1:15–23 24
1:18 200
1:27–28 46
2:4 140
2:8 90
2:9 102, 200
2:9–10 101
2:21 168
3:1 93
3:9–10 163
3:11 46, 126
4:2 208

1 Thessalonians

4:3 81
5:17 59, 169, 208
5:18 19
5:19–20 19

2 Thessalonians

2:13 185
2:16–17 86

1 Timothy

2:5 200
2:9–10 162
3:2–3 162
4:7–10 208
6:11 191, 192
6:11–16 208
6:15–16 25

2 Timothy

1:9–10 187
1:10 70
2:11–12 192
2:25–26 142
3:10–11 191
3:16 58

Titus

1:1 142
2:9–10 163
2:10 179

Hebrews

1:1–2 62
2:10 115
6:5 187
8:8–12 60
10:15–17 146
10:22 205
10:32–36 190
11:1 199
11:8 62
11:10 110
12:1 64, 114
12:1–2 191
12:2 30, 64, 115, 187
12:11 207, 209
13 201
13:15 59

James

1:2–4 190
1:12 190
5:16 83

1 Peter

1:1–4 108
1:15 104
2:5 113
2:9 113
2:10 116
2:11 217
3:4 162
4:12–5:11 45

2 Peter

1:4 95, 99, 244 n. 26
3:11 192

1 John

1 60
1:1–4 30
2:1 61
3:1–3 99
3:16 85
4:12 25
4:16–18 97
4:19 97

2 John

9 189

Jude

24 193

Revelation

1 201
2:4 97, 100
3:10–11 192
4:2 97
4:11 186
5:9 46
11:15–19 62
11:19 97
22:21 205